Taking New Zealand Seriously

Taking
New Zealand
Seriously
The Economics of Decency

TIM HAZLEDINE

HarperCollins*Publishers* New Zealand Limited

For
all of us

First published 1998
Reprinted 1998

HarperCollins*Publishers* *(New Zealand) Limited*
P.O. Box 1, Auckland

Copyright © Tim Hazledine, 1998

Tim Hazledine asserts the moral right to be identified as the author of this work.

All rights reserved. No part of this publication may be reproduced, stored in a retrieval system or transmitted in any form or by any means, electronic, mechanical, photocopying, recording or otherwise, without the prior written permission of the publishers.

ISBN 1 86950 283 3

Designed and typeset by Chris O'Brien
Cover image a detail from *Another Time*, Jeffrey Harris (1975, oil on hardboard) from the Collection of the Museum of New Zealand Te Papa Tongarewa, B.42076
Printed by Publishing Press Limited, Auckland

I do not dream of Sussex downs
or quaint old England's
quaint old towns —
I think of what may yet be seen
in Johnsonville or Geraldine

Denis Glover, 'Home Thoughts'

When the trout rise like compassion
it is worth watching

when the hinds come down
from the hills
with a new message

it will be as well to listen

Brian Turner, 'The Stopover'

Acknowledgements

Thanks to my colleagues at the University of Auckland for their encouragement and support. Thanks also to Ian Watt, Sue Page and Lorraine Steele at HarperCollins. And my heartfelt appreciation goes to my family and friends (especially M.V.), for being my family and friends.

Contents

Introduction: A Different Point of View   9

Myths

1 Alternatives   19
2 The Albania of the South Pacific?   26
3 Market Myths   36
4 The Great Free-Trade Con   44
5 The Tyranny of TINA at the End of History   52
6 Yes, We Have No Nirvanas   60
7 Who Will Drive the Buses?   69

Morals

8 Behaving Well is the Best Reward   81
9 Social Capital: the Next Big Idea?   92
10 Life at the Margin: the Meaning of Markets   102
11 True Stories from the Labour Market   110
12 Shock Collapse in Managerial Productivity!   118
13 Deconstructing the Rich List   127
14 The Good Things in Life   138

Means

15 Doing Our Own Thing in a Sovereign Economy   151
16 A Decent Day's Pay for a Day's Decent Work   161
17 Susan of Parnell: a Story of Work and Family   175
18 The Welfare State: a Modest Proposal   184
19 Schools, Health, Housing, Crime . . . It's the Economy, Stupid!   193
20 Virtue Ethics and Big Business   203
21 The Do-it-Ourselves Economics of Decency   215

Endnotes   228

Introduction
A Different Point of View

When Kevin Costner was making his epic movie *Dances With Wolves* someone asked him how a mere actor could have the temerity to think that he could direct a major motion picture. 'I may not be the smartest guy in Hollywood,' Costner replied, 'but I do have a point of view, and that's worth something in this town.'

That's a good attitude, and it's the attitude I bring to this book. I don't profess to offer certainty, salvation, total solutions. We have had too much of that sort of nonsense in New Zealand. What I have to offer is just a point of view; but one which I hope is stimulating and useful. And I'm well aware of the sting in the tail of the Costner story: flushed with the success of *Dances With Wolves*, Hollywood — and maybe Mr Costner himself — began to believe that perhaps he *was* the smartest fellow in town after all. Result: the two hundred million dollar fiasco *Waterworld*. We should all have such problems!

Enough of movie-star metaphors. This book is about economics. Just what point of view could give us useful insights into our economic predicament? In two words, it is this: *process matters*. The way we behave, the terms on which we deal with others, are, I will argue, as important in economic affairs as they are in life generally. Indeed, I believe it wrong and foolish to attempt to disentangle the economy from social and cultural concerns. Hence the main title of this book: we New Zealanders should take ourselves in our social and cultural context seriously when working out how we want our economy to function.

This point of view contrasts sharply with what has been orthodoxy in New Zealand over the last decade and a half. Known as 'economic rationalism' or 'neoclassical economics', the currently dominant doctrine cares nothing for how things are done. All that matters is the outcome in terms of economic efficiency, meaning changes in gross domestic product, narrowly defined. Process is unimportant; concepts of culture and even society, meaningless. Like Margaret Thatcher, the rationalists 'don't believe in' society, maintaining that individuals are the building blocks of the efficient economy.

Of course there is no such thing as a truly asocial, acultural, amoral economic model. Rationalism is rooted in particular notions of short-term self-centred behaviour that have strongest currency in Anglo-American — especially American — cultures. It is a matter of vigorous debate just how suited rationalist doctrine is even in these contexts, and other variants of market capitalism in Asia and Europe seem to give superior outcomes, on many criteria.

But it is not my point that we should switch from the Anglo-American model to the Japanese model, or the French, or the German, or the Singaporean. What I am proposing is that every society has to work out its own model, its own 'rules of engagement' governing the management of its economic affairs. New Zealand in fact did this for many years with some success. Now we are told that this is impossible, that we must succumb to the weight of TINA ('There Is No Alternative'), like it or not. I think this is rubbish. I believe that we can control our own economic destiny, and that we must try to do so if we are to build a decent society for all New Zealanders. I won't be arguing that all the changes in this country over the last decade or so have been for the worse. Much would have, and should have, been done as part of the normal processes of change and development. But what we have had is not reform but revolution — a wrenching of our economic lives out of our control and, fundamentally, away from decency.

My point is this: get the processes right and the outcomes will look after themselves. Ends are not independent of means. This is a conventional proposition in many fields of life. Marriage, child-raising, social intercourse, sports, education, international relations are all expected to prosper if people behave well, and fail if they do not. They are rooted in norms, rules and moral codes. But it is a surprisingly novel proposition to make in the economic context.

It will take the rest of the book to argue the point, but let us begin with examples of how some important economic issues might look from a different, process-oriented point of view. Start with the basic rationalist line that has been rammed home remorselessly since 1984: 'New Zealanders must change to fit in with the new economic policies.' Well, I will suggest: *Economic policies must change to fit in with New Zealanders.*

What policies? We are told: 'In the new competitive environment people must be prepared to accept whatever wage employers can afford to offer, if they expect to work.' Instead, try: *Jobs must pay enough to support a household in decency. Employers who can't pay such wages shouldn't expect to get workers.*

And at the other end of the income scale: 'There is a world market for the services of top executives and university professors. Therefore, we must be prepared to pay (higher) world prices to attract such people.' How about: *Remuneration should not depend on the world market but on what we in New Zealand can afford and what fits our notions of a decent distribution of income. If we hire from abroad, it should be people who want to live here, not who are attracted by money alone.*

Take this familiar line: 'It is essential that New Zealand throws itself open to foreign investment if we are to secure the capital needed for growth.' Well, dare to be different: *It is essential that we retain control over our own resources and development. There is plenty of investment money available internally. If a project is not attractive to New Zealand investors, then perhaps it isn't such a good project after all. We should invest and grow at our own pace.*

Continuing with international matters, try turning around the orthodoxy 'We need to export more to pay for increased imports' to: *We import so much because we export so much. It would be better if we produced more for ourselves.* Let us take a specific example. New Zealand's biggest export industry now is tourism. We are told that tourism is terrific because it 'earns' billions in foreign exchange, and 'generates' hundreds of thousands of jobs. Well, it seems to me that growth in tourism is raising serious issues of sustainability, fairness and control over our economy. As for the foreign exchange and the jobs, look at it this way: *All those foreign dollars tourism earns are needed to* pay for imports to replace local goods that aren't produced here because the people who would produce them have been sucked up by the tourism sector. In the long run, no particular industry or sector creates employment; they just divert resources from some other use.

Focus on the core of economic rationalism, its obsession with 'efficiency'. Here is a quote from one of the architects of the new regime: 'SOEs [state owned enterprises] account for 12 per cent of GDP . . . the need for SOEs to be efficient is thus hardly a matter for debate . . . [in the old days] there was terrible confusion from the mixture of commercial, social, regulatory and policy advisory functions.' In the new New Zealand, the managers of these enterprises, whether corporatised or privatised, are 'accountable' for only one thing, the maximisation of profits, this being the commercial yardstick of efficiency. But what if the 'confusion' arises not from political muddle but because the world really is quite complex; because commercial and social and other concerns cannot be torn apart; because dealing with them is a messy, 'political' business; and because interfering in the name of efficiency weakens democracy and is (as I will argue) actually counterproductive, even on its own terms? To raise these points is not to assume that everything in the old New Zealand was perfect. Of course it was not. All institutions should be open to scrutiny and to reform. But allowing them to be turned inside out in the cause of a narrow ideology is something quite different.

In the name of market efficiency, New Zealand has been transformed from probably the most, to now the least, regulated of the mature capitalist economies. Our regulatory institutions to deal with the great network industries, such as telecommunications, are virtually non-existent; our policies to safeguard pluralism and competition feeble in the extreme. The current line goes like this: 'In the new international market environment New Zealand firms need full freedom if they are to be competitive. If this means that they can earn vast profits from domestic consumers, or that industries become dominated by just two or even one major player, then so be it; such is the price of efficiency.' But try this: *Capitalism works best when firms choose, or if necessary are required, to take account of the wider interests of the communities in which they operate. This means that networks and natural monopolies should be explicitly regulated (as they are everywhere else). And perhaps our firms should be smaller rather than larger, the better to fit into the relatively small New Zealand economic environment.*

Rationalists love winners. They say things like: 'In the modern world only the best will survive. There is no place for those who are inadequately motivated, or who just aren't smart enough to contribute to competitive market life.' Similar outcomes are predicted by people who might not consider themselves to be economic rationalists. Some of them believe that in the new 'information age' only those workers capable of being highly trained (and continually retrained) will find jobs. Others push the centuries-old (and always wrong) line that technological change means work will be done by machines, rendering full employment impossible. I'd like to propose an alternative view: *Economics isn't everything, but the economy is inextricably intertwined with everything else that matters. Full employment is essential to the survival of the civil society. It is the right and the duty of all adults to participate in the economic process, on terms of decent wages and conditions. We can't all be All Blacks, but we all have to play the game.*

The essence of the debate can be captured in the hoary old metaphor of gross domestic product as a pie or cake. The textbook rationalist position has two tenets: first, all that matters is baking the largest possible cake; second, the way to do this is to let the best bakers take charge and be rewarded accordingly. If less skilful bakers don't do very well, and — for reasons that the rationalists aren't very good at explaining —about one person in ten doesn't do any baking at all, then so be it; such is the price of baking big cakes.

Where rationalists disagree amongst themselves is what to do with the cake after it has come out of the oven. Nice rationalists may argue that the rich bakers should hand over a fair share of their cake to the less well-off, if only so that the children of the less well-off have a fair chance at becoming rich themselves one day. Nasty rationalists are more likely to follow the line of a Thatcherite journalist with the only-in-England name of Peregrine Worsthorne, who, at the height of the excessive eighties, wrote: 'Class war? Of course there is a class war. And our class is winning!' Let the poor eat crumbs; it's all they deserve.

But the common ground all rationalists share is this: baking cakes is separate from who gets to eat them; production is separate from distribution; efficiency from equity; outcomes from process. The only thing to worry about is that if the most efficient bakers have to hand over too large a portion of their cake to the less efficient ones, then their incentive to bake well may be diminished.

Now, the point of view offered in this book will have it otherwise: *How the cake gets baked is more important than how big it is when it comes out of the oven. It is important that everyone participates in the baking process, and that they are decently rewarded for so doing. This is essential for the well-being of the not-so-talented bakers, and it won't do the champion cooks any harm either. They might just come to enjoy it, and their children surely will. And, because the 'social' side of economic life (teamwork, loyalty and so on) is a lot more important than the rationalists realise — well, who knows, the cake to which everybody contributes might even turn out bigger and better than the specialists' free-market cake. But whether it does or not, the basic point is this: get the process right, and the outcome will look after itself.*

You'll be getting the idea by now. What I am hoping for from the reader is not suspension of disbelief but enough openness and curiosity to give a different point of view a fair hearing. Try applying the *process matters* perspective to issues you are particularly concerned with. It's fun — serious fun. And it needs to be done. Many New Zealanders are deeply concerned about the state of the economy and society. They accept that changes had to be made, and can see many benefits from the new regime, but worry that things have gone too far, maybe even got out of control. They aren't proud to learn that inequality of incomes has increased more in New Zealand than in any other country. They are disturbed — even frightened — by the prospect of a permanent underclass of the underprivileged, especially the brown-skinned underprivileged. They appreciate that shops and restaurants are better now, but have an itch of guilt that working conditions on the other side of the till may not be what they used to be. They worry about whether their own jobs are secure, and what the future will hold for their children. They — we — are right to be worried, and right to want to do something about it; and if you are one of these people, then you are probably attracted to at least some of the points of view that you have sampled above.

But how would we do it? Does curtailing the excesses of the market economy mean a return to Muldoon-style interventionism? Certainly not.

So if salvation is not to be found in the invisible hand of the market or in the high hand of government, where is it? I suggest that it is right under our noses — in ourselves. The key is to strengthen the unseen ties that bind people in trust and loyalty: what a perceptive economist, the late Arthur Okun, once called the 'invisible handshake'. It is these ties that enable markets and governments to function at all, and that account for most else of what matters to us: love, friendship, honour, fun, fulfilment.

Belatedly, economists are coming to appreciate the value of the 'social capital', the empathy and sympathy found in relationships between people (including relationships within geographically defined communities such as countries, towns and neighbourhoods, and the cultural communities of kinship, class, hapu and iwi) and also in the broader sense of shared attitudes and goals. Neither democratic government nor 'free' markets can thrive without these relationships. It is also true, I believe, that the radical commercialisation of New Zealand since 1984 has, in essence, been feeding off our stock of precious social capital, with consequences at best mixed right now, but possibly disastrous in the long term. We need to rebuild our social capital. This doesn't mean we all have to go off and live in communes. It doesn't mean that economic policy will be run from town halls and county councils (though they have their part to play). It means we must take those intangible networks — based on trust and forbearance — that still have remarkable strength and resilience, and strengthen them further, in recognition of the utterly central role they play in our economic lives. That is really what this book is about.

I have written the book in three parts: myths, morals and

means. The first part clears up some widely held misconceptions about markets, trade, growth and the 'old' and 'new' New Zealand. The second part builds a framework for understanding how a successful, modern, civilised market economy can function. The final part of the book fleshes out this framework with specific proposals for implementing the economics of decency in New Zealand/Aotearoa.

Myths

Chapter 1
Alternatives

Was there — *is* there — an alternative to the massive programme of economic liberalisation that apparently transformed New Zealand in the decade after 1984? Would we *want* an alternative? That depends on how one sees the reform process panning out.[1] Contrast these two following interpretations of our recent economic history:

> By 1984, decades of heavy-handed state interference in the economy culminating in the wretched excesses of Robert Muldoon had left New Zealand as an economic basket-case, the 'Albania of the South Pacific'. The bold and sweeping programme of reforms begun by Roger Douglas effected a remarkable transformation of the economic landscape, transforming New Zealand from the most to the least regulated economy in the OECD.
>
> The results have been truly impressive. There was, of course, an initial period of adjustment to be worked through, but New Zealanders responded with impressive speed to the opportunities offered in their new, open, market-oriented environment. Since the last of the major reforms (the 1991 Employment Contracts Act), real GDP has increased by more than 20 per cent, unemployment has been slashed, from around 11 per cent to 7 per cent, consumer price inflation has been virtually eradicated, productivity has increased, and the government accounts have swung from massive deficits to substantial surpluses, used to pay down overseas debt ahead of schedule. Even including the adjustment period, economic performance in all these variables since 1984 has been markedly superior to the preceding decade.
>
> New Zealand is now firmly set on the path of sustainable supply side-driven economic growth. There is, however, no place for complacency. The recent falling away in the pace of growth — though no doubt temporary — reflects a slackening in the pace of the reform process since 1991, as well as the surviving

unconstructive resistance to the new era on the part of a small minority of leftish politicians and ivory-tower academic scribblers. But there is truly no alternative to New Zealand taking its full place in the modern, competitive world economy, and the great majority of workers, employers and consumers have wholeheartedly embraced that new world.

Now this:

Modern New Zealand history is divided into two periods. The first, covering the thirty years from the end of World War II, can be called *the years of external shocks*. After the high export prices of the Korean War boom, our terms of trade trended downwards, with wild year-to-year fluctuations, reflecting both the limited range of our exports and of our markets. In face of these difficult external conditions, the country performed remarkably well, maintaining throughout the period extraordinarily low unemployment rates, while building for the future more diversified and competitive primary and manufacturing industries.

Industrial development in New Zealand, as in other small or medium-sized economies (Canada, Australia, South Korea), was fostered by protective policies (tariffs, import controls) which in the New Zealand case were particularly important, given the very small size of the domestic market. However, as manufacturing industries matured, protection was progressively reduced, in a process which continued until overtaken by the sweeping liberalisations of the post-1984 regime.

Economic growth was lower than in other, less lucky countries struggling to catch up from underdevelopment or the ravages of war. But the key element of the 'wage earners' welfare state' — high-wage full employment — allowed New Zealanders to build decent lives for themselves and their children with what now appear rather low levels of assistance from the state. How this would change!

The second period, of about twenty years from around 1976 to the present, can be called *the years of internal shocks*. In these decades, what happened to us was largely determined by what we did to ourselves, or — more accurately — what we allowed to be done to us by a sequence of determined, wilful individuals — Muldoon, Douglas, Richardson, Brash — who exploited the smallness and unicameral politics of the country to basically capture the policy process.

Alternatives 21

The external auguries were relatively good, in contrast to the earlier era. The terms of trade index trended upwards at nearly 1 per cent per year, and its variance was only half that of 1956–76. The diversified agricultural and manufacturing tradables sector built up in the previous decades should have been well-placed to take advantage of these favourable external conditions, and indeed did manage impressive increases in export performance, in particular to the newly opened manufacturing markets of Australia.

But overall, economic performance in the second period has been woeful. Unemployment has gone from virtually nothing to average nearly 7 per cent for the twenty years. Economic growth was nearly halved, to just over one percent per year. Productivity has stagnated. Inflation was either too high or too low, and averaged 9.1 per cent. Government expenditure has doubled in real terms, though most citizens would say that the quality of public services received has deteriorated. Most miserably, real wages — the purchasing power of ordinary citizens — trended steadily downwards.

What on earth went wrong? The ordinary, orderly progress of economic affairs was continually being massively disrupted. First came the authoritarian excesses of Muldoon (Think Big, National Super, SMPs . . .), which wrecked the macroeconomic ratios and distorted investment incentives. Then came the ideologically driven excesses of Rogernomics and Ruthanasia — ruthless shocks to economic and social life in the name of a so-called free market dogma. Even the long delayed cyclical recovery of the mid-1990s was quickly flattened by exchange and interest rates driven up to cruel levels in the name of price rigidity and blind openness to foreign investors and speculators, leaving an emerging balance of payments crisis symptomatic of the gutting of the productive sector in the name of consumer efficiency.

Are the writers of these two passages breathing the same air? Well, yes they are — I wrote them both. And I used the same set of economic statistics as the basis for both.[2] The first passage could be a distillation of dozens of pro-reform pieces; the second is written from the heart. Let us deconstruct them — first the rhetoric, then the economics. The first passage uses modifiers to frame the reforms in the most appealing way. The old state was 'heavy-handed', the ensuing reforms 'bold' and their results 'remarkable' and 'impressive'. Even the word 'reform', the use of which has been conceded by many critics of the post-1984 events, is heavily loaded: my *Concise Oxford* defines it baldly as *removal of abuses, esp. in politics*. A more accurate and neutral noun would be 'revolution': any fundamental change or reversal of conditions.

'Adjustment' problems — the wretched financial and property boom/bust of the 1980s and the wrenching recession of 1988–91 that destroyed one manufacturing job in three — are framed first as inevitable ('of course'), and then in a positive light as something to be 'worked through', which 'New Zealanders' did with 'impressive speed' (implying unanimous support). The judgements embodied in these epithets may or may not be accurate, but they are not (of course!) supported by any evidence in the text.

Much is made of the post-1991 recovery. Changes in GDP, employment and unemployment are maximised by dating them from the very trough of the recession, and, in different narratives, one will find them serving multiple duties to justify various policies — here ascribed to the Employments Contracts Act, there to the Reserve Bank Act, somewhere else to the slashing of welfare benefits. The current 'slowdown' (by now of four years' duration, with no end in sight) is actually turned to advantage by a brilliant rhetorical ploy: anything unsatisfactory about economic performance must be *because the reforms have not been taken far enough!* There is the obligatory sneer at the doubters, especially in academia, though this can backfire, since we (few) may thereby be emboldened to think that our opposition actually has an impact. But we are outnumbered by the 'great majority' of our countryfolk striding confidently off to join the magnificent brotherhood of 'modern, competitive' nations.

The second passage is at least as rhetorically loaded as its precursor. You'll be able to tease out the tricks. Note in particular one sly use of statistics — government expenditure 'doubled' — but over what period, and what about *per capita* expenditure?[3] At least the number referred to is 'real' — that is, corrected for changes due to inflation.

So let us move on to the economic substance underlying these two different points of view. The key is the common ground — nobody wants to claim Muldoon. Both passages refer to his 'excesses', and consign his regime to their unfavoured period — one to the past, the second to the present. To the pro-reformers, Muldoon's blunderings were just the culmination of decades of government meddling in the economy, preventing the natural state of affairs — laissez-faire, unregulated 'free' markets — from having its head.

My own view is rather different. I emphasise the social foundations of economic activity and the damage done by upheaving those foundations. In the years up to, say, the mid-1970s, New Zealand had many rules and regulations and considerable protection of the domestic economy from foreign competition. This provided a stable and secure framework within which the people — society — got on with the job of stitching together a serviceable set of economic arrangements. Though not always 'efficient' in the rationalist microeconomic sense (for example, cars were assembled locally more expensively than they could have been imported), this system was, as noted, remarkably effective at delivering high-wage jobs for everyone who wanted them,[4] and it was also — an important but little-known fact — very efficient in terms of what economists call 'transaction costs', which are all the costs of coordinating and controlling economic activity and market exchange.

Then along came Muldoon, followed eventually by Douglas and so on, with their massive disruptions of the received order. These were not only terribly wasteful in their own right — billions of dollars down the tubes forever from the mistakes of Think Big, from the over-hasty privatisations, from the share and property market boom and bust, from the great recession of 1988–91 — but also wasteful in an indirect sense, as they destroyed the guideposts, the focal points that facilitate the conduct of economic affairs. The symptoms of this are a substantial increase in transaction costs (see chapter 12) and the rise of apparently endemic unemployment.

Thus, from my perspective, Muldoon and the more-market revolutionaries who overthrew him can be lumped together as purveyors of disruptive shocks to the body economic. So-called deregulation is as much a state-sponsored intrusion in the economic lives of the citizens as are regulation and other direct interventions. However, the substance of those shocks is also material. Muldoon was scornfully anti-theory (though, of course, this is itself a theoretical stance), but the rationalists have been relentless in imposing their theory on us — microeconomic efficiency to be generated by rigorously self-seeking, opportunistic behaviour in markets. And it is in the inadequacies of that theory that we should look for the fundamental causes of what, after more than a decade, seems a persistent failure of the economy to perform as planned.

Perhaps opportunism is not so opportune after all. New learning in economics is finding that apparently irrational behaviour, such as cooperation with strangers (people we don't know), can in fact pay off in the long run for all parties. Were we better at cooperating with strangers, and at other economically productive strategies, under the conditions of the 1960s than those of the 1990s? Perhaps the clue to the discovery of the alternative path to economic rationalism is in our own recent history.

The next chapter digs into this history. There are some myths to root out. It isn't just a matter of whether the 'old' New Zealand was better than the 'new' (or vice versa). It is a question of understanding what the old New Zealand really was, and where it was going. There is a good piece of advice for anyone making comparisons. It is this: beware the counterfactual. Rationalists often talk as though the only alternative to their model was continuation of the blunderings of Muldoonism. This is foolish and unfair. When I claim that the revolution has been a failure I have in mind an alternative which, at the very least, continued the path of moderate reform that began well before Muldoon and was actually continued by him (e.g. Closer Economic Relations with Australia). We didn't need to turn the economy inside out in order to get a good meal in a restaurant or a decent latte. These and many other enhancements to the quality of our lives were coming anyway. The macroeconomic crisis inherited by the incoming Labour government in 1984 did not itself justify a massive upheaval of our microeconomic institutions — rather, the reverse.

Still, the revolution happened, and its consequences must now be lived with. What is really needed is some serious analysis about where we could go from here to reclaim sovereignty over our economic lives — as individuals, as communities and as a nation. If we do not learn from the mistakes of history we will be condemned forever to repeat them; but if we do take seriously the good and the bad of the past half-century then I do not doubt that we can make some genuine progress.

Chapter 2
The Albania of the South Pacific?

In September 1995 the Toronto *Globe & Mail* — Canada's national newspaper — ran a long feature story about New Zealand. Titled (rather feebly) 'Can the Kiwi fly?', it dealt at length with the events of the past decade, in which Canadians take a lively and perhaps nervous interest. Will they be next for the economic revolution?

I was in Canada when this article appeared, and a number of people asked me about it. They were particularly intrigued by a list of curiosities about the old New Zealand, under the heading 'Believe it or Not'. This had been assembled by the Canadian journalist Timothy Appleby, who had made a quick trip to this country. Here is Mr Appleby's list:

- It was illegal to drink alcohol in a restaurant or to manufacture carpets out of anything but wool.
- Buying margarine required a prescription from a doctor.
- It was against the law to truck goods commercially more than 40 miles without permission from the railways.
- A permit was needed to subscribe to an overseas journal.
- To invest abroad, a New Zealander had to renounce his citizenship.
- There was once a wildcat strike in a meat-freezing plant because the men's lunchtime French fries were burned.
- Union membership was compulsory for almost everyone, and contracts were binding on far-removed companies that had had nothing to do with negotiations.

Weird place, huh? But this list is mythical, in two important senses. The first is the matter of whether these anecdotes are 'true', either literally or in the sense of not being misleading. I will come back to that.

The second is connected with the running theme of the *Globe & Mail* article, and of many others like it, published abroad and in New Zealand. This is the notion that, in 1984 when Roger Douglas took over, the country was in a seriously stupid and disfunctional state which fully justified the radical measures introduced.

Why is this mythical? Because *every one* of the serious items on the list (that is, the ones which aren't mythical in the first sense) had been dealt with, or at least begun to be dealt with, before the fourth Labour government and Roger Douglas came to power. Margarine appeared in the consumer price index by the mid-1970s. Liberalisation of the importing and production of synthetic carpets began in the early 1980s with the tendering system for import licences. This was part of a sustained and well-paced programme of trade liberalisation that can be traced back to the 1969 National Development Conference, and of which the centrepiece was the Closer Economic Relations (CER) free-trade agreement with Australia, implemented in 1983.

As for drinking wine in restaurants, licensing began in the early 1960s. The excellent BYO custom goes back as far as I can remember, and remains the prime reason why mark-ups on restaurant wine lists are so reasonable in this country — a nice little example of how unexpected side-effects of policies can be beneficial.[1] In the important transportation and labour relations sectors, major legislation liberalising trucking and making unionism voluntary was introduced in 1983, by the Muldoon government, after years of preparatory work.

Finally, that wildcat strike over burnt chips — well, why not? Who knows what miseries of repeated bad cooking drove the men to finally make a fuss?

The other items are mischievously mythical in the first sense, i.e. of not containing much truth. The one about permits needed to subscribe to journals implies censorship and the 'thought police'. It is true that import licensing (largely abolished by

1984) covered books and journals, like just about everything else, but the key point is that the licenses for these crucial items were granted. Our libraries do not have great gaps in the runs of their foreign journals for the licensing period. Nor did private citizens miss out. As a boy in Dunedin I used to give some money to Frank Dubbo, the local newsagent, who would then pass it on to the distributors, Gordon & Gotch (or 'Grizzle & Grouch', as Mr Dubbo called them), who then would presumably apply for a licence or whatever, and in due course, once a month, my copy of *Road & Track* would turn up, mailed directly to me from California.

As for the one about having to renounce New Zealand citizenship to invest abroad: well, there were quite irksome rules and regulations limiting our access to overseas funds and of course these rules did not apply to the rest of the world — over whom we can hardly claim jurisdiction — but thousands of New Zealanders held shares on foreign stock exchanges.

There is a serious point behind all this. When we are evaluating the state of the country today — whether we are gung-ho for or agin the economic revolution — we have to have a counterfactual to compare it with. We have to establish what New Zealand would be like under the most reasonable alternatives to Rogernomics. What is utterly illegitimate is to compare New Zealand now with some semi-mythical stereotype of the nineteen-fifties. It is quite true that consumer goods and services (for those consumers with the income to buy them) have improved a lot. Shops, restaurants, wine, even beer are better in 1997 than they were, say, in 1984. But they were better in 1984 than in 1974, and better then than in 1964. *And they are better now in Canada and Britain than they were in those places in 1984 or earlier.*

Much of what has happened in New Zealand is not unique. The Anglo-Saxon countries in general were pretty grey places for a decade or so after the war, when austerity was the necessary order of the day. The 'swinging sixties' broke things open in England — in music, clothes, interior design, entertainment — and the colonies came to the party a little later. But come we did, and things have continued to improve ever since. The incoming regime in 1984 did inherit from the Muldoon administration something of an economic crisis, but it seems fairly clear now that Douglas and Treasury used this as an excuse to ram through their programme, not as its true *raison d'être*. The recent book and television series *Revolution* was stunningly revealing about this. Here is the then Minister of Finance, Roger Douglas, recalling events:

> It [the post-Muldoon crisis] was undoubtedly a great window of opportunity. It got the ball rolling and in a sense I made every endeavour to make sure the ball didn't stop rolling. I had the principle that it was much harder to shoot me down if I kept one pace ahead.[2]

As Marcia Russell puts it, 'Behind the scenes Roger Douglas had stolen the ball and was running with it.'[3]

So it is no longer credible, if it ever was, to claim the *force majeure* of Muldoonism as justification for the one hundred swingeing policy initiatives that came crashing down on us, and it is quite plausibly argued that the revolution actually made things more difficult. Muldoon left a legacy of massive public debt, due to his wilful and foolish spending initiatives: subsidies for farmers; over-generous superannuation; the disastrous 'Think Big' megaprojects. These mistakes needed to be corrected and debt paid down by prudent fiscal policy over a long time. But the spending side is only half the picture. Revenues matter, too. If you wake up one morning with the realisation that you have a substantial debt to pay off, you don't decide: 'Well, from now on I am only going to work four days a week' — you work *harder*.

Yet a four-day work week is, in essence, what New Zealand went on after 1986, with instability and deflation combining to induce the worst recession in our post-war history. One in three manufacturing jobs disappeared in about six years, and the tax base from which debt is repaid shrank accordingly. Even in 1996, at the end of a belated cyclical recovery, the number of full-time equivalent jobs only just surpassed its level of ten years before, when the population was more than 9 per cent smaller.[4]

New Zealand before the 1984 revolution was not a society in stasis. Here we need to confront the second myth that underpins the Canadian journalist's little list. This is the myth about what the old New Zealand really was. Were we, in the picturesque phrase, the 'Albania of the South Pacific' — a rigidly closed, regimented, non-market economy? This is certainly the impression given by the *Globe & Mail*'s list (and by the text of the accompanying article, in which we are referred to as having been an 'economic basket case') and by much of the local literature on the revolution, with its persistent rhetoric of referring to what happened as the 'reforms'.

When I was giving seminars about the New Zealand revolution to Canadian audiences, I was able to introduce the idea of querying the myth in a rather sneaky way. As it happens I lived in Canada for seventeen years, working as an agricultural economist for about half that time, and I know a lot of their little secrets. So, I would first show the slide of the *Globe & Mail* 'Believe it or Not' list. The audience would laugh and shake their heads. What a quaint place this Kiwiland must have been. But then I would put up another overhead: a Canadian 'Believe it or Not', no less. This was it:

- Most Canadians still have to buy their alcohol in sordid Soviet-style state-monopoly stores. And you want your wine chilled? Forget it!
- It was illegal in Canada to colour margarine yellow. And tens of thousands of Canadian dairy farmers are millionaires at the consumers' expense thanks to highly protectionist government-issued quotas.
- Prairie grain farmers were forced for more than sixty years to rail rather than truck their produce to market.
- It is illegal to patent a new variety of wheat in Canada. Only the government can do this.
- Canadian carpenters are not able to work in the town where they live if their trade certificate is issued in another province.
- It is illegal in Canada to display the actual (tax inclusive) price to be paid for any good or service, except on taxi meters and newspaper coin boxes.
- In Halifax, Nova Scotia, municipal workers staged a wildcat strike because the new snow shovels they were issued with set their teeth on edge when they scraped the sidewalk.

This list just about matches, topic for topic, the New Zealand list. Everything on it is 'true', except for the story about striking over snow shovels, which I made up. (Well, in the thousands of real-life labour disputes in Canada there is sure to have been one at least as silly as striking over burnt chips.) When I put the list up on the screen in my seminars the Canadians, who are good sports, would chuckle ruefully and sometimes contribute another item.

The point was taken. No one would think of calling Canada the 'Albania of North America', but it has its share of odd practices and seemingly strange regulations. An essentially anecdotal list that focuses on these is mythical, in that it presents a misleadingly skewed view of reality.

Yet we have been conditioned in New Zealand to accept the Albania myth about ourselves, by what amounts to a relentless string of misleading anecdotes. The myth has power because from a certain frame of reference it seems quite plausible. It is true that, for a quarter-century or so, New Zealanders had to operate in the context of an unusually (by the standards of other capitalist countries) large number of government regulations which appeared to 'protect' us from outside influences. And if your frame of reference or 'model' or world-view ascribes considerable importance (for good or ill) to government's role in the economy, then you might place great weight on all those rules and regulations, even to the point of letting pass an exaggeration like the 'Albania of the South Pacific'.

But you would be wrong. Unlike Albania (Communist or post-Communist), New Zealand had a well-established system of private-property rights adjudicated by a sophisticated and uncorrupt judiciary and administered by an undeniably honest and capable public service.[5] Most transactions were negotiated voluntarily between individuals. We were, in short, a capitalist market economy; one that seemed to function, by international standards, rather poorly in some dimensions (economic growth) but spectacularly well in others (full employment). We were a trading economy faced with an unfavourable market environment: a long-term decline in our terms of trade, coupled with short-term instability, which we were struggling to cope with by building up our manufacturing sector and diversifying our export markets.

What the revolution of 1984–91 did was rip apart the institutions and procedures that had been developed over the previous three decades, in the name of an extreme and simplistic ideology. Those revolutionaries who weren't in it primarily to feather their own nests were blinded by the 'Albania' myth to the reality of what they were tearing apart.[6] Their one hundred major policy changes amounted to qualitatively much more than a simple acceleration of the genuine reform process that had been making quiet progress since at least the 1960s. They were — in the true spirit of revolutionaries everywhere, from Marxists to Maoists to Muslim fundamentalists — a massive attempt to reshape the very personalities of their people: in our case, to turn us into sharp-as-a-tack, rigorously opportunistic, 'commercial' entities in place of our supposedly sleepy, unenterprising former selves.

Revolutions never go according to plan (because such grand but simplistic projects are always unworkable), and ours has been no exception. The challenge now is to take something positive from the experience; to use it to understand better what we were and what we could be. To underscore the need for re-evaluation, let us set the scene with some figures. We look at forty years of New Zealand's economic history, divided into two two-decade periods — 1956–76, called, as explained in chapter one, the 'years of external shocks'; and the 1976–96 period of the 'years of internal shocks'. The latter is the period when first Muldoon and then the Treasury/Douglas/Richardson/Business Roundtable cabal got stuck into our economy and society, literally wrenching it apart with ambitious schemes and destabilising projects. Table 1 shows what happened, summarised by annual averages or trends for some important economic variables. The first two rows set the external scene. In the first twenty-year period New Zealand's terms of trade (basically, the prices we get for our exports divided by the prices we have to pay for our imports) was trending down and was about twice as volatile as in the next twenty years, which have, on average, given us a nice recovery in the trend as well.

In the first period we suffered nasty surprises such as collapses in wool prices, loss of preferential access to the United

Kingdom market for our dairy products, and oil price hikes. These shocks forced a long and determined process of diversification of our exports — markets and products — that has paid off in a lower variability of the terms of trade: we have also, in the last twenty years, been quite lucky (or smart) in the prices we have received. The shocks in the latter period have been largely self-induced.

The next two rows summarise two of the most important macroeconomic indicators. The trade ratio measures the total value of trade (exports and imports) as a fraction of total gross domestic product (the total value of economic output produced in the country). It has increased somewhat, but is still not very high by international standards. Other countries of our population size have much larger trade ratios — Ireland's, for example, is over 70 per cent. The reason is that our awkward location makes trade quite expensive. International trade is vital to New Zealand, but we should not rely on it as our salvation — production within New Zealand for New Zealanders must be the backbone of our economy.

The size of government, in terms of the share it spends of the GDP, has actually risen. The old New Zealand was a welfare state, but it was what has been called a 'wage earners' welfare state'.[7] With every household having at least one person in a decent job, people were able to cope by themselves with many of the social problems that increasingly now fall upon the state welfare sector to deal with.

The comparison is rammed home most vividly with the next item on the table — the unemployment rate. This was virtually zero for all the first twenty years — an extraordinary achievement given the unfavourable external environment. Unemployment is, sadly, one variable in which our performance has become truly world-class — in the nasty recession of 1988–92 our unemployment rates actually exceeded the OECD average for the first time.

Economic growth in the first period did not seem very spectacular at the time, at about 2 per cent a year. This still is not impressive, but even less so is the paltry 1.05 per cent a year achieved on average since 1976, despite (or because of) the repeated doses of shock therapy administered to the economy

Table 1: The New Zealand economy, 1956–96

	The Years of External Shocks	The Years of Internal Shocks	
	1956–76	1976–96	
Trend in Terms of Trade	–0.6%	0.8%	annual percentage exponential trend in terms of trade index (export prices/import prices)
Standard Error of Terms of Trade	0.121	0.061	standard error of terms of trade exponential trend
Trade Ratio	0.20	0.23	average of exports and imports divided by GDP, annual average
Government Expenditure Ratio	0.31	0.38	government expenditure divided by GDP, annual average
Unemployment Rate	0.2%	6.9%	number of registered unemployed divided by total labour force, annual average
Economic Growth	2.0%	1.05%	average annual percentage rate of change of real per capita gross domestic product
Inflation	5.7%	9.1%	average annual percentage rate of change in consumer price index
Trend in Real Wages	1.4%	-1.6%	annual percentage exponential trend in real wages (nominal wage index/CPI)

Source: Dalziel and Lattimore, *The New Zealand Macroeconomy: A Briefing on the Reforms*, Melbourne, Oxford University Press, 1996, for 1960–95 data. Other years from Statistics New Zealand databases.

in attempts to jolt us into growing faster.[8] I actually think this obsession with economic growth is fundamentally misconceived, but more on that later.

Two more variables are needed to complete this setting of the scene. Since the war we have always had inflation. Over the fourteen years from 1974 to 1987 the consumer price index annual inflation rate increased by less than 10 per cent only once. Since 1992 inflation in New Zealand has been very low, as it has elsewhere in the world. These low rates are not unprecedented, though: the average for the first ten years, 1956–66 was 2.8 per cent

Finally, what is indeed the 'bottom line' for many families — the trend in real wages. This is a summary measure of workers' purchasing power — the level of actual (or 'nominal') wages divided by the consumer price index. The table shows that, whereas the first twenty years saw a slowish upward trend in real wages, this has been more than completely reversed since 1976. It is hard to take these rather disturbing figures at their face value. Perhaps the consumer price index really does fail to pick up many of the improvements in product variety and quality, as critics allege, though with little hard evidence. But unless there has been a marked deterioration in the reliability of the CPI — which is possible — it seems hard to avoid the conclusion that our first twenty-year period was better for wage and salary earners than the second.

All these numbers add up to a strong case for a fundamental re-evaluation of the New Zealand experience. The old New Zealand performed better than it should have, according to current orthodox wisdom; the new society has been a grave disappointment, whether one focuses on the last twenty or the last ten or so years. Could it be that wrenching our country off its path of gradual reform and piecemeal liberalisation, first with the authoritarian excesses of Muldoonism, then with the ideologically driven imposition of the rationalist revolution, was a mistake?

To answer this question we need to roll up our sleeves and dig down into the basics of what it means to live in a 'market' economy, which involves discarding a lot of myths about what markets don't mean. Chapter three initiates the analysis.

Chapter 3
Market Myths

Thirty years ago, in stage one economics at Otago, our professor explained why he believed markets worked better than central planning. He told us a story about Soviet Russia, where they used physical targets rather than the profit motive to allocate resources. There was a bolt factory, somewhere in the provinces. At first the factory's production target was set by the planners in Moscow in terms of quantities — so many million bolts per month. The plant managers were savvy enough to realise that the easiest way to meet this target was to produce very small bolts, and this they did — many more small bolts than were needed, and, of course, not enough medium- and larger-sized bolts. Frustrated, the central planners changed the target to tonnes — so many hundred tonnes of bolts per month. The managers' response was to switch production to making a small number of huge bolts, this being the easiest way of meeting a target based on total weight.

We laughed at this fable, and agreed that it most excellently demonstrated the superiority of capitalism over communism. The sovietologist Alec Nove tells a rather similar story which reveals that the failings of the Soviet system were not unknown to those at the top.[1] Party Secretary Nikita Krushchev, no less, would point to the enormous chandeliers perilously overhanging the tables in state banquet rooms, and explain that their ungainly and dangerous bulk was due to the chandelier factory's target being set in tonnes.[2]

One wonders how the Russians survived. But survive they did; even, for a while, flourish. While the capitalist economies were mired in their great slump, the Soviet Union grew through the decades of the 1920s and 1930s at a terrific rate. These twenty years 'belonged' to the USSR at least as much as the first two decades after the Second World War belonged to the USA, or the 1970s and 1980s were the era of economic triumph for Japan (and the 1980s and 1990s for China).

It seems apparent that Russian middle- and lower-level managers developed all sorts of stratagems to get their jobs done through the morass of central planning: informal networks with their peers in supplying and purchasing organisations; 'slush funds'; inaccurate reporting to their superiors; use of perks and other incentives to motivate their employees — in fact, all the tricks and ploys well known to their capitalist counterparts. Indeed it has been argued that the distressing failure of the Russian economy to cope with its new market system since 1990 may be because the sudden shock of its radical reforms swept aside the old informal networks without replacing them, and it was these networks (not central planning) that had been the real glue holding everything together. Could the disappointingly painful and slow response of the New Zealand economy to the radical changes imposed on it have similar symptoms?

In any case, it is clear that the ideologues' convenient dichotomy between 'centrally planned' and 'market' systems is woefully simplistic, because it focuses on who owns and controls the physical and financial capital in the economy while neglecting the important social capital (the trust and forbearance built in to informal relationships), which is 'owned' neither privately or publicly, in the conventional sense.

That said, there is still a big difference between bolt factories in market and planned economies. Whereas the latter operates within the terms of some clumsy and possibly absurd physical production quota, the market firm is subject to the constraint of commercial viability — to make a profit, which means choosing your bolts carefully so that the revenue they bring in exceeds the costs of producing them.

The profit motive is a marvellous force for ensuring that the shelves in the hardware store are stocked with bolts in the shapes and sizes we want, and for dealing with thousands of similarly mundane but vital matters involving the allocation of society's scarce resources. But it ain't quite that simple. Markets are worldly, human institutions, imperfect and not perfectible.

Even the make-a-profit constraint, which sounds so sensible, depends crucially on the prices at which costs and revenues and thus profits are calculated being the right prices. Market prices reflect only the private valuations of buyer and seller. When there are 'externalities' — other people affected who are not involved in the transaction — such prices will not necessarily result in the best outcome. Externalities matter in many important areas: health, education, natural-resource use, the environment, consumption of alcohol and other drugs, as well as anywhere (which may be just about everywhere) that social capital is at stake.

The purity of the supply/demand story is also sullied when the parties don't have all the information needed to make good decisions. When production follows price with a time lag, markets can generate wasteful 'cobweb' cycles of over and under supply. A high price now induces too much production, which eventually results in a glut and a collapse in price, which then drastically discourages supply, which in turn leads to shortages and a too-high price, and so on. The market traces a cobweb-like pattern around the supply-and-demand curves, never homing in on the equilibrium where the curves meet.

Asset markets are particularly prone to massive price instability as their 'true' value is determined by their future earnings, which of course are impossible to predict with certainty. One of the most startling numbers I have ever seen was in 1991, at the peak of the Tokyo boom, when the land around the Emperor's Palace — about three quarters of a square mile of unused real estate — was worth about as much as *all* the land in Canada or in California![3]

A true market devotee might say well, so be it, that must be what the land is really worth. But it isn't; not now. The bubble burst, creating, as part of a trillion dollars of bad debt, the 'world's poorest man' — a doctor who lived out every doctor's dream of becoming a property speculator, and ended up with a net worth of *minus* $1.8 billion.[4] This fellow lived on in luxury, owing so much that it was quite impracticable for his creditors to foreclose. A story like this adds a few zeros to Keynes' old maxim: 'If you owe your bank a thousand pounds, you are in trouble; but if you owe it a million pounds, your bank is in trouble.'

An almost equally startling and disturbing number in the other direction is that, at the level of privatisation vouchers as of November 1993, the whole of Russian industry — the entire productive capacity of one of the largest economies in the world — was valued at about the same sum then being offered for the Hollywood studio Paramount Pictures.[5]

These crazy 'market prices' are a worry not just for Japanese and Russians, but for all of us, since they distort prices and investment decisions made for other assets, including foreign investment in little countries like New Zealand. They call seriously into question the doctrine that absolute openness to international capital flows is necessarily the best thing for a small economy.

In a mature capitalist economy — at least of the Anglo-Saxon variety — the stock market is where most assets are bought and sold. Is this reassuring? The blind greed that fuelled New Zealand's share-market boom in the mid-1980s floated dozens of new ventures. Few of these companies remain listed on the market, and the principals of some of the failures have been jailed as fraudsters. After the Great Crash of October 1987 57 per cent was wiped off the 'value' of New Zealand-quoted companies in four months[6], and the property market collapsed as well, leaving still-enduring scars in downtown Auckland's empty sites and parking lots, where fine old buildings once stood. I don't know what we can do to prevent these vicious boom and bust cycles, but at the least they should inject some healthy scepticism into our analysis of the market-knows-best thesis.

Even for mundane consumer goods it is rare to find the sharp-as-a-tack pricing assumed in the supply/demand market model. One of the best-known market puzzles is the enduring discrepancies in the prices of new automobiles in Europe. Despite the fact that for many Europeans (who tend to rent their housing) a new car is the biggest purchase they will make, and so worth the effort to get the best deal; despite the fact that cars are highly portable, and so susceptible to arbitrage (unlike, say, services or groceries); and despite the absence of tariffs or other border barriers within the European community, there are substantial and persistent price differentials across national markets. The locations of the best and worst deals do seem to change: once the most expensive market was the United Kingdom and the cheapest Belgium; now Germany and Italy have the highest and lowest prices, in most cases. For seven popular models sold in all of six countries surveyed recently, the difference between high and low tax-free manufacturers' recommended prices was as much as 43 per cent (for a Rover 214), and not less than 20 per cent (for a BMW 316i).[7]

Consumer groups and some economists get quite cross about these discrepancies. Why aren't they arbitraged away? What is 'wrong' with the market? But no one seems to be able to do anything about them. Perhaps they should just be accepted as further evidence that there is a lot more to market transactions than price; and that for both consumers and producers historical, cultural, social and economic factors all matter to their market behaviour, so that even in an unusually free and competitive market situation outcomes can differ significantly across countries. The single, unique market is almost always a myth. Even with open borders, prices of new cars and of thousands of other goods and services show substantial variations from one place to another.

Prices can be distorted by market power. When one or two big firms dominate an industry they can push up prices charged to their customers and push down prices they pay their suppliers. The resulting profits don't necessarily signal efficient use of resources but rather unequal distribution of power. Many New Zealand industries are now dominated by just one or two firms.

The source and disposition of oligopoly ('few sellers') profits are serious political and economic issues, not solved by laissez-faire. This has concerned the most influential prophet of 'free' markets, Milton Friedman, who once called 'fundamentally subversive' the notion that business has a social responsibility (to other 'stakeholders', as we would now say) other than to maximise the returns to its shareholders.

What is most interesting about this statement is that it needed to be said at all. If Friedman's ideal world of perfectly competitive market capitalism were true in reality, then there would be no excess profits for stakeholders to squabble over. Competition would ensure that each firm, large or small, earned no more than it needed to remain in business and renew its capital stock. The pursuit of individual self-interest — private profit — unequivocally serves the public good only when private agents have no market power, so that the only sources for increased profits are useful activities like improving the product or producing it more efficiently. But the managers of large oligopolistic corporations have additional choices, including manipulating the market (through, for example, tacit pricing agreements with their supposed competitors and predatory behaviour to keep out new firms), and manipulating what goes on inside their firm (including their own remuneration schemes). There is no presumption, in economic theory or fact, that the invisible hand of free markets will benignly guide these self-interested managers to act in the overall interest.

This is not an argument for central planning, but a plea for recognition of the pervasiveness of what John Kenneth Galbraith and others have called private planning — a national and global system of large corporations with some discretionary power that they use to plan and control their market environment.

In big bureaucratic firms there is plenty of room in this process for plans to go awry. The type of person who succeeds in struggling to the top of a private-sector bureaucracy may well be motivated by self-interest (personal ambition and greed, if you will) to an unusual extent, but aligning that interest with the wider social interest — or even just the interests of the shareholders — remains a major problem of corporate governance. Many business decisions, especially the really big ones involving the purchase of other large businesses, seem to have been motivated not by the rational pursuit of reasonable profit but by hubris, egotism, megalomania or just fantastic whimsy: the boys must have their toys to play with, and the bigger the better.

Spectacular recent examples are in the entertainment business, where star-struck CEOs compete to see who can spend the most money taking over a movie studio or television network. Time and Warner Brothers merged for $US15 billion, and are still struggling under a $US19 billion debt load. In 1995 Disney took over the ABC network, for $US19 billion. Disney chairman Michael Eisner burbled about 'reflecting what this country stands for' and 'synergies under every rock'. Sometime songwriter Edgar Bronfman, bored with running Seagram — the family liquor business — had them spend $US5.7 billion to buy 80 per cent of Universal Pictures. An analyst summarised what was happening as a 'nervous frenzy'. Japanese firms' attempts to buy into glamorous US entertainment businesses (such as Sony's takeover of MGM) and other property and financial investments have resulted in losses of more than $US320 billion between 1986 and 1993.[8]

Huge mistakes can be made within business bureaucracies. A story in the *Economist* (November 1995) put the value of the mistakes made by General Motors in its attempts to counter the threat from Japanese imports — basically, investments that did not pay off — at about $US50 *billion*. It is easy to get 'zeros-shock' at the size of these numbers. To put them in perspective: the geniuses at General Motors lost as much as is produced in one year by the entire population of New Zealand — about one year's GNP.[9]

New Zealand has produced its own list of value-subtracting enterprises, even in addition to the Equiticorp and other monsters of the share-market boom. Brierley Investments Ltd spent too much money on acquiring a large British hotel chain, Mount Charlotte, and compounded the mistake by pumping managerial resources that might better be occupied with other projects into the hotels in the hope that they could eventually be sold again at a price that saves face. The chief executive responsible for this mistake, Paul Collins, was given a $4.75 million hand-out so that he wouldn't feel too upset when he was finally relieved of his position. What sort of market incentive is this supposed to be? It makes me sick.

In the 1980s diversification was all the rage, and companies leveraged themselves to the hilt to assemble conglomerates of unrelated businesses. Now, in the 1990s, the herd is stampeding back whence they came, stripping down to 'core' businesses, 'sticking to the knitting'. Perhaps even as I write some new nostrum is sweeping through the boardrooms. This susceptibility to fads really does not instil any confidence that the principles of sound business management have been discovered and learnt.

Of course, any adage to the effect that 'power stuffs up' cannot be confined to the private sector. The New Zealand economy has suffered terribly from hubris and hastiness in its public-sector decision making, especially when government has messed in the market. The early 1980s gave us the Muldoon/Birch 'Think Big' megaprojects — macro- and microeconomic disasters estimated to have cost us a staggering $7 billion[10] — which bring to mind the Canadian economist Sylvia Ostry's line: 'governments aren't very good at picking winners, but losers sure are good at picking governments'. Then came the Douglas/Prebble dogma-driven privatisations of the late 1980s, which saw valuable national resources such as our forests tossed over to the private sector at prices which, then and now, seem billions of dollars too low, despite the $120 million that Treasury spent on consultancy advice.

So what have we learnt from all this? What is the best way to run a bolt factory — which is where the plan-versus-market debate started in this chapter? We can probably agree that private planning guided by the profit motive beats central planning on this one. But it isn't as simple as all that, and extrapolation from stories about the nuts and bolts of the economy to prescribing 'more market' as the solution to every problem is dangerously simplistic. Planning, at all levels, is an integral part of economic life, and if we are to make intelligent use of market forces, we need to develop a fair degree of sophistication — even scepticism — about just how far and how effectively market forces can extend. This is particularly true of international trade, to which we turn in the next chapter.

Chapter 4
The Great Free-Trade Con

You are at home, preparing dinner for your family, when there is a loud knocking on your front door. Wiping your hands on your apron, you go to open it. Two big fellows in dark blue suits barge in, sniffing the air.

'We smell cookin'!' says one of them, in an American accent. 'Where is that?'

Without waiting for an answer they head for the kitchen, where your casserole is simmering succulently on the stove.

'So what's going on here, fella?' they demand.

'I'm just cooking my family's dinner,' you answer, weakly.

'*Just* cooking dinner!' they exclaim, exchanging significant looks. Business cards are proffered, which reveal one of the Americans to be the President of the Ete-2-Xcess international restaurant chain, and the other his attorney.

The attorney takes over:

'My client wants to know why he wasn't given an opportunity to bid on this job. All we ask is for a level playing field; transparency in regulations; free competition. My client has a restaurant in your neighbourhood offering a full range of family dishes at competitive prices. We believe that my client can supply cost-efficient nutritional services to your family. Unless, of course, you are *competing unfairly*,' he adds, peering around the kitchen suspiciously. 'How much rent do you pay on this joint?'

'I own this house. I don't pay any rent,' you admit.

'Definite case of unfair, subsidised competition,' says the attorney, making notes. 'And who does the dishes?'

'My children do, when I can catch them.'

'So how much do you pay them?' the attorney wants to know.

'We don't pay the children to do chores in this household,'

you reply, by now getting somewhat cross. 'We consider it their family duty.'

'Duty-schmooty!' scoffs the American. 'It's a clear case of exploiting child labour. Even we pay more than that. This is seriously unfair competition and the US government may be forced to retaliate with a Section 301 countervail on your pathetic kiwifruit exports to our great country. You will be hearing from us unless you provide my client with a fully specified Request-For-Tender to supply comprehensive cooked food services to your family by the end of the week. Good day to you, Sir!'

A silly scenario? Perhaps, but writ large it is an accurate parable of the world trading system, with its pervasive but dodgy rhetoric of 'free' trade, 'level' playing fields and 'contestable' markets. It *is* a system clumsily manipulated by the United States government in the interests of its multinational corporations, with others hanging on to Uncle Sam's coat-tails, none more keenly than little New Zealand. We, the nation that boldly and successfully stood up to the Americans on the issue of nuclear warships, have been complete and willing patsies on the trade front.

The myths and distortions woven into international commercial policy would take at least a book to unravel[1], but here we can at least make a start. We need to deconstruct the banal but powerful metaphor of the level playing field that dominates the discourse on international trade policy. The Americans say: 'All we want is a level playing field for everyone to compete equally on. What could be fairer than that?'

'Well, what if we don't want to play?'

'You must play; it's the law!' (You can't cook your own meals.)

'Well, what game will we play? What rules?'

'American rules, of course. What a silly question!' (Our attorneys will prepare the contract.)

'Who will be the referee?'

'Don't worry, we'll find someone suitable.'

And they will, and do. Good examples of these attitudes in action are always being thrown up in the disputes between the two economic superpowers, Japan and the United States. The Japanese understand the Americans, and don't like what they see. The Americans just don't understand. Take automobiles. After a few false starts, Honda and Toyota and the others worked out what it took to sell cars in the US market and did it, with enormous success. In contrast, US manufacturers have never been able to export more than a trickle of their cars to Japan. The reasons are simple: American cars are too big for Japanese conditions and their steering wheels are on the wrong side. You would think that they might have figured this out and at least sent over some right-hand drive vehicles. But they didn't. Instead *Ford and Chrysler seriously demanded that the Japanese change (in Japan!) to left-hand drive, thereby removing what they claimed was an unfair trade practice, deliberately discriminating against American-made cars.* The gall of this is almost sublime. President Bush himself led a delegation of American auto executives to Japan to demand better 'access' — a misconceived venture that ended in humiliation when the president vomited at an official banquet.

More recently, the United States government and auto industry have been getting vexed about the difficulties they are having in bidding successfully on supplying new parts to the Japanese car companies. Their 'keiretsu' system of strong but unwritten long-term linkages between suppliers and purchasers is claimed to be difficult for foreigners to break into. The playing field is not level; the market not fully 'contestable'. And nor is it. But whose fault is that? The American system relies on two quite different methods for mediating transactions between buyers and sellers: they either use short-term written contracts negotiated by lawyers, or they internalise the whole transaction by vertically integrating. Japanese don't like the first system (they don't want to have half a million lawyers, like the United States), and they don't need to resort so much to vertical integration because they are so good at managing informal relationships based on trust and mutual forbearance between firms.

The result is that whereas Toyota produces in-house just 25 per cent of the value of a car bearing its name and purchases, with the other 75 per cent coming from outside suppliers, for General Motors the ratios are reversed: 75 per cent in-house; 25 per cent bought on the market.[2] Just consider what this means: most of the Toyota parts-buying transactions judged insufficiently contestable by the Americans are, back home in Detroit, *completely incontestable*, because they are carried out within the firm. But does Toyota demand that GM divest itself of, say, its huge Fisher Autobody Division, to give Toyota a chance to bid on building Chevrolet bodies? No, it wouldn't waste its time. But, really . . . .

The list of aggressive trade practices at which the United States is undisputed world leader is lengthy: unilateral retaliation (through their notorious 'Section 301'), extra-territoriality (punishing foreign companies for 'violating' United States sanctions on third countries), obstructive use of private anti-dumping suits (used more than in all the rest of the world put together), simple failure to obey edicts from the World Court and other international organisations.[3] This is the truly lopsided international playing field on which New Zealand is so keen to play: *'Pick me for your team, sir, please!'*

Now the moral of all this is not that the Ugly Americans should somehow be made to behave. Other countries have what could be called 'barriers' to free trade as well. The key point is that they are *different* barriers, reflecting real and important differences in social and cultural structures across countries. The Americans' special sin is that, being bigger and stronger than everyone else, they want to impose their way on everyone else, hardly understanding that anyone who isn't a knave or a fool could have a problem with that.

We don't want the Americans to be beaten, we want them to back off. The Japanese don't want to lose their keiretsu system; the Americans don't want to lose their half a million lawyers. We in New Zealand should think seriously about what we don't want to lose, too.

There are clear signs that the global *Pax Americana* has been pushed further than other countries are comfortable with. These signs are seen not just in the new, contentious extensions to the 'level' playing field — to intellectual property, to access to resources, to cultural activities, to multinational investment — but even in the traditional mainstream business of reductions in import tariffs. Nations emerged from the Second World War with very high tariffs — the legacy of a desperate and unsuccessful round of 'beggar-thy-neighbour' protectionism in response to the pre-war Great Depression. Maynard Keynes taught treasuries and central banks how to avoid another worldwide slump, and thus set the stage for multilateral tariff-cutting negotiations — the successive rounds of the GATT (General Agreement on Tariffs and Trade).

For about three decades this liberalisation process went pretty well, as tariffs were cut from 30 per cent or more to around 10 per cent by the 1980s. But the most recent push towards zero tariffs has induced a flurry of compensatory non-tariff barriers. The free traders get very huffed and puffed about these, but perhaps they should pay more respect to the real and possibly legitimate forces that might underlie resistance to fully open markets.

The strength of these deep-seated domestic preferences has been vividly — even spectacularly — demonstrated in some recent research by a Canadian economist, John McCallum.[4] McCallum uses what is known as a 'gravity model' to explain the sizes of trade flows between regions. This model is borrowed from the physical theory of the gravitational attraction between two bodies being directly proportional to their masses and inversely proportional to their distance from each other. In the trade version, mass is proxied by GNP, and distance is distance.

The model works well statistically — embarrassingly well, since it makes no use of conventional economic concepts such as relative prices and comparative advantage. John McCallum gets the model to work even better by allowing for an additional factor — the preference people have for dealing with other people like them. For example: the Canadian province of British Columbia and the US state of Washington are of about the same economic mass (GNP) and are about the same distance from the Canadian province of Ontario. But trade between Ontario and BC is about *twenty times* larger than trade between Ontario and Washington. The difference is particularly striking because the two countries are integrated to a greater extent than just about any other country pair: they have the longest joint border; their bilateral trade flows are the largest of any in the world; there have been virtually no tariffs between them since the Canada-United States free-trade agreement of 1988, and their similarities in language, culture and so on are marked.

What John McCallum's results demonstrate so vividly is the height of the 'invisible barriers' between nations; barriers which when converted into 'tariff equivalents' are rather larger than the customs duties so assiduously bargained away under the various rounds of the GATT.

What should we do about this? The free traders' gut response is to go for 'deep integration' and attempt to bulldoze away the remaining non-tariff barriers to a 'free' globalised economy. But can you bulldoze something that is invisible? Should we try? It all depends on the source of the invisible barriers. If they are just dirty tricks and sly stratagems played by protectionist governments at the behest of vested interest groups in their electorates, then, yes, there is a case for further liberalisation through international treaties and the like.

But what if — as indeed the scale of the McCallum numbers in the already highly liberalised Canada/United States setting, and the success in general of the gravity trade model, strongly suggest — national preference is the manifestation of deeper and more serious forces: the greater empathy and trust people feel in dealing with others of their own tribe? This is not just a matter of sentiment — though sentiment is legitimately important — but also of efficiency: the *transaction costs* of dealing with people whose motivations and cultures are similar to your own may be significantly smaller. Tracking the movement of goods across national borders gives us a rare opportunity to spot these transaction costs in action: it is startling how huge they are. More on this in chapter 12.

Now surely there is more to be said in favour of free trade than I have let on here. Doesn't economic theory strongly support it? Well, it would like to. In the conventional model tariffs are 'distortions', the removal of which will, in theory, improve overall efficiency. But by how much? This is what Paul Krugman calls economists' 'dirty little secret': the theoretical gains are really embarrassingly small. For example, the elimination of a 10 per cent tariff yields an improvement of about half of one per cent (of the value of the trade).[5]

Some economists have searched for something more to show for their faith in trade liberalisation. There is a lively but unresolved debate about the extent and meaning of a correlation between economic growth and the degree of 'openness' of an economy. A well-publicised recent paper by the Harvard economists Jeffrey Sachs and Andrew Warner shows, for an impressive cross-section of 117 countries, what appears to be a strong correlation between openness and growth.[6] But there are fundamental problems with these correlations, stemming from the basic problem of inferring causation from correlation when there are other determining factors at work, and when these other factors differ in important ways between countries (a key point of this book).

For example, one end of the spectrum is littered with hopeless basket-case economies (African and Latin American) which so mismanage their political, economic and social affairs that not only do they show poor growth performance, but they are incapable of dealing with the rest of the world with any degree of openness. There really isn't much a country like ours can learn from Zaire or Nigeria.

At the high-performance end, Sachs and Warner show unscientific signs of knowing what answers they want to get. Korea — a definite star in the growth stakes for their data period — is classified as open, whereas others would see it as a striking example of successful application of protectionist principles.[7] There is no weighting of the data for country size, but it is a fact that most of the billion or so people who have experienced high economic growth over the past fifteen years live in the People's Republic of China — then and still a communist country![8]

Even if we restrict ourselves to the smaller economies in the sample it is tricky drawing inferences that are relevant to New Zealand. Singapore and Hong Kong, the two geographically tiny 'super-trading' economies (with trade shares larger than 100 per cent of GNP), are really just life-support systems for strategically placed free ports. Nothing for us there. Ireland is in many ways similar to New Zealand (same population, language, etc). It has a high trade share (more than 70 per cent of GNP) and has recently grown quite quickly. But it is a dubious model for long-term development. The Irish have basically taken advantage of their membership in the European Union to turn themselves into 're-exporting' specialists — using favourable tax and wage rates to encourage multinational firms to import semi-finished goods from other Union countries, add a small amount of value to them, and send the result back into the European market. This sort of strategy (which has also been followed by Malaysia) has resulted in 'de-coupling' of the labour market (so that unemployment in Ireland is above 10 per cent), and is in any case hardly available to New Zealand given our South Pacific isolation.

So we should be sceptical of crude 'free trade' recipes for economic success, especially when there is a strong American flavour to the ingredients. But this does not imply retreating to some isolationist opposite. The family in the story that began this chapter should be able to eat their home-cooked casserole in peace. But they would be dull dogs if they ate at home every night. Most families enjoy 'importing' meals on occasions — if not from Ete-2-Xcess then from McDonalds or the local fish-and-chip shop, if they still have one, or getting Chinese take-aways or a pizza. And many families 'export' to others — someone from the household may work as a chef or a waiter. It's a question of getting the right balance between home production and trade. Families can easily sort this out for themselves, but it needs a bit more thought at the level of the nation. Imports may be the spice of life, but they aren't the meat and potatoes of a healthy national diet. Close study of modern international trade reveals how different nations are, and how much that matters. These differences should be taken seriously, not suppressed in the name of a simplistic ideology that serves interests that are not ours.

Chapter 5

The Tyranny of TINA at the End of History

In 1989 a Japanese/American Rand Corporation analyst named Francis Fukuyama proclaimed the 'End of History'.[1] What he meant was that the great modern struggle between socialism and capitalism had finally ended with the fall of the Berlin Wall and the impending collapse of the Eastern European communist regimes: the Western market model had triumphed and that was that. No more 'history', meaning no more ongoing conflict between regimes and ideologies.

It was as though history — since the French Revolution, at least — was a giant tug of war between the teams of the left and the right. The outcome of this battle had only very recently seemed clear. In our century the triumph of the Bolsheviks in the 1917 Revolution in Russia had added a powerful new player to the socialist side, and with the debilitation of the capitalist countries through the futile slaughter of the 1914–18 'capitalists' war' and the worldwide depressions of the 1920s and 1930s, it seemed to many that history in the modern age was leaning to the left. For decades after the Second World War, most of the world's people lived under communist (China, USSR, Eastern Europe) or socialist (India and many other developing countries) systems. But the East fell behind the West, and the 'South' — the very poor countries — stagnated under central planning. The right began to regain ground, and then, with the catastrophic suddenness of a tug-of-war, the left side collapsed, leaving the market-forces team triumphant, if in a dishevelled heap (it really has taken quite a time for the victory in Eastern Europe to be consolidated).

New Zealand reached the End of History ahead of everybody else, in a remarkable late run from well back in the pack. Using the excesses of the last Muldoon administration as cover, and with TINA ('There Is No Alternative') as their figurehead, our 'reformers' — Finance Minister Roger Douglas, with Treasury pushing him, the Big Business Roundtable pulling him, and his Prime Minister not paying much attention — rammed through their hundred and one major policy changes, which left this country more thoroughly globalised, homogenised and internationally user-friendly than any other.

This chapter focuses on the intellectual foundations of New Zealand's revolution. This is a matter conceivably of more interest to the professional economist than to the general reader, and I won't be offended if you jump ahead to the punchline of the chapter.

The theoretical underpinnings of the End of History are strictly economic: specifically, the modernist 'neoclassical' economics which, in my lifetime (since the publication in 1947 of Paul Samuelson's great treatise *Foundations of Economic Analysis*) has virtually conquered the mainstream of economic theory and practice. Modernism, in economics as in literature and other fields, focuses on the individual, alone in their universe, and universal in the narrowness of their self-obsession: the rational self-seeking opportunistic optimising economic agent, in our jargon.

This doctrine is essential to the End of History. It provides a theoretical structure — stamped with all the authority of mathematics — in an attempt to prove the superiority of market over socialist systems. And it offers practical rules of implementation — basically, tough macroeconomic policies (on inflation and government budgets) along with laid-back or 'liberal' microeconomic attitudes to behaviour in markets, which have been codified in what the economist John Williamson has dubbed 'The Washington Consensus' — a set of precepts for orthodoxy reflecting the views of the United States government and the Washington-based United States satellite institutions such as the World Bank and International Monetary Fund.[2]

The universality of neoclassical economics is crucial to its general applicability: one size fits all situations and societies and stages of development. It is hard to conceive of a less 'social' social science than modern economics; nor one more reductionist of human nature and experience than a theory in which people in all times and places differ only in matters such as whether they prefer pink to blue toothbrushes.

Even quite recently in its history, economics as a discipline encompassed schools of thought that reflected particular historical and geographical concerns: the Canadian 'Staples' model of development based on natural resources; the British Free Traders; the American Institutionalists struggling to understand the great new corporations being created in their country. But now the very thought of such regional qualifiers would be laughable to the well-trained economist. There is just good economics ('rigorous', meaning based on the mathematical implications of individual optimisation) and bad economics (everything else).

Good economics is by now a thoroughly Americanised enterprise. It is defined by, and disseminated from, the top twenty university departments in the United States, through publications in academic journals and teaching in their PhD programmes. The brightest students from all over the world are sent, almost without exception, to these top departments, or to one of a very few international clones of them, such as the London School of Economics. A quite open ranking of departments, set by numbers of publications and citation counts in the best journals,[3] determines, and thus is in turn determined by, where the newly minted PhDs get jobs. Only the very best or very worst schools will hire their own graduates, but departments line up in a strict pecking order with the top ten recruiting only each other's best students, the others going to the next tier, and so on. The clearing house for matching supply and demand is a vast travelling 'job market', which sets up in hundreds of hotel rooms and suites early every January at the meetings of the American Economic Association. The *lingua franca* of these job interviews is always the same: orthodox neoclassical economics as ordained by the Big Ten.

I once noted the academic qualifications of members of the three best Canadian economics departments — Queen's, Western Ontario and the University of British Columbia, which would rank somewhere in the middle of the top fifty worldwide. There happened to be one hundred assistant, associate and full professors, nearly all of them men. Most had American PhDs. *Not one* had a PhD from a Canadian department other than Queen's, Western or UBC themselves, even though some of the professors had qualifications from second-rate United States schools or even (in the case of a couple of senior profs) no PhD at all. Earning a doctorate in economics from a lesser Canadian university is a positive handicap, a complete waste of four years of your life, if you aspire to a decent university job within North America. This situation would be almost inconceivable in another social science such as political studies, where rival schools of thought coexist (not always happily), and where having some local training is regarded as an advantage, not as a sure signal that someone was not bright enough to get into MIT or Princeton.

In New Zealand academic economics things are somewhat different. We have a wider mix of qualifications — European, British, Canadian and American. We still sometimes hire our own PhDs, something I am North American enough to regard as rather unprofessional. We still have a number of middle-ranking lecturers without doctorates — many of them very useful academic citizens indeed — though we no longer hire such people at entry level. There is some pressure to latch onto third-rate neoclassical theorists (all we can usually get, since the good ones are snapped up in North America), rather than go for the best people we can attract, no matter what their field of interest, which I think a more sensible strategy for New Zealand. We do encourage, for their own good, our smartest masters graduates to enrol if they can in a top-ten graduate school in the United States, though if this is not an option, I for one recommend the more humane atmosphere of a decent Canadian campus, such as Queen's, UBC or Toronto, over its academic equivalents in the States.

As a result of our reasonably eclectic approach, economics departments in New Zealand universities generate a diversity of points of view from a range of academic backgrounds — something that infuriates the Big Business Roundtable but which should be moderately reassuring to just about everybody else. But the academics do not make economic policy in this country; and, in particular, we were not responsible for

Rogernomics and the New Zealand economic revolution. Perhaps some of us should have put up more of a fight against it. There is a meekness and mildness about New Zealand academic economists, which is not to our credit.

In any case, the blueprints for the revolution were largely imported: embodied in the overseas training of Treasury officials, and in a procession — which continues today — of expensive (though usually undistinguished) American and British consultants and speechifiers, paid for by Treasury and the Business Roundtable to goad us into further excesses.

The substance of the blueprints — 'free market' economics — will be dealt with in the second part of this book, where the powerful but narrow insights of neoclassical economics will be placed in a broader and more realistic theory of society and the economy. New learning in economics is giving the lie to the crude nostrums of neoclassicism.

Perhaps I should make my own position clear. While I am a critic of orthodox neoclassical 'American' economic theory, I believe that economists and economics have a useful role to play in the decent society. I also have great respect for the energy, intellect and creativity of most of the very top (mostly American) economists. *These men and women do not themselves espouse a narrow neoclassicism!* Ahead of that game, they are deeply interested in how the world actually works.

The most prestigious prize in economics (apart from the Nobel itself) is the John Bates Clark Award, made only every two years to an economist under the age of forty working in America.[4] The last four winners were David Kreps, Paul Krugman, Laurence Summers and David Card — three Americans and a Canadian. These four are true *wunderkinder*. Kreps is quietly fomenting a 'revolution' in economics, querying the fundamental axioms of 'greed, rationality and equilibrium.'[5] Krugman — whom we met in chapter 4 — is a marvellously insightful and iconoclastic analyst of world trade. Summers, when still a student, collaborated in a study which fundamentally changed how we look at unemployment. Card is subverting the old dogma on minimum wages.

Though thoroughly trained and adept in orthodox theory, none of these economists, nor others on the cutting edge of the discipline, are hidebound neoclassicists. The new learning they are developing underpins most of the ideas in this book. But this is not what gets taught in the graduate school — yet. It takes time for new ideas to percolate through to the mainstream, and it behoves all of us to be properly conservative in what we press upon the impressionable minds of young grad students. Certainly, the economics learnt by Roger Douglas's Treasury advisers in their stints at US business schools and economics departments in the late 1970s and early 1980s would have had a strong neoclassical bias — the strongly anti-Keynesian, pro-laissez-faire Chicago School was then in ascendancy. But this now seems narrow, quirky stuff, that has notoriously failed empirical testing. Maynard Keynes' famous quip about practical men being the slaves of some defunct economist, of 'madmen in authority . . . distilling their frenzy from some academic scribbler of a few years back',[6] is so sadly true of New Zealand.

Reports of the End of History have been much exaggerated. The Washington Consensus is already crumbling, if it ever really existed.[7] What was to have been its crowning glory — the Multilateral Agreement on Investment — has been stalled, perhaps stopped, by a remarkable international grassroots campaign disseminated through the Internet. Nations do differ persistently in their paths to economic success and it is inevitable that they should. The End of History is a myth.

True, it is a powerful myth, because it is vastly convenient to the most powerful economic interests in our lives: to those who want the world (and our little piece of it) to be a safer place for the great multinationals to roam. But globalisation is a political force in the service of the *Pax Americana*, not an inexorable consequence of the laws of economics. Very interestingly, the End of History idea has been in effect abandoned by one of its leading intellectual architects — Francis Fukuyama — who has since produced an extraordinary book on the importance of social and cultural factors to economic performance, *and just how much those factors differ across nations*: the very opposite of the we-are-all-becoming-Americans message of the End of History.

There is a danger here. Rejecting one myth carries the risk of exposing us to another; one to which well-meaning politicians are particularly susceptible: that the rest of the world is a wonderful source of free 'lessons' we can learn; of easily transplantable fix-its for perceived domestic problems. If only we trained our young people like the Germans do, or our unemployed like the Swedes, or did as much R&D as the Americans, or guided industries like the Japanese, or saved as much as the Singaporeans, or subsidised exporting like the Koreans. If only we were *like them.*

But what if there are *reasons* why some countries do one thing and others another? In one sense exploding the myth of the End of History does not necessarily spell the end of TINA, for there may indeed be, in the long run, no alternative to following the dictates of our own, unique social and cultural heritage. But what is truly mythical and mischievous is the proposition under which New Zealand has laboured for more than a decade: that our society and culture are economically meaningless; that there is no alternative to imposing on ourselves a crude universalist dogma that may not even be appropriate to the country that spawned it, much less so anybody else.

One thoughtful Japanese critic of the End of History, Eisuke Sakakibara, calls instead for an 'end of progressivism' — the typically 'Western' or American belief that there is only one ideal end.[8] He notes that Western civilisation does not 'own' modern technology, much of which has its origins in discoveries made by other civilisations and cultures. He notes the gathering problems of the Western system: its impact on the global ecology, its propensity to slumps and political instability, its growing polarisation of incomes and wealth, its apparent inability to eradicate mass unemployment (particularly in Europe), its so far highly unsuccessful shock-therapy application to Russia (in contrast to the greater success of China's indigenous approach to industrialisation).[9]

Sakakibara seeks the peaceful coexistence of civilisations, and their coexistence with nature — an image of harmonious cohabitation rather than conquest and growth. It is not, in his view, a matter of retreating to premodernism, but rather of moving forward to a plurality of civilisations in a postmodern age which 'can and should share [modern] neutral technologies and institutions while retaining diverse cultures and traditions'.

This is perhaps a romantic vision, though it may be grimly realistic to foresee that the current programme of Western dominance over nature and other cultures is not sustainable. Alternatives must be explored. These will involve, in my view, going beyond just tolerance of cultural diversity as something worthy in itself but essentially separate from technology and economic institutions, towards appreciating that economy and culture — society in its broadest sense — need to be treated as an organic whole if we are to make progress in dealing with the malaise of modernism. For an economist, this must mean a critical reassessment of the assumptions of neoclassical doctrines, of the myths of market economics.

Chapter 6
Yes, We Have No Nirvanas

NZPA Press Release: Wellington, April 1, 2001: *Roll Over Beethoven! Kiwi Breakthru Stuns Musak World!* Maestro Frenzi, Line Manager: Performance (formerly conductor) of the NZ Symphony Orchestra announced today yet another productivity breakthrough which confirms this now Hong Kong-owned institution as a world leader in music technology. Following the earlier programme of labour-saving innovations which have seen the orchestra's staff cut from more than eighty to just three — one operator on each of the woodwind, brass and strings synthesizers, with Maestro Frenzi himself working the drum machine with his foot — the NZSO has now achieved a shattering breakthrough: they have cut their performance time of Beethoven's Fifth Symphony — the world-accepted benchmark of orchestral productivity — to just *four minutes* — one-third as long as their previous best time of twelve minutes, and well below the previous world record of ten minutes held by the London Cacophonic.

Maestro Frenzi modestly attributed the breakthrough, in his charming Austrian accent, to 'gut old kivi ingenuity'. It is in fact a masterpiece of lateral thinking; an idea so simple (like all great ideas) as to seem obvious in retrospect. As Maestro Frenzi explained: 'We asked, why play the movements *ein, zwei, drei*, one after the other? Zo linear! We play them *all four all at once!*'

This brilliant innovation is expected to eventually allow all nine of Beethoven's symphonies to be performed at one concert — a terrific saving in time. Although the NZSO no longer has audiences at its concerts, today's record-breaking effort was witnessed by the Cultural Attaché from the Chilean Embassy, who was observed to take copious notes.

Loony tunes, no? Well, yes, but that is a lot of what economic 'progress' is all about: labour-saving innovations. And the absurdity of breakneck-Beethoven highlights one of the limits to growth that we are not yet confronting. The present dominant economic metaphor is of exponential — limitless — economic expansion. All our political parties promise to increase the 'rate' of economic growth, and confidently expect problems of poverty, unemployment, inequality and so on to melt as a result. But in ignoring the inexorable limits, they risk actually *worsening* the problems. To document this perhaps startling assertion, we need to examine the three limits to growth: 'services', 'servicing' and 'social'.

Limits to growth: services

Much of what we usually think of as the process of economic growth involes producing more 'things' — material objects such as food, clothing, shelter. This has been achieved by giving one of the necessary inputs to thing-production — labour — more and better of one of the other inputs — machines (what economists call 'capital stock'). The results over the past two centuries have been spectacular, especially in agriculture but also in our manufacturing industries, in terms of the quantities of labour input needed per unit of commodity output. But the improvements in our living standards, though very substantial, have been much less spectacular.

The reason is simple: We do not live by bread alone. We also 'consume' *services* — the direct output of other people — and the scope for productivity improvements here is inherently limited. We neither know nor care how much labour goes into baking a loaf of our daily bread, but we care very much how much goes into performing a Beethoven symphony: up to a point, the more people the better (larger orchestra), and as for the amount of time it should take, this is a matter of taste, but few would want to hear a performance in less than thirty or so minutes, which is the fastest time currently available on CD. *The whole point of a service is that it does take time! The input is the output.* A long back-rub is better than a short back-rub, and the human input is essential — having one's back rubbed by a robot would hardly be the same experience.

This means that even if our rate of improvements in ingenuity at thing-production continues unabated, the rate of growth in total productivity (GNP) *must* drop back. Consider a simple example. Suppose we start with an economy divided 50:50 between production of things and production of services. Over a period of years there is a doubling in thing-productivity, meaning that only half as much labour is required in this sector as before: this labour can now be used to produce services. Assuming a constant total labour force[1], total output in real terms (that is, measured in base period prices) will have increased by 25 per cent[2]

Now another similar period of time passes, and through strenuous application of new technologies and capital investment, the thing-sector achieves a further doubling of its productivity. Will total economic output increase by another quarter, or 25 per cent? No, it will not. Because only half as much labour is now released from the half-as-large thing-sector, aggregate GNP increases by much less — just 10 per cent.[3] This process will continue until no labour is left in the thing-sector. All material goods are now produced by robots, and everyone is engaged in supplying personal services to everyone else (we are all giving each other back-rubs). Growth has ended in nirvana.

But there is a problem with this process at the personal level. So long as there is some productivity growth, every person can have their standard of living improved from the fruits of those productivity improvements. But once the process stops, one person can only have more if another has less. The income distribution has become a zero-sum game. Each person, striving to improve their living standard, can succeed only if others fail.

We accept that we cannot all live like kings or queens with forty concubines or gigolos and four hundred servants: it just doesn't add up. But it stops adding up well short of such imperial decadence. The economist Lester Thurow reports that three decades of Gallup Polls in the United States — covering a period in which average real incomes (that is, after adjusting for inflation) increased substantially — found that the answer to the question: 'What is the smallest amount of money a family of four needs to get along in this community?' has stayed roughly constant *in relative terms* at between 53 and 59 per cent of whatever was the average income in the year the question was asked.[4] The pattern holds internationally. Thurow cites another paper, by Richard Esterlin, which surveys evidence from many studies and reports that a person's happiness is apparently 'almost completely dependent on his relative income position within his own country and almost not at all dependent on his absolute income'.[5]

The reasons for this are partly subjective: we assess ourselves in terms of how well we are doing relative to our peers. Good old-fashioned envy no doubt plays a part — known to sociologists as the theory of relative deprivation.[6] But there is also a sound objective basis for shifting standards of acceptable incomes. As average incomes rise, so will the incomes of the people producing services. But their incomes are also their price — what they charge for their service — so that a constant money income will buy fewer services than before. It is truly better to be poor in a poor country than poor in a rich country.

None of this means that from an individual point of view it is futile to try to 'get on' economically. If you personally work harder or smarter or luckier or meaner you will get richer, if that's what you want. Fair enough. But we can't all do it, and that should perhaps give us pause. If as a nation we accept various sacrifices in the name of economic growth, and if most of this ends up cancelling itself out, then were we being so smart in the first place?

The basic problem — limit to the time available — hits even harder with the other great finite resource, 'land' or, more generally, natural resources. Here things are exacerbated by what is probably the ultimate source of all problems, political, social and economic — population growth. More warm bodies means more people to supply labour services as well as to demand them, but it means less land available per person.

Two or three generations ago, the holiday cottage — 'crib' south of the Waitaki, 'bach' everywhere else — was something accessible to New Zealanders of just about every income group. Sited, often without formal title, on land near sea, river or lake; cobbled together on family working bees from demolition materials; furnished with urban cast-offs and tasteful shell collections — the bach was quintessential Kiwiana, what would now be called a 'lifestyle', but then just what you did over long weekends and summer holidays.

The bach still is part of the Kiwi lifestyle, but only if you are lucky enough to have one in the family, or can afford the $80–$100,000 or more now needed to get a plot of land within a bike ride of a decent beach. For most lower- and middle-income New Zealanders, owning a bach or 'country cottage' is as unattainable as it is for their counterparts in the crowded countries of Europe. Such are the more bitter fruits of economic growth and population growth.

Limits to growth: servicing

Limits to growth set by the finiteness of the services of labour and land are becoming well appreciated, even if not yet well integrated into our thinking about economic growth and policy.[7] Less well understood are what I call the 'servicing' limits to growth. Suppose we did achieve the rather inhuman nirvana of everyone having their own robot to give them back-rubs and perform other personal services. Terrific, but *who will repair the robot when it breaks down, as it inevitably will?* Not another robot — it is incredibly difficult to devise machines that can reproduce or repair themselves.

Automation is extremely labour-intensive — a paradox that induced the leading car manufacturer Toyota to retreat from using robots to assemble the RAV4 recreational vehicle when it built a new plant. Faced with the problem of prosperity — high labour costs — Toyota had been at the frontier of developing production techniques using supposedly labour-saving robots (automation). But it found two unpleasant side effects: the number of maintenance personnel escalated[8], and the remaining 'line', or production, workers, no longer able to work with or understand the new machines, were less able to contribute to the *kaizen* system of continuous improvement which has been so important to Toyota's success.[9]

The tendency for things to break down is the inexorable consequence of the Second Law of Thermodynamics: the 'entropy law', which tells us that every physical system is constantly tending to revert to a state of randomness or disorder. It appears to apply too to social systems, especially large hierarchical organisations. It is only by the application of an external energy source — the sun (in daily doses and liberated from the past through fossil fuels) — that we can keep entropy in check. But directing that energy is itself a highly labour-intensive activity: basically, it is a service activity, with the inherent limits of available time that we have noted above. It is rather remarkable how little attention has been paid to the consequences of the entropy law for economics. Once we realise that machines tend to break down, and that coping with this requires labour input, we can see at once that economic growth based on giving everyone more capital to work with must end.

The same is true of 'human capital' — the knowledge and skills stored in our brain that enhance our productivity. You can invest in acquiring human capital through education: the more time you spend doing this, the less time — by an exactly equal amount — you have to actually produce something. Diminishing returns are an obvious consideration — everyone's capacity to usefully learn is finite, which limits the amount of human capital each of us can build up. And entropy is a terrible intruder into the process: *the more you learn, the more you forget, and at an increasing rate as you get older and entropy attacks the grey cells!*

More than a decade ago, I wrote my first book on a stylish little Olivetti manual typewriter. The capital required was modest: just a desk, the Olivetti, and the human capital I'd invested in learning to touch-type years ago during an underemployed university vacation. Basically, I sat down each morning and started typing. If I didn't type anything, it was because I couldn't think of anything to write, not because of any difficulties with my capital stock. Now I type onto one of two expensive computers (one at home, one at the university). Unlike my manual typewriter, which still works as well as ever, my computers have to be replaced every two years with ever more powerful models needed to cope with the ever greater demands of the software, the latest version of which has just been loaded onto my machines. As a result, I spent the first half-hour yesterday morning not writing this book but trying to figure out how to eliminate the large empty border at the top of the screen. With the space taken up by this and by the rows of 'toolbars', there was little room left for the actual text. Today, it was twenty minutes trying to recreate a feature that I knew how to use on the previous version of the software but which seemed to have disappeared from the new, improved edition.

I did work out how to do these things, which leaves about ten thousand more bells and whistles to come to terms with. With each of these, if I don't use them often (and of course I can't use them all often — there isn't enough time: that finite resource), I'll forget what to do (entropy again) and have to relearn. Computers are marvellous and fun, but do they *really* make me a more effective worker? There is certainly a big statistical puzzle here. As the Nobel economist Robert Solow put it: 'Computers show up everywhere in the economy except in the productivity stats.' To put it all onto a more exalted level: does anyone seriously believe that Shakespeare would have written greater plays if he'd had access to a PC loaded with Microsoft Word?

Limits to growth: social

The fattest and funniest man of early nineteenth-century England was the Reverend Sidney Smith: the 'Smith of Smiths', as Lord Macaulay appreciatively called him.[10] Towards the end of his long and busy life (1771–1845) Smith marvelled at the improvements he had witnessed: gas, steam-boats, railways, McAdamised roads, wooden pavements, the police force, cabs (taxis), umbrellas, braces, quinine, carriage springs, (gentlemen's) clubs, the penny post, plus 'humane laws, the sobriety of the gentry and the safety of the streets'. Smith was 'utterly surprised that all these changes and inventions did not occur two centuries ago'.

That was a very good point. It shows that Sidney Smith did not subscribe to a myth which has perhaps become more pervasive over the years: that progress depends on exploiting the latest science and technology. While Smith was surely optimistic in supposing that the applied arts had progressed far enough in Tudor times to permit the harnessing of steam power for locomotion, just about all the improvements he listed were well within the boundaries of known technologies when they were introduced.

Thomas McAdam's improvements to the once appalling British roads are a wonderful example. McAdam's crucial insight was simply that the stones being used on the roads were too big. After careful observation, he worked out that the point of contact between the wheel of a coach and the road was not more than one inch in length. If the road surface had stones larger than this, the coach wheel would in essence have to push them out of the way, resulting in slow, bumpy progress and eventually potholes, ruts and many fatal accidents. Smaller stones, on the other hand, would be compressed and consolidated by the passage of traffic, yielding a smooth, fast and safe surface. When this insight was accepted, the big job was organising the resources to rebuild the roads. McAdam pursued this with relentless energy, and by 1837 'England got the best road system since the fall of the Roman Empire'.[11]

The science in this enterprise was mundane (though clever); the big implementing effort was a feat of *social* organisation, as it was for many of the life-enhancing improvements of which Sidney Smith was so appreciative — not least, humane laws and the safety of the streets.

And so it still is. It is easy to think of improvements which depend on as yet undiscovered technology. Perhaps electric cars are a good example — we just don't yet know how to make portable batteries light enough. But even here it should be pointed out that we already have a well-proven technology for electrically powered transportation — trains. We have chosen to organise our affairs around the use of personal transportation systems (cars and roads), but this *is* a choice, and one that it would not be inconceivable to reverse. It is a social, not a scientific, matter.

Scientific 'breakthroughs' are perhaps most eagerly awaited in medicine: there is no surer headline-grabber than the announcement of a possible new cure for cancer or AIDs. But what are we waiting for here? There are two facts to be faced: first that we are all going to die of something eventually — there is no earthly nirvana — and, second, that making this regrettable truth temporarily more tolerable is largely a matter, not of science and medicine, but of how we organise our social and personal affairs: good public health, eradication of poverty and responsible lifestyles can postpone some causes of sickness and mortality (lung cancer, heart disease) and eliminate others (AIDs).

People seem to have a fascination with utopias, be they nirvanas ('no more work') or nightmares ('no more jobs'). My colleague John Deeks writes of a late nineteenth-century book by Edward Bellamy, *Looking Backward 2000–1887*, which promised elimination of the 'four wastes' of competitive capitalism (mistaken undertakings, hostile competition, gluts and crises, idle labour and capital) through authoritarian, centralised organisation in accordance with scientific principles.[12] Bellamy's book sold 650,000 copies in ten years! I'll be happy if my book sells half that many.

If we accept the limits to growth, then we have a chance to make some progress on the things that really matter: things like Sidney Smith's safety of the streets, humane laws and an end to poverty. Pursuing the myth of exponential growth is to chase the pot of gold at the end of the rainbow. It diverts our efforts from the mundane but achievable goals of the decent society. Yes, there are no nirvanas — but who cares? There is plenty of useful work that can be done within our earthly limits.

Chapter 7
Who Will Drive the Buses?

People with more education are more productive, or at least earn higher incomes, true? Yes, true, on the whole. So if we want our economy to be more productive, should we encourage our citizens to get more education or training? No, not necessarily, for two reasons.

First, education and training have costs to be weighed against the benefits — the direct costs of buildings, teachers and so on, and the opportunity cost of earnings foregone whilst the student is in training. Nowadays, new university lecturers may be thirty years old when they start their first job. And second, just because the people who have taken extra education or training earn more, it doesn't mean that the people who chose not to were making a mistake, or that those with advanced education would have done better if they had trained even more.

The point — which is so often missed in policy discussion about the contribution of education to economic growth — is that in a reasonably free and fair society the people who get more education are *inherently different from* those who go into the workforce with fewer formally learned skills. If people have good information about educational and training opportunities and good access to them, then they will tend to sort themselves out. Those with the aptitude or need for education will get it; those otherwise inclined will not, and the result could be quite efficient. Forcing more training on those who would not choose to take it for themselves may be actually counterproductive — the additional benefits will be exceeded by the costs of the exercise.

The point is one of logic and is widely misunderstood, often with distressing consequences. Let us illustrate it with a medical example. Apparently, women who have babies very late — in their late forties — tend, statistically, to live longer than average. Does that mean that a woman in her forties who wants to lengthen her lifespan should do everything possible to have a baby? No, it does not. Apart from the cosmic selfishness of such an act, it misses the causal point. People who are unusually strong and healthy will for that reason tend to live longer than average. And also because of their natural vigour, they will, if women, be more likely than average to have a baby rather late in the piece. Hence the correlation. But another woman of ordinary constitution who sets out to become pregnant after her normal child-bearing years could thereby *harm* her health and lower her lifespan, because of the stresses and strains of late pregnancies.

This causation caveat should be widely applied at all levels, especially at the level of economic policy, when by copying some attribute of a successful nation another nation hopes to replicate its high economic growth rate, not appreciating that it is some non-replicable and fundamental difference that accounts for both the supposed cause and the effect.

And so it is in education. We should not assume that people cannot choose for themselves an appropriate level of skills and training. But having said that, it should be conceded with concern that, in New Zealand, access to tertiary education is probably not as free and fair as it used to be, largely for economic reasons such as mass unemployment and pressure on low-wage jobs, which limit young people's ability to pay their way. I discuss this issue in chapter 19. Here, though, I would like to analyse — in a sceptical spirit — why we are so keen on education in the first place.

About twenty years ago, there were hopes that education would turn out to be the Holy Grail of economic growth; the missing link in the chain of reasoning to explain why some countries grew faster than others. Economists had previously understood economic growth in terms of physical capital — the land, machinery and buildings necessary for production. But it turned out that physical capital could not explain the great quarter-century of growth that followed the Second World

War. So attention turned to the concept of intangible human capital — the productive potential in each of us as enhanced by education and training.

But here too the search has come up short. In its 1993 *Survey* of the New Zealand economy, the OECD paid special attention to education and human capital. In order to motivate the issue, they cited a study by Psacharopoulos which uses the standard 'growth accounting' methodology to tease out the various contributions to increases in GNP.[1] The OECD reports (p. 74) the results of this study: 'improved labour quality due to education contributes up to one-quarter of the rate of growth of national income, with an average contribution of just under one-tenth'. Is one-tenth supposed to be a lot? On this evidence, even the OECD's muted conclusion that 'empirical testing . . . would seem to offer support for — or at least be consistent with — the importance of human capital development for economic performance' would seem too strong.

The OECD does not report a particularly interesting feature of Psacharopoulos's results, that three countries (Canada, the United States and the United Kingdom) with relatively low post-war economic growth performance show amongst the highest percentages of this growth supposedly explained by education (25 per cent, 15 per cent and 12 per cent, respectively), whereas three brilliant performers — Germany, France and Japan — show very low contributions (2 per cent, 6 per cent and 3.3 per cent). This is consistent with the proposition that education is a blight on growth. A more temperate inference would be that the resources spent on education have some pay-off, but this does not help us understand the really important *differences* in international performance.

There are plenty of these correlations around. In a survey article the economist Andrew Weiss notes that more education goes with higher wages (and lower unemployment), and also with better health, less likelihood of smoking, drinking or taking drugs, and lower absenteeism.[2] But, again, beware causation. Take the education/health link. Apparently it applies *before* the education takes place![3] That is, people who will eventually get more education are healthier anyway. It isn't the schooling that teaches them good health practices, but something innate — perhaps longer time horizons in their personal life planning — which results in those people looking after themselves better and taking the trouble to get educated.

These insights have led economists to propose what are called 'sorting' models, which focus on education as a 'filter'. It is not so much that education adds productive potential directly, as the human-capital model assumes, but that it allows employers to sort or filter people by their innate but hard-to-verify qualities such as ability, perseverence and reliability, which are what really matter to on-the-job productivity. By grinding out a degree — in Latin, or whatever — the job seeker signals that they are quite intelligent and have good work habits.

These sorting models have very interesting policy implications.[4] First, they do not support encouraging people to get more education (who otherwise wouldn't), because this could just blur the signal that links observed educational attainment with unobservable innate characteristics — it could lower the value of education for everyone.

Second, they should provoke us to ask a very fundamental question: *why* do employers find it difficult to predict those basic personal characteristics that matter so much to them? Having people sort themselves out by undertaking years of tertiary education or training is a rather expensive way of doing it. I suggest there is an interesting insight from the old New Zealand here. When our workforce was dominated by 'good Kiwi jokers' there was no need to resort to education for sorting — everyone knew just about what to expect from each other, people were spoken for by their mates, and employers themselves were socially and culturally much of a muchness with their workers. They knew what they were getting.

In terms of a concept I think is very important, New Zealand was a high-social-capital economy, meaning that economic relationships — including the relationship between employer and employee — were characterised by a high degree of empathy and trust. There are differences now: much higher participation rates of women in the paid workforce; Maori separatism; increased racial diversity from Pacific Island and Asian immigration; a widening of the income differential between worker and manager. Some of these trends are good in themselves;

some bad; some debatable. But their implications for our economy need to be faced. One of these is the possibility that the increased demand for tertiary education has at least elements of sorting about it: individuals from minority groups feeling that they need to serve time in tertiary institutions to demonstrate to increasingly bewildered employers that they 'have the stuff' to be good workers.

Of course post-school education does have direct economic value. It imparts useful knowledge and teaches useful skills. It also, for most students, improves their general employability, socialising selfish and undisciplined teenagers into people with reliable work habits. And I am not saying that you can become a doctor or a carpenter without training. But I am suggesting that we do not necessarily need to train more doctors or carpenters, or train the doctors and carpenters more, or persuade would-be carpenters that they should become more highly trained doctors instead. There just isn't the evidence to support the proposition that the supposed ailments of slow-growing economies is due to their inadequate investments in human capital.

The point continues to elude most commentators on policy issues. Typical of these is the *Economist* magazine of London, which reports a study showing lower numbers (particularly of craftsmen) qualifying in engineering and technology in Britain compared with France, West Germany and Japan. It concludes that this 'links, pretty convincingly, Britain's productivity figures to its persistently poor training record'.[5]

In fact, British productivity — properly measured — would more likely be *reduced* if more training was forced on its workforce. That is because, compared with the Germans, *the British aren't very good at being trained!* In the clothing industry, for example, there are fifteen times more machine-operator trainees in Germany than in Britain, who learn in two months what it takes *two years* for their British counterparts to pick up. That is, there is a very good reason why the Germans train more — training has a higher pay-off there. This is not because Germans are more intelligent than Brits, but because they have a different *attitude* to investing in their own human capital and towards taking the sorts of pains needed to do precision-skilled work. In economists' terms, the British tend to have a different work/leisure trade-off. Loading extra training on unwilling hands will just waste their time and risk ruining some expensive machinery.

These deep-seated cultural differences between nations should be taken very seriously, as should the cultural and attitudinal differences between individuals within a society. Individuals with the appropriate attitude and aptitude can better themselves through further education or training, and a decent society should be anxious that none of these people are prevented from fulfilling that potential through family or early schooling disadvantages. But this is not a universal panacea, and it will not make everybody better off. One of the many studies of returns to education compared Australia and the United States and found that, after controlling for ability and family environment, returns to schooling were about twice as high in the United States as in Australia.[6] The reason? Differences in the income distributions of the two economies. In the United States, a tertiary qualification is needed to pass into the higher-paid occupations; in Australia (and probably New Zealand) this is true to a much lesser extent.

That is, it is the income distribution that determines the returns to education, not (or not simply) the other way around, as is ordained by human-capital models, which would predict a much more similar international pattern of returns to education. Just to ram home the point, consider a study by one of the leading specialists in the field of labour economics, James Heckman of the University of Chicago, who calculated that, even based on the higher returns to education in the United States, it would take a gigantic, quite infeasible, investment in human capital to pull wage differentials back to their 1979 levels (which therefore were not historically to be accounted for in terms of human capital endowments).[7]

So the solution to the great mystery of the determination of income and its distribution must lie elsewhere. I will suggest that it is in fact a quite mundane matter, right under our noses. Take the case of someone who everyone will agree is a most useful member of the workforce: the bus driver. Consider all the attributes required by such a person. She or he must be reliable and honest — she is responsible for perhaps sixty passengers and a piece of mobile capital equipment that could be worth several hundred thousand dollars. She must have energy to keep that big bus pushing on through the rush-hour traffic. She should have good interpersonal skills. She must have the moral authority and leadership qualities to maintain order in her bus. She must be self-reliant and show common sense when things go wrong. Oh, and yes, she must have a qualification — a heavy-vehicle driving license, and some training.

Since most of us can drive, we perhaps don't always appreciate the level of skill involved. In fact, for some people, an ordinary driver's licence is the most advanced skill qualification they will ever get. But it is not a tertiary degree. It does not require years or even months of further education. To qualify to take the wheel of a big bus takes from six weeks to four months of training (depending on whether you ask the bus company or the union). This fairly brief bout of 'education' is an indispensable, but really rather small, part of what it takes to be a satisfactory bus driver, yet it is the only part of that package of qualities that shows up in measures of human capital. So it perhaps should not be surprising that human-capital statistics cannot account for much of economic growth or of the distribution of the fruits of that growth.

Of the other qualities, some are innate: determination, energy, flair. Most people can drive but some are better at it than others. The other qualities are all, in one way or another, about dealing with other people: honesty, reliability, leadership, empathy, sympathy. These matter even for non-professional drivers. The reason driving in New Zealand is so unpleasant (compared to, say, Australia) is not so much a general technical incompetence, but an effusion of inconsiderate anti-socialness that emerges from us when we grab the controls of a motor vehicle.

These social qualities are certainly very important to our moral standing as human beings. We all know that. What has not until recently been widely appreciated (except by good old Adam Smith, who worked it all out more than two hundred years ago) is their *economic* importance. Indeed, only in the last few years has the concept of social capital emerged in economics, as a summary of the stock of empathy, trust and goodwill in an economy, to rank with physical and human capital as one of the 'factors of production'. Social capital is even more intangible an entity than human capital, and not much progress has yet been made in quantifying it. But it is there, and it matters a lot. The importance of social capital is an underlying theme of this book and it is discussed more fully in chapter 9. It informs both analysis of the old New Zealand (which performed better than it should have according to conventional physical and human-capital models) and of the new 'reformed' economy, which has been rather a disappointment.

An aspect of the new economy which New Zealand supposedly shares with the rest of the world is the increased importance of 'information' processed and transmitted globally by the ever-changing technologies of computers and telecommunications. It is fashionable to trumpet the imminent arrival of the 'information economy', staffed by 'symbolic analysts' — highly trained desk workers who send symbols (information of various sorts) back and forward to each other. Arguably, such work depends more on physical and human capital than social capital, since many information transactions don't involve any direct interpersonal contact at all.

But it is wise to be sceptical. When presented with claims of the 'information sector' making up most of the economy,[8] one is tempted to ask: 'but what will all the information be *about*?' On closer examination, many of the workers assigned to the information sector turn out to be engaged in control and monitoring functions — accountants, clerks, lawyers, bureaucrats — rather than in producing information for its own sake. The numbers of these control, or 'transaction', workers has indeed increased rather alarmingly in New Zealand, as documented in chapter 12. This is a phenomenon I attribute to the erosion of social capital (which reduces the need for explicit control mechanisms) that has accompanied the more-market 'reforms' in this country.

But the demand for information for its own sake must be limited. How many more newspapers or television programmes do we need to read or watch? The best of luxuries for most of us are the direct services of another human being, which by their nature cannot be automated or processed into impersonal information. And nor can most of the mundane tasks of everyday work and life: childcare, housework, teaching, repairing, building houses, driving the buses, and so on. It is reported that even now in the United States there are one-and-a-half times more janitors than all of the bankers, brokers, lawyers, accountants and computer programmers put together.[9]

So we need to put formal training and tertiary education in its place: necessary for many jobs, but not for all of them. And we should not undervalue the qualities that are not necessarily imparted in the classroom — common sense, emotional intelligence, reliability, empathy — nor fail to reward decently those whose work requires and contributes to these qualities (the social capital), even if they do not have the formal academic aptitudes of the fabled symbolic analysts. *The men [and women] who simply do the work for which they draw the wage.* Their contributions should be valued and paid for.

Morals

Chapter 8
Behaving Well is the Best Reward

To the economic rationalist — whose ilk has ruled the roost in New Zealand since 1984 — behaving well is strictly a leisure-time activity, to be undertaken at home by consenting adults and their children. The concept of decency — even of morality — has no place in the 'real' world of the market economy. The basic postulate that underpins economic rationalism is this: every individual acts totally and solely in their own self-interest. In the jargon, individuals are rational, self-seeking, optimising, opportunistic 'agents'; in more everyday language, *Homo economicus* is a selfish shit.

In this model there is no place for empathy or altruism, and none for basic moral concepts like honour and decency. Selfish shits are ruthless opportunists, acting only to please themselves (though their egoism is such that they bear no malice or any other negative feeling to anyone else). This is a behavioural assumption, not a normative one; a statement on how the world works. If you remonstrate about it with an economic rationalist, he or she will just smile sadly, shrug their shoulders and say, 'So sorry, but — apart from you and me, of course — the world *is* full of selfish shits — rather, rational opportunists — and any policies that don't take account of this will be chasing fools' gold; just making things worse than they need be.' Thus, for example, the rationalists' programme to minimise the role of the state, on the assumption that non-crassly opportunistic behaviour cannot be expected from politicians and public servants. Nests that can be feathered, will be feathered.

In the rationalist view of the economy, there is no *possibility* for anything other than selfish behaviour. Under competitive conditions, every agent is small and powerless to influence their environment. Anyone who sentimentally undercharged their customers or overpaid their workers would go out of business, swept aside by more 'rational' competitors. There is a unique 'equilibrium' outcome, where all agents are just making enough to stay in business, with nothing left over to waste on altruism.

Now, far be it from me to suggest that people never behave selfishly, or that policy should not take into account the possibility that they do. Nor should I fail to point out that there are wide tracts of economic behaviour where pursuing self-interest is not selfish, it is just minding one's own business. But as an overriding creed for the conduct of the economy, the selfish-shit model is not only repugnant morally, it is also *bad economics*. The insight here really belongs to John Maynard Keynes, the only great economist of our century, though you can trace the core idea back to Adam Smith (surely the greatest economist of any age). Keynes' cruder critics maintain that Keynesianism is all about government 'spending its way out of recession', but his message is actually a lot more subtle and interesting than that.

Keynes argued that it is wrong to claim there is a single outcome or equilibrium for the economy. Instead, *depending on how people behave*, there is a wide range of possible outcomes, of which some (e.g. full employment) are better than others (mass unemployment).

The point is often now illustrated by the famous 'prisoner's dilemma' analogy. Here is the story.[1] A murder is committed. The police have absolutely no evidence, but desperately need a successful prosecution to get their conviction rate up. They round up two of the usual suspects, and put them in separate cells. Each suspect is told: 'We know both of you were in this heinous crime, but the other guy isn't saying anything. If you finger him, we'll throw the book at him for not cooperating, and he'll get life. But we'll arrange a reduced charge for you — you'll only be in for a year.'

'What if he fingers me as well?' asks the prisoner.

'We'll get both of you then: standard sentence, ten years in the slammer.'

'So what if we both stay silent?'

'Fat chance!' snorts the interrogator. 'But if you did, we'd have you both for obstruction of justice: three years.'

Why is the policeman so sure of getting the prisoner's testimony? Consider it from Suspect No. 1's point of view. What he should do depends on what No. 2 does. If the other guy talks, then No. 1's best action is to talk, too — ten years versus twenty five. But if the other stays silent, then it is still better for No. 1 to incriminate him: he gets just one year in jail instead of three. So, even without knowing what No. 2 will do, talking is the rational action for Suspect No.1. Equally, it is the rational action for No. 2, who will be going through the same thought processes in his cell.

Therefore, each will get ten years in jail by being 'rational', even though there is a feasible course of action — both remain silent — which would yield them much shorter sentences of three years. Rational man is, in Amartya Sen's telling phrase, a 'rational fool'.

Now, the relevance of this analogy is that just about every economic encounter between two or more people has elements of the prisoner's dilemma. The key ingredient is that there be some freedom of manoeuvre in the situation of which one participant can take advantage at the expense of the other. Say you hire someone to paint your house. Once the job is underway, there are opportunities for each party to 'hold up' the other. Despite having promised to paint your house at all possible speed, the painter could wander off to other, more lucrative jobs, just returning to your house when it is convenient, knowing that it will not be worth your while at this stage to pay them off and get in another contractor (who would probably just do the same thing, anyway). For your part, even if the job is done well, you could withhold the last 10 per cent of payment normally due on completion on some spurious grounds of inadequate performance, betting that the painters will not find it worth the trouble to make a fuss.

The dilemma is particularly acute in 'lumpy', one-off situations, such as you might face if you went overseas for a while and had to do something with your house. Why should a tenant on a short-term lease look after your place, or pay the rent on time or even at all?

If these problems cannot be resolved then we will see costly, inefficient outcomes. You may decide to paint the house yourself, thereby reverting to a primitive, pre-market situation that forgoes the benefits of the division of labour. You may just close up your house instead of renting it, or go to the expense and hassle of storing all your belongings to reduce the opportunities for damage by renting it unfurnished. Markets are not working well.

These 'dilemmas' pose their own acute dilemma to economic rationalists. On the one hand they cling to their basic assumption that people are selfish shits — self-seeking opportunists. But of course they want to be able to prove that the outcome of such behaviour gives you the best of all possible worlds. Much effort and ingenuity has gone into resolving the dilemma, to some effect.

One possibility is to turn to the legal system, using enforceable contracts as the means of committing both parties to optimal behaviour. Written contracts are certainly very useful things, but there is a clear trade-off between covering the contingencies that provide loop-holes for opportunism (leading to prisoners' dilemmas) and the costs in time and legal fees of negotiating and writing the contract. In fact no contract can ever be absolutely watertight, if only because contingencies depend on unknowable future events, and this can open up whole new avenues for opportunism. Look at the USA, where there are more than 500,000 practising lawyers (more than in all the rest of the world, apparently), of whom it has been said that one half are occupied in drawing up contracts, and the other half in exploiting loopholes in them.

A second approach, much favoured by theorists, takes advantage of the existence of a future, of a time dimension to economic activity; specifically, that many interactions between economic agents are repeated, so that there may be an opportunity to punish opportunistic behaviour by retaliation in subsequent meetings. Suppose, in our example, we add the possibility of the prisoners' friends outside the prison taking terrible revenge on anyone who 'talks and walks'. Keeping one's mouth shut may then become the rational thing to do. In technical terms, the pay-off matrix has been altered to make the mutually most beneficial course of action (keeping silent) the rational choice for each prisoner.

The study of interactive situations is called 'game theory'. It was introduced in a famous 1944 book by the great mathematician and all-round genius John von Neumann in collaboration with the economist Oscar Morgenstern,[2] in the hope of finding a general theory of social behaviour that would match in predictive power the theories of the 'hard' sciences. Game theory has become, over the past decade or so, the hottest field in economics. It offers seemingly limitless opportunities for that fine display of arcane mathematical technique that is the initiation rite of the well-trained young economic theorist. But results, in terms of practical utility or predictive power, have not matched the intellectual fire-power trained on the subject, and this may have something to do with the inherent handicap of retaining an emphasis on purely 'rational' — i.e. opportunistic — behaviour.

Difficulties abound. Suppose the repeated interactive situation (known as a dynamic game) is finite, meaning that the players know that they will meet for a last time. The rational thing to do in that last 'endgame' will be for each player to cheat on the other, since there is no possibility of future retaliation. But knowing this, each would want to cheat on the last-but-one meeting, and so on, by backward induction, back to their first meeting. Cooperation unravels at once.

If we blur the finality of the endgame by making the future uncertain or discounted (not valued so highly as the present) we also blur the outcome of the game. Now we have the notorious 'folk theorem'[3] which says, more or less, that just about any outcome, including cooperative behaviour, is possible: predictive power equals zilch.

So this isn't much help, and it may be that the theorists need to broaden their behavioural horizons beyond narrow rationalism to make real progress. As a first step, they could, while retaining if they must the assumption that individuals care directly only about their own utility or happiness, bring in *sympathy* — the idea that the utility of one is (partially) dependent on the utility felt by certain others. My happiness partly depends on you being happy too. Suppose, for example, that the two suspects in the prisoner's dilemma are 'brothers', either literally or as members of the same gang. Then the distress each would suffer at the thought of the other incarcerated for a long period could be sufficient to stifle any desire to 'sing', moral considerations aside.

But why suppress moral considerations? Why not take the next step, from sympathy to morality. If each prisoner has a moral code which simply proscribes 'squealing' to the police, no matter who the other suspect is, then both will get off with the shortest sentence. Rigid adherence to an 'irrational' behavioural rule yields the best results. Such codes are indeed prevalent even amongst criminals: the police often have great difficulty in getting witnesses and evidence in cases involving violence between gangs.

It also matters whether the players have *empathy*, in the sense of understanding each other; and having a good notion of how the other will respond to the game situation. Such understanding is naturally easiest to achieve when the players share a belief and value system. Then each can feel some confidence in predicting how the other will respond, which should help them reach the mutually beneficial outcomes.

Some intriguing laboratory experiments by economists and psychologists throw light on the importance of sympathy and empathy.[4] In what is called the 'ultimatum game', subjects — usually impecunious undergraduates — are divided into pairs. One person — the Proposer — in each pair is given a sum of money and told to make an offer to the other (the Responder), dividing it between them as the Proposer sees fit. The Responder can either accept or reject this offer. If accepted, the split goes ahead; if rejected, no one gets anything. There is no come-back — the game is not repeated.

Now, according to crude rationalism, the Proposer need only offer the smallest possible amount — one cent — because it is 'rational' for the Responder to accept this rather than go away empty-handed. But crude rationalists do not do well at this game. What various experimenters have found, typically, is that the most common (modal) offer is actually a 50:50 split; that, on average, offers are in the 30–40 per cent range, and that offers much less than that are usually rejected. This holds up even when the game is played for a pretty serious stake — $100 (this is a 'real' game — the players actually pocket the money). With fifty pairs playing, four Proposers (perhaps MBA students?) did have the nerve to offer only $10: three of these were turned down flat. Even two of the five $30 offers were rejected by indignant Responders, who preferred to go away with nothing rather than allow their Proposer to profit from what they considered to be a mean bid.

These experiments are particularly interesting for demonstrating the difference between altruism and morality as the basis of economic behaviour. Crude rationalism does not fail here because people are altruistic rather than selfish. If that were so, then Responders would accept low offers, altruistically getting pleasure from the Proposer's prosperity. That they mostly do not accept low offers tells us that altruism is secondary to morality in this situation: that it is regarded as simply 'bad manners' to offer a low share, and bad manners must be punished, even at some cost to the Responder.

What is clear is that there is a broadly (though not universally) accepted moral code about what is a fair and reasonable allocation of the windfall, and that players who abide by this code do well at this game, whereas players who ignore or break it do poorly. Though both author and reader of the above are now ineligible to play the ultimatum game, because we know about it, it is interesting to wonder how we would have played it. I think that I would have offered a 60:40 split, giving me a significant but not greedy premium for my good luck in being chosen as Proposer. I hope I would have, anyway. What would you have done?

The ultimatum game emphasises the importance of empathy, of people being on the same wavelength, whatever that wavelength may be. Morality is a cultural concept, and if the culture supports, say, an 80:20 split, and everyone knows this, then such offers will be generally accepted — a more opportunistic environment will be sustainable. Indeed, in the lab it was found possible to generate such a culture by rewarding those who had the lowest accepted offers with the chance of making some more money by playing the game again. Low accepted bids became the norm, thus showing how imposing a 'competitive' structure on the game can actually alter the sort of behaviour needed to succeed. We have seen a lot of this in New Zealand recently.

But is such behaviour really functional? A major problem with all these experimental games is that they themselves are legally constrained by a moral code not found in the real world: the human subjects must not be made worse off as a result of playing. The students who 'lose' don't actually lose anything, they just don't win. But of course the economy is not so kind and gentle, and players have the opportunity to do real harm to each other. Faced with this possibility of loss, people may simply chose not to play at all — not to do business with each other — *unless they can trust others not to behave opportunistically*; trust them to offer a tolerably decent split of the pay-off should they happen to find themselves in the role of 'proposer'. Thus, empathy needs to be supplemented with the deeper morality of fairness; of a shared willingness to behave decently.

I had the opportunity recently to be game-master myself. A colleague and I were taking a group of twelve policy analysts and managers from the Ministry of Health in Wellington on a short course on the latest developments in economics and how these might apply to the health sector. As a bit of light relief (though with some seriousnesss of intent) we had them play the following game. Everyone was given a stake of $5 and asked to divide it into two portions. Portion A they would receive at the end of the game. Portion B would go into the pot, and along with everyone else's portion Bs would be doubled by us and then distributed evenly amongst the twelve in the group.

So, to maximise the total payout, each person would assign all of their $5 to the common pot and would get back $10. But there is of course a prisoner's dilemma situation here. Each individual can maximise their own reward by pocketing all their stake (setting portion A at $5), and taking their share of the pot — freeloading off the others. This is the 'smart' (opportunistic) way to behave, but if everyone does it there will be nothing in the pot and total returns will be just $5 each, instead of the $10 achievable by unselfish behaviour. Now, when this game is played in laboratory situations a strong tendency emerges for people to use a 50:50 rule — they divide their stake equally into the two portions, implying a sort of compromise between opportunistic and altruistic behaviour.

So what happened with our health policy professionals? It was very interesting. The average division was indeed quite close to 50:50. But this was not the modal division — that is, the most popular — and in fact none of the twelve actually chose a 50:50 allocation. Our dozen players were actually bi-modal — four of them kept everything for themselves, and five put their entire stake into the common pot, to be doubled by my colleague and I. There was about $30 in the pot, doubled to $60, or $5 each, which is all that the altruistic folk received, whereas their selfish colleagues got this plus their portion A stake of $5 (and these payouts were real money).

Can we account for these marked differences in generosity? We shouldn't be able to, because the experiment was supposed to be anonymous, but I devised a cunning way of identifying the players (thereby no doubt transgressing the rules for experiments on human subjects). The group happened to be evenly divided between women and men, and it was this division that just about perfectly explained the differences in playing strategies. All but one of the people who put their all into the pot were women; all the 100 per cent-selfish players were men. I told the class this: the men seemed quite unabashed; the women rolled their eyes and said: 'Well, what do you expect?' Everyone had a bit of a laugh (this was a good-humoured bunch who seemed to get along quite well with each other) and we carried on.

We then ran another little contest which perhaps revealed how little empathy there is between professional economists (my colleague and I) and everyone else. We asked everyone to write down on a piece of paper a number, this being their guess of the price of a bottle of sparkling wine we had already purchased, and which would be given to the person whose estimate was closest to the actual price paid. That price had been set the night before over a beer — my colleague and I had each written down what we thought we should spend on the wine, and agreed to take the average. I proposed $20, my colleague — a notably generous person — $30, so I purchased the best sparkling wine I could find for $24.95.

And who guessed this? No one did. All the estimates were less than $24.95 — the winner predicted $20. Some of the numbers were lower than I thought it possible to purchase wine for. Perhaps they were just having us on.

These little experiments and games do not prove anything. Nothing *proves* anything. But they and many others add up to something substantial. We do have some rethinking to do. A Chicago economist once said that 'economics economises on morality'. He was probably thinking, as many others have, of the famous passage from *The Wealth of Nations* by Adam Smith to the effect that it isn't because of altruism that the baker bakes us our bread or the brewer brews our ale, but because it is in their economic interest to do so. We pay them for it, as we in turn are paid to provide our own services to others.

This is a marvellous and powerful insight into the miracle of how things get done in a decentralised market society, and the point that it would be foolish to *rely on* non-economic motives to get our bread baked or beer brewed is well taken. But morality and decency are crucial here, in sustaining the invisible web of mutual trust that emboldens a society to make the giant leap from self-sufficiency to the division of labour; from everyone for themselves to taking up a trade such as baking bread in the confidence that a market will exist where the bread can be exchanged (via the medium of money) for the thousand other items that the baker's family needs to survive and flourish.

Adam Smith, who himself plied the trade of professor of moral philosophy, knew this far better than many of those who have since vulgarised his insights into simplistic slogans for laissez-faire and 'free' markets. Here is a quotation from his other great book, *The Theory of Moral Sentiments*, which is explicit about the need for a general code of behaviour that limits egotistic opportunism: 'general rules of conduct . . . are of great use in correcting misrepresentation of self-love concerning what is fit and proper to be done in our particular situation'.[5]

The notion that *behaving well is not just good — it is good economics* is a powerful idea, with important practical implications. It helps us understand why the New Zealand economic revolution has been such a flop (relative to predictions), based as it is on a cynical view of human nature. It leads us to seek some 'space' — economic sovereignty — within which the crucial bonds of empathy and sympathy can be strengthened for the common good. It turns us away from the vastly expensive managerialist model — in which everyone, including the managers themselves, has to be continually monitored to ensure they perform to plan — towards a more economical 'virtue ethics' process of simply trusting good people to behave well.[6] It emphasises the importance of process itself, as opposed to a focus on outcomes, narrowly defined. Behaving well really is the best reward.

Chapter 9
Social Capital: the Next Big Idea?

In 1997, the journal *Daedalus* published a special issue commemorating fifty years of change and upheaval in four major academic disciplines — philosophy, English, political studies and economics.[1] A few months before, the *New Yorker* magazine had commemorated the fiftieth anniversary of the death of John Maynard Keynes with an article, 'The Decline of Economics', deploring the shrivelling of what in Keynes' time had been a real-world, policy-oriented discipline into sterile mathematical formalism.[2]

In yet another anniversary of perhaps more immediate moment to New Zealanders, *Landfall* came out with its fifty years celebration issue in November 1997. I was delighted to be asked to contribute to this, and I wrote an article on the *Daedalus* special issue, reviewed along with two recent New Zealand books on the reforms, by Jane Kelsey and Brian Easton.[3] I noted the big difference between the recent history of economics and the other three disciplines. English, especially, was riven by 'theory wars' and 'cultural revolutions' in the 1960s and 1970s, as a result of the racial, sexual and political upheavals suffered or enjoyed in those years, leading to what is now called 'deconstructionism' — the breaking down of the hallowed 'texts' of (mostly) dead white males into (mere) cultural artifacts, meaning different things to different readers; all depending on cultural context.

Economics emerged unscathed from the cultural revolution, crouched under its protective carapace of calculus. But there are, at last, some hopeful signs of change from within. In chapter 5 I talked of the very relevant and interesting work of four winners of the John Bates Clark medal — the prize given every two years to an economist under the age of forty. One of those four is the Stanford economist David Kreps, who represents the younger generation of economists in the *Daedalus* volume. Kreps is a brilliant microeconomist, secure in his technical achievements. He is secure enough to admit, without shame, that he is writing a book *with a sociologist*! And the exchange of ideas is at least mutual — not the usual colonisation process whereby the neighbouring social and managerial science disciplines are impregnated with 'greed, rationality and equilibrium', as Robert Solow, who represents the senior generation in *Daedalus,* summarises the core assumptions of neoclassical economics.

So just what can economics learn from sociology? Well, what do we need to know? Rather a lot! We have a great hole at the core of economics, what Solow drily calls 'the measure of our ignorance'. We don't know why some nations are much richer than others; nor — which amounts to the same thing in the long run — why some grow faster than others. The measure of our ignorance (and Bob Solow got his Nobel Prize for pointing this out) is the difference between the growth that actually occurs and that which can be explained or predicted by increases in the measured inputs to production — labour, 'land' (including all resources) and physical capital (buildings, machinery, computers). The usual suspects fail to confess to the mystery of growth.

Of course economics does have a model of the economic system — the neoclassical model that underpins the doctrines of economic rationalism that rule the roost here these days, this being based on untrammelled opportunistic individualism (greed, rationality, equilibrium). The rationalist all-purpose 'McModel', as I call it, struggles to explain the facts of post-revolutionary New Zealand: higher rather than lower transaction costs; little improvement in efficiency; mediocre macroeconomic performance. But it struggled before, too; notably, being quite inadequate to explain the most striking economic fact of the old New Zealand, the quarter-century through the late 1970s of almost no unemployment — anomalous to a model that requires a 'natural' buffer stock of unemployed labour to prevent inflation.

Also intriguing is the relatively compressed income distribution of the post-war period — an era when a responsible but not particularly skilled working man could bring up a family in something like middle-class comfort and security. This shouldn't happen under rationalism, which has earnings determined by individuals' endowments of 'human capital' (skills and abilities), leading to rather larger skilled/unskilled pay differentials.

Here it will be suggested that the rationalist model needs not so much supplanting as supplementing. The new learning in economics — not so new in other social sciences — is discovering that the recipe for a successful market economy needs to add another ingredient to the rationalist's emphasis on opportunistic individualism.

The sociologist James Coleman developed in 1990 the concept of 'social capital',[4] defined later by Putnam *et al.* (1993) as the social structure which facilitates coordination and cooperation. This term is inherently attractive to economists. We are accustomed to attributing an economy's capacity to produce flows of goods and services to its stocks of the various assets or 'capitals' — physical capital (land, buildings and plant), human capital (ability and skills) and technological capital (the state of the applied arts and sciences). Since none of these capitals can account for a society's ability to produce more goods and services by behaving cooperatively rather than opportunistically, it is natural to impute this capability to some new (or newly recognised) asset, for which 'social' capital is an appropriate name. It is our capacity to trust each other and it stems, I believe, from the prevalence of two qualities in society: empathy and sympathy — understanding the motivations of others, and wishing them well.

Social capital raises two interesting issues in the New Zealand context. First, by their very nature, the returns to social capital are not just pecuniary, to be measured in gross domestic product. Behaving well to others is its own reward in that it is intrinsic to the existence of a decent, civilised society.

Second, and also by its nature, social capital cannot be privatised. It is created by everyone who plays by the unwritten rules — with predictable honesty and willingness to refrain from crude opportunism — and so its fruits must be shared by all participants in the system. How is this done? My hypothesis is that, especially in pre-revolution New Zealand, returns to the social capital were distributed through the earnings distribution, which, as noted above, was rather unusually compressed until quite recently. That is, in addition to being rewarded for their productivity resulting from individual talent and skills, workers were also rewarded for being steady hands, good parents, solid members of the community — all social-capital-enhancing characteristics from which others benefit. Since these characteristics are rather more evenly distributed than are talent and skills, the earned-income distribution was flatter than would be predicted by the private-property-based human-capital model.

Of course this system is quite different from the asocial rationalist world of individuals and the state, in which 're'-distribution occurs only through the confiscation of private property by the tax system. 'Nice rationalists' are those who favour a limited amount of such redistribution to those who 'through no fault of their own' are incapable of putting enough human capital into the pot to get a living wage in return; 'nasty rationalists' would let the private-property chips fall as they may.

From a social-capital perspective, rationalists — nice and nasty — are missing the point. Their narrow obsession with government as the only impediment to the exercise of private-property rights exaggerates the power of the state, for good or ill, especially to redistribute income. Once the wages and salaries and bonuses and rents and dividends have been paid out, it may be too late to significantly change outcomes through taxation. The rich avoid tax; the middle classes pay up, but then use their social skills to extract in return a disproportionate share of the things that government buys with tax revenues.[5]

It is perhaps easy in a small country like New Zealand to confuse state and society. New Zealand's (formerly) marvellous free national education system is correctly seen, I believe, not as a collectivist institution imposed, top-down, by central government, but as a genuine manifestation of *social* will, in the cause of safeguarding the social capital, by enabling all children, wherever they live and whatever their parents' income, to get what they need to become useful members of society. The health system once played a similar role, as well as fulfilling an insurance function against the financial consequences of an unlucky accident or illness. Pensions were not a grudging handout to those too feckless to accumulate a sufficient store of private property to see them through their declining years, but rather a willingly offered reward for the years spent tending and extending the social capital in the workforce and community.

As for unemployment benefits, these were offered — on quite generous terms— *but never accepted*! The weekly (unemployment or sickness) benefit entitlement for someone married with children in New Zealand in 1962 was 55 per cent of the average weekly wage, as opposed to approximately 42 per cent today. Yet in March 1962 the number of sickness beneficiaries was 4346 (now more than 34,000) and the number of unemployment beneficiaries a tiny 232 (now 140,000). The benefit system was purely an insurance against an eventuality which —for twenty-five years — just didn't happen. It is interesting to compare New Zealand with Japan, a much larger economy which also achieved very low (though not zero) rates of unemployment for long periods. In Japan, this is usually attributed to the *nenko* system operating within large companies, which virtually promised an employee a job for life in exchange for loyalty and restraint. Superficially, New Zealand differs: job turnover rates have always been quite high — most workers were not 'loyal' to a single employer. But if we suppose that the relevant social organisation within which mutual trust and obligation generates full employment is not the large company but the small country, the apparent difference disappears. A New Zealand worker switched between employers just as the Japanese salary-man was switched between divisions of Toyota or Mitsubishi: always a job, *even if he wasn't particularly competent or useful* — this being crucial to the functioning of the whole system.

Social capital is quite a new concept, and it hasn't settled down yet. It still means different things to different people, which is fair enough, but it is important to be clear on what we are talking about. One coinage of the term that has had some recent circulation in New Zealand amounts to a sort of self-help community-spirit thing, possibly obviating the need for so much state assistance for the poor and unemployed. I am not going to knock community spirit, which has many fine features, and which would clearly benefit from the stability and security of a high-wage full-employment economy. But I don't see the causation working the other way around. That is, I don't see community spirit, or communitarianism in general (as this movement is properly termed), helping us much with *achieving* high-wage full employment. And too much of the drawing-up-the-wagons, them-and-us community spirit may actually hinder economic development, because it limits the commercial horizons of entrepreneurs. I have heard a Maori leader noting wryly that an obstacle to the growth of prosperous enterprise in close-knit communities can be an excess of the spirit of communal obligations — basically, giving away the product cheap or free to the whanau, which rather reduces the profits available for reinvestment in the business.

The social-capital concept that I think is really useful is quite different from communitarianism. At the risk of oversharpening the distinction, I would put it like this. Whereas communitarianism is about (only) trusting people you know, social capital is *all about trusting people you don't know*! And this is the breakthrough concept that may provide the missing input to the growth equation.[6] Economies thrive when people are prepared to do business with people they don't know, because only then can the full potentialities of specialisation and the division of labour be realised.

We are actually back to the business of behaving well stressed in the previous chapter. Behaving well with people you know is not such a big deal. You may like them, and even if you don't there is the strong possibility you will meet them again, so you have an incentive not to get too far out of line for fear of retaliation. This is the game-theory approach, and it has some applicability. But it doesn't explain the great miracle of economic prosperity, of people rubbing along with each other, trusting strangers, doing things together that make them and others better off.

Of course, social capital is a truly social matter, not just an economic asset like a back-hoe. One of the main points of my argument is that economy and society should not — indeed, cannot — be separated, and that the current dogma, which is doing its best to wrench them apart, is profoundly misconceived. The terms on which we live with each other matter at all levels of human existence, including business and economic affairs; and it is worrying indeed that a consequence of rationalism has been that those terms have been declining in quality.

A personal example. Growing up in Dunedin, I lived some miles from school (Anderson's Bay Primary School). Yet, from a very early age, I travelled to and from school on my own, by bus or bike, and played after school until tea time without getting permission from home. In allowing me this freedom my parents were very trusting, not so much of me — I was too young to be dependable — but of the adults and older children in the community, whom they expected — correctly — would keep an eye on me and my playmates, dealing with any accidents or trouble, and, of course, policing our tendency to commit mildly illegal acts. We would ride our bikes on the footpath and take short cuts through private property, but we never questioned the authority of an adult, even one unknown to us, to 'tell us off' for so doing.

Anderson's Bay was — probably still is — as quintessentially *middle*-middle-class a community as has ever existed anywhere in New Zealand or the world. Every weekday morning, all the men went off down the hill by car or trolley bus to something their children called 'the office': this was to me an utterly mysterious concept (my father was a doctor), which I did not fathom until my teens, when I took a holiday job with what was then the National Mortgage Company and discovered for myself the true tedium of the office existence.

Our family lived in an upper-middle-class enclave on our own hill, separated from Anderson's Bay by the flatland lower-middle-class suburbs of Tainui and Musselburgh — mildly dangerous territory to cross, but nothing too alarming.[7] The secure freedom I had to roam these neighbourhoods taught me something about life, developed my self-reliance and was great fun. A tiny triumph of social capital in action!

Now, I hope that most Kiwi children can still find their

own way to and from school. But I know that many do not, especially upper-middle-class kids. Walking in the morning to the university from my house in Parnell, I see tense-looking adults driving cars, frustrated by the traffic congestion to which they are themselves contributing. In the back seat sit one or two prim children, often in uniform, being chauffeured to school. I think what a waste of the adult's time, and what a waste of the children's opportunity to live more in the world around them, to draw on the social capital and, by their own participation in society, *to do their bit to contribute towards sustaining the social fabric, rather than insulating themselves from it*. I do understand that Auckland in the mid-1990s is not the same as Dunedin in the 1950s and 1960s, but I regret that — in this instance if not in all others (after all, I choose now to live in Auckland rather than the city where I grew up).

Many New Zealanders are aware of, and worry about, the decline in what I have called social capital. But they may not have connected it with economic matters, partly because it is a rather new concept in economics, and mostly because we have all been rather brainwashed into accepting the notion that untrammelled self-seeking behaviour is the essential ingredient for prosperity in the 'new' economy. I argue to the contrary: there is never any shortage of opportunism; what is needed are the customs and protocols that temper self-seeking behaviour for the eventual greater good of all, including (most of) the self-seekers. This is the real source of the 'rising tide that raises all boats' — not rampant individualism.

The situation may be even worse than it appears. We may as a nation have been living off our social capital; depreciating it without devoting energy and resources to replenishment. Think again of the basic metaphor of the prisoner's dilemma game, in which cooperative behaviour yields a better total outcome than does narrow self-seeking. Writ large in the real economy, the 'game' is played many times by many people. In this situation it is always possible for a few jerks to 'defect' — to play the self-seeking strategy — because for the rest of us it is not worthwhile to jeopardise the success of the whole game by retaliating against the 'free-riders'. As the number of defectors increases this will remain true, but only up to a point. Beyond this, the burden of the free-riders becomes insupportable, and the cooperative outcome collapses. We are then all forced into narrow opportunism, like it or not.

Could such a collapse be on the cards for New Zealand? I hope not, but there are reasons for concern. Economic rationalism is only a decade or so old here, and most of the current workforce grew up and learned how to behave under the old regime. But what of the young people who will replace us? I worry about both ends of our notoriously widening income distribution: unbridled greediness at the top, which mocks the willingness of those with economic power to 'leave something on the table' (a key ingredient of the old social contract); economic incompetence and demoralisation at the bottom, with the emergence of New Zealand's first generation of kids from families in which it has been normal for the fathers not to be in steady legal employment.

And what of those in the worried and defensive middle classes? Each bright middle-class kid who is pulled out of the state system and cocooned in a private school, each retreat from a mixed neighbourhood to the 'security' of a new private-estate development, represents another tug on the social fabric; another weakening of the ties that bind, or bound, us together as nation and society.

This is not a simple matter. The changes for the worse cannot all be blamed on economic rationalism, and nor should we fail to celebrate those changes that have been for the good. New Zealand really is more fun to live in now than it used to be, in most (though not all) respects, if you have a well-paid, secure job. And the difficulties of achieving cooperative outcomes have been exacerbated by three major trends — increased 'competitive' pressures, especially from foreigners; breakdown of the old Pakeha dominance of society; and breakdown of the old division of labour between men and women. The first of these makes cooperative behaviour seem more expensive; the other two mean that people are less sure about how others will react, and they have less empathy and less sympathy with other players in the economic game.

I think we can do something about the pressures of competitiveness. But I do not mourn monoculturalism — indeed I expect that Pakeha economics can learn a lot from Maoritanga, to which the concept of social capital is surely intrinsic. And I believe that if a woman wants to share the burden of paid work she should be able to do so on the same terms as the men, and that feminism has a lot to teach economics and economists.

In Part III I will make some suggestions about how we could go about regenerating our social capital. First, though, there is more to be uncovered on the mysteries of markets — social capital in action.

Chapter 10

Life at the Margin: the Meaning of Markets

Returning to live in New Zealand in July 1992, I was faced with an empty house to fit out, having given away all my 110-volt appliances in Canada. My new neighbour came upon me as I was about to set out for the shops. 'Where are you going?' she asked. I said I was about to hit the stores for home appliances.

'Buy them all in one place,' she advised. 'Then you'll get the best deal.'

'Deal?' I said, surprised.

'Oh, yes,' she insisted. 'You must bargain over the prices.'

'How primitive,' I thought to myself. 'They haggle in shops in this country.' But, being a confident, competitive male, I actually enjoy haggling, and so I set off hopefully to the store recommended by my neighbour.

The procedure that followed can be observed in bazaars in poor countries the world over. I went around the shop with the salesman, pointing at things: washing machine and dryer (New Zealand-made, of course), television, vacuum cleaner and other stuff. We went back to the counter and he added up all the list prices. He told me what it came to. I asked what sort of discount he would give me on the lot. He immediately took 10 per cent off the total. I then asked if he could 'manage it' for a round-number figure, somewhat below his offer (a 'focal-point price', in economic lingo). The salesman looked solemn and said that he would have to go back to the office and do some sums. He disappeared to the back room, no doubt to do no more than close his eyes and count slowly to twenty. In the meantime, I noticed a few other things I needed — extension cords; a toaster. The salesman returned from his notional calculations, all smiles. Yes, they could just oblige me with that price. Okay, they would throw in the extension cords and the toaster. Sure, they would accept payment by credit card.

And so the deal was struck, and I went off home with my booty, happy to have saved hundreds of dollars and grateful, of course, for my neighbour's fortuitous intervention.

But, in retrospect, I am not quite comfortable with this episode. I'm not worried that a more skilful and aggressive haggler than I could have got an even better deal (this particular store did shut down soon after my visit). Rather, I wonder where the money came from to fund my discount. Retailing is a mature business, with a well-known and easily replicated technology. The market should be 'thick', the supply of retailing services 'elastic', as economists say. Competition should keep prices pretty close to the minimum needed to sustain a business. There should really be no room for haggling. Everyone should pay the one low price. But they didn't — my discounts were subsidised by other customers paying full list prices, and those list prices must eventually be higher to cross-subsidise the good deals granted to the hagglers like me.

We can have both efficiency and equity concerns with an economy based on haggling. On the efficiency side, there are the resources used up in the actual bargaining process, and the erosion of the informational value of the price mechanism (when listed prices aren't 'real'). Plus, by doing all my buying in one store in order to maximise my bargaining clout, I missed out on the range of products available if I had looked around. My 'free' toaster, for example, works terribly — I'd have been better off paying proper money for a good toaster at a specialty kitchen store.

As for equity, we have to consider the sizeable group who, for reasons of ignorance, timidity or just distaste for the process do pay the full list price, which has been driven up to compensate for the lower margins on sales to hagglers. Nor can we expect that lower prices will go to those who need them most. There is plenty of evidence that when there is a range of prices in the market, *the poor pay more*! Rich folk get the best deals (that's part of how they got rich), and the middle classes, with their financial reserves, mobility, confidence and social skills, do better than the lower orders. A haggling economy breaks through the protective anonymity of thick markets to squeeze the surplus (little though there is) out of the poor and desperate.

There was an interesting illustration of this 'price discrimination' in action in a recent study of bargaining for a new automobile in the United States. New cars are so expensive and so heterogeneous (models and options) that even in very rich societies like Europe and the United States it is quite common to haggle. So who gets the best deal?

The researchers in this study trained a group of presentable-looking, smart, youngish people to use an identical, scripted bargaining strategy, and sent them out to see what prices they could negotiate for a new automobile.[1] Some of them were white, some black; some male, some female. Each unwitting car dealer would receive two visits, several days apart. One ostensible customer would be a white male; one might not be. More than three hundred cars were bargained over, from more than 150 dealers — a good-sized sample.

Results were striking: white males got the best deals, followed by white females, black females and, well behind, black males. The researchers calculated that dealers' profits would have been *three times* larger from their final offers to black males than from the deals offered white males.

What explains these differences? The researchers are properly cautious in interpreting their results. But simple racial animus — ill-will towards blacks — doesn't seem to be the culprit: black 'customers' did not do significantly better at black-owned dealerships. It is suggested that the dealers base their own bargaining strategy on inferences about the knowledgeability and willingness to search of their customers.[2] Whatever the reasons, the results certainly support the authors' conclusion that 'the discrimination uncovered in this study stands squarely in the face of earlier analyses that reject the possibility that discrimination can persist in a competitive market'.

Open price discrimination is in fact quite a common commercial practice. Students, for example, get cheap rates for cinema and airline tickets. The rest of us don't mind this — at least, I don't — but we might not be so happy if students also got cheaper groceries at the supermarket. What's the difference?

It is this. In the cinema or on the plane, the students are using seats which would otherwise be empty. The marginal cost is low. We non-students can see the sense in this, and appreciate that filling those seats lowers the businesses' costs of supplying services to the rest of us, from which we can expect to benefit. But it is not cheaper to supply students with groceries, and doing so would necessarily mean that the rest of us would have to pay more. Also, such practices would encourage wasteful and unfair arbitraging, which is less likely with discounted cinema or travel tickets. It would be easy to pay a student to buy your groceries for you, but it would rather miss the point to have them see the movie for you, and it is difficult to travel under someone else's name.[3]

In many countries overt price discrimination is illegal unless it can be justified by demonstrating different costs of supplying different types of customer. This is as it should be. But covert, or 'systemic', discrimination is much harder to root out. You can find out that, say, blacks pay more than whites for new cars, but what can you do about it? The private sector can do something. When, a decade ago, General Motors created a new, stand-alone corporation called Saturn to 'build and sell small cars in a new way',[4] they did end up with something special, but this was not the car itself — generally judged to be rather ordinary — but rather the transactions involved — between management and workers, and between dealers and customers. Part of the latter is a rigid 'no-haggling' policy, which has appealed in particular to woman buyers. This is not because women are wimps when it comes to bargaining, but perhaps because they are less likely than men to be attracted to the zero-sum, I-win-you-lose characteristic of the haggle, and prefer a cooperative, service-based approach to retailing.[5] In any case, the results of inculcating the 'Saturn spirit' have been rather extraordinary. The company invited all owners and their families to a 'homecoming' at their Tennessee plant: 44,000 turned up in their Saturns!

This is good stuff, but not necessarily applicable to all car makers and all car buyers. And much of the problem of people in a weak economic situation being exploited in the market is not because there is (illegal) discrimination at point of sale —

at the cash register in the supermarket or department store — but because the poor have poorer information about, and less physical access to, stores where prices are low.

What is needed are markets in which a plurality of competent sellers compete for the custom of confident, well-informed buyers, with the result that a product is sold at the same sharp price to everyone with the minimum of fuss. Achieving this desirable state of affairs is not so easy. The main requirement for an efficient market is that it be 'thick'. A thick market is one which anyone can get into — on the supply or demand side — without affecting the price. If there are many buyers and sellers, the addition or subtraction of one of them is too small an event to shift the market significantly.

There is much to be said for thick markets. Stability of price gives participants the confidence to make long-term commitments and investments, which pay off in even more efficient outcomes in the future. With very many players, price discrimination is difficult to sustain so everyone pays the same price. And this price is determined by the 'marginal' customers — the ones who are most willing to shop around. Who are these keen, knowledgeable customers? We all are, in our chosen fields of special interest and expertise, and in thick markets there are enough such specialist buyers to keep sellers 'honest', meaning offering good products at sharp prices.

Thus, we can do most of our shopping without spending a lot of time and money searching around for the best deal, confident that in a thick market someone else — the specialists — will be doing this, and thereby will ensure that prices are as they should be. In contrast, an exchange system based on bargaining between buyer and seller loses much of the efficiency of thick markets. Marginal participants will take the trouble to get themselves good deals, but there is no automatic mechanism for extending the benefits to everyone else. Each buyer, each seller, has to fend for themselves. The outcome is more costly in direct transaction costs, and, as noted above, is likely to be inequitable, in that weaker players will do poorly.

Thick markets can never be taken for granted. They are human artifacts, not inevitable outgrowths of the natural law of the invisible hand. Indeed, we must appreciate just how fragile is the achievement of a well-functioning market system; and how vulnerable it is to being undermined *from within*.

One problem is this: thick markets are good for consumers at large, and they are good for small businesses needing access to customers. But they are not good for big business, and therein lies the tragic flaw of laissez-faire capitalism: big business *hates* thick markets, and is devoted to destroying them. It sees all the 'surplus' — the difference between what we pay and what things are worth to us — going to the customer and thinks: what a pity! Wouldn't it be better if *we* could extract that surplus for ourselves? A small businessperson need not waste their time with such thoughts, since they are constrained by competition from dealing at anything other than the marginal price. But the corollary of bigness is fewness, and when sellers are few in number, they have a chance to break away from the constraints of impersonal competition and indulge in some serious surplus extraction. In little New Zealand, there is a lot of fewness around these days — a lot of markets dominated by just two or even one large seller or buyer.

That is certainly something to worry about, but we should look at ourselves too, at the consumer-obsessed, go-for-the-deal attitudes that now permeate our lives and culture. If we have become a nation of inveterate hagglers, we can't really blame it all on multinational monopolies. We do need to appreciate the importance of restraint and forbearance to market life. One example: in 1993 there was a sharp increase in world prices for logs, tempting some New Zealand foresters to divert trees to the export market, or demand that local sawmillers pay the high world price. This was very upsetting to the trade. The director of the industry association talked about 'irresponsible' supplier behaviour during what turned out to be just a 'spike' in prices (i.e. they dropped back again quickly). He said: 'We had a fright and the relationship broke down.' Taking opportunistic advantage of short-term supply-and-demand conditions eroded the long-term viability of the market.

Another example. At lunch recently in Vancouver, a Canadian colleague told a group of us economists about something surprising he had just read in a journal. 'A survey was carried out in California and in China,' he said. 'The same question was asked: "Is it fair that sellers should put up their prices when demand increases?" What proportion do you suppose answered "no" in each country?'

Jim Brander, my colleague, had been startled by the answers, but I was not. I guessed that proportionally more Californians than Chinese would think putting up prices unfair, and I even got quite close to guessing right on the proportions answering no: I suggested that 70 per cent of the Californians and 40 per cent of the Chinese would disapprove of price-raising opportunism in this circumstance.[6]

Why was I so smart? Well, partly because I had already come across a few other studies in this vein.[7] But mainly, I think, because the shock of coming back to the new New Zealand has sharpened my insights into the meaning of a market economy and what it takes to function well. I guessed that even though Californian teenagers may tend to be unusually hedonistic and individualistic in a nation of hedonists and individualists, the fact that each of them has been steeped since earliest childhood in market life would have instilled in them a sense of the 'rules of the game', of the morals of the market; of the self-restraint required of market participants if the system is to function smoothly. The mainland Chinese, on the other hand, still live under a rough mix of the two extreme regimes of highly centralised planning and highly decentralised one-on-one haggling, each of which encourages — indeed, requires for survival — ruthlessly opportunistic behaviour. They have not yet learnt market manners, the rules of *doux-commerce*.

A market is an institution for the exchange of goods or services between willing participants. Actual physical markets — places with stalls and vendors and haggling — are really a very primitive form of exchange institution, of some residual social and cultural value, but quite incapable of sustaining the volume of transactions required in a successful economy. These bazaar-type institutions are what the mainland Chinese have known, and what they will need to develop beyond as they seek to approach developed-nation status.

Meanwhile, New Zealand is charging off in the other direction — back to the bazaar; back to the zero-sum, one-on-one, beat-each-other-up haggling economy.[8] It is rather bizarre;

another Kiwi paradox: the 'free market' revolution has actually subverted the market system in its full sense. The point is this: a civilised market economy is truly an excellent thing. When it is really going well we can almost take it for granted, doing our buying and selling with a minimum of fuss, confident that we are getting or giving a fair price for a product of decent quality. But like everything else that matters in human affairs, markets are social and cultural institutions. They only behave well if we who make them behave well. They need widespread honesty, tolerance, forbearance and trust. Unfortunately, these qualities do not trade at a premium in the new New Zealand.

Chapter 11

True Stories from the Labour Market

Not long before the 1996 election two New Zealand parliamentarians were in Australia, addressing a conference on economic reforms. One MP, an architect of the 1991 Employment Contracts Act, spoke glowingly of the success of that radical piece of labour-market legislation. 'There have been enormous productivity gains,' he claimed.[1]

'No, there haven't,' said the other MP. And he was right, and had the figures to prove it. Wriggle and twist and distort though the proponents of the ECA may (and do), they cannot in the end escape the cold truth: it has been a washout in terms of labour productivity — less than one per cent growth per year in this decade, well below the growth achieved in previous decades in New Zealand and over the same period in Australia.

It is quite a puzzle. At the micro-level, anecdotes of productivity improvements abound. And in surveys, employers tend to attribute productivity gains to the new flexibility allowed by the ECA, instead of the old (usually union-mediated) collective agreements that covered all workers in the same trade or industry. But the good-news stories just don't show up in the macro data, which reveal mediocre productivity performance, even more mediocre real-wage growth (so that income distributions are widening), and increased insecurity of work. Not much fun for most participants or would-be participants in the workforce.

Now this is very interesting to a professional economist as well as very important to everybody else. Of all the hundred-plus major 'reforms' that have been imposed on us since 1984, the ECA is perhaps the biggest and the purest, in a scientific sense. It really does offer a fairly clean test of a specific economic theory. And the theory fails this test (as it has failed in New Zealand before — our great post-war miracle of zero unemployment is impossible, according to the economic model behind the ECA).

The journalist Patricia Herbert wrote a long and thoughtful review article on the Employment Contracts Act in the excellent periodical *New Zealand Books* (August 1996). She began and ended her piece with the productivity puzzle, but left it unexplained. It doesn't fit the theory: something must be wrong with the assumptions of the theory. But what could it be?

Herbert leaves a clue. She tells about late-night stake-outs waiting for the outcome of the trend-setting metal-trades wage negotiations, when she was a young member of the parliamentary press gallery in the early 1980s. Her interest in this was personal as well as professional: in those days journalists had a relativity wage linkage with core fitters: 'What they got, we got.'

'It was, of course, economically absurd,' she writes. 'But it was also socially cohesive. My interest in the wage fortunes of the core fitter diminished substantially when the link between us was severed.'

Here's the clue. To solve a puzzle we usually have to think laterally, to query some unexamined assumption. *Why was it 'of course' economically absurd that journalists and metal workers had linkages in their wages? And might not 'social cohesiveness' have something to do with productivity?*

The ECA is above all an instrument for destroying social cohesiveness. It does this by fostering one-on-one negotiations between employer and employee. The theory is that productivity is the result of individual effort and enterprise, so workers should be rewarded individually, to maximise their incentives to perform. Well, what if productivity performance is not solely an individual effort? What if *cooperation* is key to getting things done in the workplace? Such cooperation can take many forms, few of which have anything much to do with top-down management: 'showing the ropes' to a new worker, fixing other people's mistakes before they get serious, sharing tasks efficiently — basically, all the things we call 'teamwork', or social cohesiveness at the work site.

Now — and this is the big insight — if productivity depends on the effort of a team, then the efficient thing is to reward the team collectively, not individually. That is, if output goes up, everyone should get a pay increase, not just a few selected individuals, so that all the individuals in the team will have that incentive to contribute to their joint effort. ECA-type single-worker contracts discourage this, because if you do something to help another worker, they reap the benefits, not you. But old-style collective bargaining agreements do provide the structure within which teamwork makes economic sense.

Even the national awards referred to by Patricia Herbert are consistent with this. Of course, the type of teamwork I have been talking about here functions at the level of the organisation or the work site (though national 'team spirit' is important, too!), but a well-performing work site can be rewarded through bonuses and from the long-term job security that goes with belonging to a successful operation. The key is that two people with the same skills on the same job should not be paid differently.

This does not mean that individual ability and effort go unrewarded. The most energetic and able members of teams are recognised as such, first by their team-mates and then by their supervisors and managers, whose ranks they will eventually be invited to join, at a higher salary. But there must be a balance between individual and team. It is this balance that has been radically disturbed by the Employment Contracts Act, and we should therefore be unsurprised to see the effects on lower productivity growth. In crude supply/demand terms there is certainly no mystery here: make an input cheaper, and more of it will be used, and less of other inputs (such as training and capital), so that the cheaper input becomes less productive. Puzzle solved?

Collective and, especially, national wage awards are efficient in another important sense: they economise on what are called 'transaction costs' — the actual time and effort devoted to settling the price of a good or service, such as providing wage labour. With economic growth, the size of the total economic 'pie' grows; this must somehow be shared out in bigger slices. How to do this? The efficient and fair way — and this is perfectly standard economics — is that the fruits of growth are distributed in a general increase in wages and salaries.

That's just what used to happen, with general wage orders and fixed relativities. Patricia Herbert got her fair share of the bigger economic pie without having to divert a minute of her time from her real, useful job of being a journalist. Nowadays that wouldn't happen. Each worker is supposed to haggle individually with their boss — a time-consuming business for both sides, and one that can be distressing, even demeaning, for the person on the weaker side of the bargaining table. This, along with increased competitive pressure from 'cheap' imports, must go a long way towards explaining one of the great scandals of 1990s New Zealand — the unprecedented sight of real wages actually declining through the 1991–94 recovery and beyond.

It is not 'absurd' that there be linkages between the wages of workers in quite different professions. People are not dead fish, their value to be set by the impersonal interplay of supply and demand in an auction room. It is the job of the 'market' to *deliver* decent standards of living for working people, not to *determine* them. Of course economic forces will play their role in the way earnings relativities evolve — with some premium paid for investments in human capital (training), and with some (though temporary) reward for skills in short supply — but in a civilised society these forces are quite tightly constrained by moral and social considerations. Instead of arguing that workers should 'price themselves into jobs', the decent economy insists that employers price themselves into workers: if they can't pay a proper wage and make a reasonable profit at the same time, then they should get out of the market and let someone else more competent make use of the resources.

It is a measure of how flexible and effective markets can be to observe how over the past century or so they have accommodated what has often seemed at the time to be dangerously radical changes in labour legislation. Not that economists have always shown great faith in this: back in 1837, for example, one of the leading scholars of the time, Nassau Senior, argued strenuously that reducing working hours from twelve to ten a day (!) would bankrupt industry because it depended for its profit on the work of the last (twelfth) hour. Well it didn't, of course.

New Zealand used to be well ahead of Britain and Europe and the United States in the business of labour reform. At about the time that Nassau Senior was spouting his reactionary nonsense, the carpenter Samuel Parnell was refusing to build a house in Petone for a merchant, George Hunter, unless his working day was restricted to eight hours. The matter was settled amicably, and Parnell went on to found the Eight-Hour Day movement. The trade-union movement got under way, in fits and starts, in the following decades, aided from time to time by parliamentary legislation such as the 1894 Industrial Conciliation and Arbitration Act and, eventually, the 1987 Industrial Relations Act, which encouraged a sensible rationalisation of what had become an overfragmented structure, with too many small, ineffective unions.

All this was torn apart in 1991 with the ECA, of which perhaps the major and intended effect was to weaken unions, whose membership has nearly halved since 1991. A major symptom of the weakening has been the collapse in strikes and lockouts — stoppages which cost about two hours' work lost per worker per year in 1990 were down to about twenty minutes per worker/year in 1995 — rates not seen here since the 1950s and early 1960s, when New Zealand's labour relations were the wonder of the western world. But there is a big difference between then and now — in the fifties and sixties real incomes were steadily rising, so there was good reason to be peaceful. What is unprecedented in modern New Zealand history is the conjunction of low levels of apparent industrial unrest with deteriorating real incomes and conditions of employment. This is not peace but pacification.

Why no fuss, no public outcry? I suspect that unions have never been really popular with New Zealanders, even amongst their members. The old stereotype dies hard of the union official as a whingeing Pommie or dour Scot with bits of his breakfast egg on his tie. But this is not the point. You don't have to be 'pro-labour' to appreciate what they have done.

The truth is that any New Zealander who has a well-paid job with good working conditions is riding on the back of more than 150 years of tough struggle by workers and unions, beginning with Parnell in 1840. These achievements are not secure.

They can be rolled back, and have been, remarkably quickly, since the enactment of the Employment Contracts Act, with very little fuss from the deliberately weakened labour movement. Not long ago I sat in on a briefing by the President of the Council of Trade Unions, Mr Ken Douglas. I was quite shocked by the CTU's attitude. Shocked by its moderation — timidity, almost. They don't want a return to monopoly, compulsory unionism with national awards. What they ask for is legislation to protect collective bargaining, which seems to me a pretty basic worker's right in a decent society. In effect, they are only seeking to reclaim labour rights as these are now in the United States. Really!

We would perhaps not have been so disappointed in the Employment Contracts Act if we had taken on board the lessons from an earlier period of our history, when, for about two decades up to the early 1970s, New Zealand operated with not just low, but literally *zero*, unemployment, year in and year out. This is quite unfathomable from a rationalist economic perspective, which perhaps explains why it has been ignored. The New Zealand economy (then) was like a bumblebee which (I have been told) cannot fly, according to aerodynamic theory. One recalls Paul Samuelson's Scottish preacher, with his advice: 'Here is a grave problem, brethren. Let us look it firmly in the eye, and pass on.'

The theoretical problem with full employment is this: in the rationalist model, labour is just a commodity like coal or computers or cars, and we need to maintain permanent buffer stocks of unused commodities to cope with unforeseen fluctuations in supply and demand, which otherwise will generate large swings in prices (as they do for commodities such as fresh produce, which do not store easily). The buffer stock of labour is, of course, unemployment, and there is a 'natural' rate of unemployment below which demand will start to push up wages and prices, leading to inflation. The apparent trade-off between unemployment and inflation was discovered, ironically enough, by a New Zealander, A.W. Phillips, though not, of course, using New Zealand data, and his eponymous Curve is probably the most famous discovery of post-war macroeconomics.

But why no buffer stock needed in New Zealand? If you ask

someone who has thought a bit about this question they are likely to respond with one or more standard answers: high wool prices; preferential access to the United Kingdom dairy market; import controls; overmanning on the railways. These factors do all have a role in the story of post-war New Zealand, but they do not explain how labour was continually being reallocated between firms and industries without having to go through an intervening spell in the unemployment pool.

My hypothesis is this: in the old New Zealand, there was a social contract between employers and labour, based on a certain code of how each should behave. Each employer felt some obligation to give work to a man seeking a job, whether or not they had an official vacancy, and to pay that man (it did not apply to women, whose participation rate was much lower than men's then) enough to support a family, which entailed accepting a rather flat income distribution, with limits on how much employers and managers would pay themselves.[2] On the workers' side, every able-bodied man felt an obligation to turn up to work (even though unemployment benefits were actually quite generous), and their unions did not endanger the full employment situation with excessive wage claims. This doesn't mean that there was no inflation and no industrial disputes — of course there were, but these were not out of keeping with the experience of economies that also needed the discipline of mass unemployment to keep labour in line, as New Zealand most clearly did not (though does now).

So long as everyone followed the code, this high-wage, high-employment situation was sustainable: the 'surplus' workers' wages would be spent, generating demand for goods and services which would, through the macroeconomic feedbacks, justify the decision to employ them. But adhering to the code at the micro-level (individual firms, workers and unions) required a high degree of empathy, which was most easily maintained in a homogeneous, stable society dominated by single-worker (male, of course) families and businesses protected from cut-throat competition. Here was true social capital at work.

New Zealand's post-war economic history has revealed a huge paradox: the old, supposedly rigid regime in fact achieved a superb balance between supply and demand for labour; the new 'flexible' market system cannot function without a sizeable margin of excess supply of workers over jobs. We cannot go back to the past — if only because our labour force is so much more heterogeneous now — but we would be fools not to take it seriously. As an economist once said: 'The invisible hand is all thumbs in the labour market.' New Zealanders have been finding this out the hard way since 1991.

Chapter 12
Shock Collapse in Managerial Productivity!

High in the hills, a storm sweeps away the conduit carrying water to the village. It will take days to fix, and a substitute source of supply must be found. Fortunately, in the gully below the village runs a stream. The village has no pump but every household has a bucket. At first, the villagers fetch their own water individually, each slithering down the steep bank to the stream, and struggling back up the hill with their bucketful, some water sloshing out on the way. Then the cry goes out: 'Form a chain!'

After some discussion and negotiation this is done. Almost the entire village is stationed at intervals down the bank, and in minutes the full buckets are flowing up the chain and the empty ones back down. At first quite a lot of water is lost in the changeovers from one person to the next, but soon, with practice and repositioning of a few hopeless clumsy-hands, the buckets arriving at the top are almost as heavy as those leaving the stream.

In just twenty minutes the old wine barrels at the top of the bank are filled to overflowing with enough water to get the villagers through the day, and they disperse cheerfully with much mutual backslapping for their energy and ingenuity, promising to reassemble at the same time the next day, when they will try to fill the barrels in fifteen minutes flat.

Our villagers have discovered — or rediscovered — two of the great techniques of modern industrial organisation: the division of labour and the assembly line. More than two hundred years ago, Adam Smith famously used the example of the pin factory to illustrate this:

> One man draws out the wire; another straights it; a third cuts it; a fourth points it; a fifth grinds it at the top for receiving the head; to make the head requires two or three distinct operations; to put it on is a peculiar business; to whiten the pin is another; it is even a trade by itself to put them into the paper . . . Ten persons, therefore, could make among them upwards of forty-eight thousand pins in a day . . .,[1]

whereas a single workman trying to make a pin all by himself would scarcely 'with his utmost industry, make one pin in a day'. Just by allowing labour to specialise, and with no change in the technology or even, necessarily, any increase in the value of tools and machinery required, great improvements in productivity can be effected.

In the village water situation, specialisation is spatial: each villager 'specialises' in standing in a certain unique spot, there to receive and pass on a bucket. No special skill is required: indeed, the chain is probably 'de-skilling', in the sense that it takes more balance and judgement to carry a bucket up a tricky path than to transfer it on the spot. Nor is the chain capital intensive. In fact, fewer buckets will be needed, and the invention of the chain could indeed have been spurred by a shortage of buckets, such that there weren't enough for everyone to fetch their own water. Nevertheless, the chain realises a vast productivity improvement, in essence because whereas under self-sufficiency buckets *and* people had to move similar distances, now only the buckets move.

But specialisation is not sufficient. A new task, not needed under self-sufficiency, is involved: coordination. In the making-pins example, what if the fellow drawing the wire decides to take the day off? And even if he doesn't, how does he know how much wire to make? Henry Ford's classic solution was to put all the specialists under one roof, lined up in order of the stages of assembly of the product. Then it is rather easy to coordinate the workers — basically, by setting the speed at which raw materials (newly filled buckets) are fed in at the start of the line. Assembly lines have disadvantages relative to more decentralised modes of production — their output rate is rather inflexible, and they are very vulnerable to breakdowns: if one person drops a bucket, this may trigger a 'chain' reaction of bumped buckets back up the line. But, functioning well, specialisation and assembly lines greatly expand the productive power of society's resources.

New Zealanders are great formers of chains. We respond to these situations instinctively. Almost without conscious coordination, New Zealand villagers would find their way to their appropriate stations: the young and limber racing down the bank to compete for the damp and relatively arduous task of filling the buckets, from which they would pause occasionally for water fights and to pluck from the stream overexcited small children who had fallen in; the tall and strong hoisting the full buckets up and over into the barrels; the wise and sedentary sorting out the distribution of water from the barrel; the rest of us taking our places in the chain and setting to our task. The old and infirm would be willingly excused duty: 'Don't you worry, Gran, we'll have that bathtub of yours filled up in no time!'

We are good at it — or have been good — because we have (or have had) the high degree of empathy and sympathy — the social capital — that facilitates sophisticated exercises in productive cooperation such as the water chain. But even with the best goodwill in the world there will need to be resources devoted to coordinating the chain which are not needed if everyone gets their own water. There will have to be facilities for storing the water, and for allocating it between users. Someone will have to decide when the chain will be operated, and will have to contact the others and, perhaps, spur them into action after the initial flush of enthusiasm wears off. Along with the division of labour and the assembly line our villagers will discover their handmaiden, what economists call 'transaction costs'.

This is the great trade-off of industrial organisation. In order to increase productivity people must specialise, but the instant they do so the need is created for someone to coordinate their specialised activities: the finer the division of labour, the fewer workers will be actually available for production, or 'transformation' activities, and the more will have to be diverted to coordinating or 'transaction' work that doesn't directly add to the number of buckets being moved. Social capital is key to determining the terms of this trade-off: a high-trust, high-empathy society will be able to literally to get its act together with less transaction fuss than a society in which the people do not share basic values, goals and social skills.

Adam Smith's famous phrase was the 'invisible hand',[2] but perhaps a more appropriate metaphor for the glue that binds together a modern market economy would be 'the invisible handshake'. Empathy with how others think, sympathy with the interests of others, and adherence to an implicit set of rules of engagement are the great catalysts of market life, reducing the need for costly supervision, monitoring, contracts, negotiations and litigation, in both the 'productive' and the 'transaction' sectors of the economy.

New Zealanders were skilled practitioners of the art of the invisible handshake. We were a homogeneous society, similar in aspirations and achievement. We were trusting and trustworthy. We were self-reliant but kind. We were willing to take responsibility for our own actions as well as (perhaps irksomely so) the actions of others. But there certainly were some serious trade-offs. The homogeneity and simplicity that oiled the wheels of commerce came at a cost. The culture was Pakeha and the economy was built around the needs of the full-time male worker. The range of consumer choice was limited, and government regulations (such as import controls) made it difficult to start new businesses in many industries. Much of the old New Zealand is just not acceptable to us any more, and rightly so.

But my point is this: the system in the 1950s and 1960s may have been dull and limited. But it functioned with little fuss: *our market system was remarkably cheap!* This does not mean that the price actually paid for goods and services was, necessarily, low. By today's standards, some costs were low: for example, housing, staple foods and running a car.[3] Other things — new cars, household appliances — seem expensive. However, the cost of 'delivering' the goods — the transaction-cost wedge between what the consumer pays and what the producer gets — was low, possibly lower than anywhere else in the world then or since. The proportion of *transformation* workers, doing stuff that other people want for its own sake, e.g. building, making, teaching, healing, fixing, to *transaction* workers, whose indispensable but not intrinsically valued task is to facilitate the exchange of useful things for money, was high.

How high? It turns out that the industries and occupations devoted to coordinating transactions are substantial users of resources in their own right in a modern market economy. There are the shops themselves, of course, but behind them is another vast network of warehousing, distribution, transportation, communications; and whole professions devoted to administering the transaction of goods and services and the security of the property rights that attach to them: managers, clerks, accountants, lawyers, auditors, bankers, insurers, police, custodians, guards.

What these people do is valuable, on the whole, but it is not valued in its own right. They do not bake bread, brew beer, butcher beef. What they do is run the markets that bring together the producers of goods and services with the people who want to consume them. I have followed, with modifications, the method of two American economists, Wallis and North (the latter a Nobel-winning economic historian) to calculate the total numbers of people involved in these transaction activities in New Zealand over the past forty years.[4] I counted all the workers in industries devoted to providing transaction services — finance, insurance, real estate, legal and other business services, guards, central government administration — plus those workers in other industries in transaction occupations (managers, clerks, administrators). I also included the unemployed in the transactions sector. These are essentially a pool of available resources, like empty fridges in a store, apparently necessary in an economy based on specialisation and decentralised markets. All other workers are classified to the transformation sector.

So, how do the numbers add up? Figure 1 shows the picture. It plots the ratio of transaction to transformation workers in New Zealand over the forty years from 1956. The trend is upwards, as we would probably expect — as the New Zealand economy has become modernised and more sophisticated the proportion of people needed for coordinating and supervisory activities is likely to have increased.

But the trend is not steady. Far from it. In 1956 the ratio was 0.36, meaning that just over one transaction worker was needed for every three shop-floor, coal-face transformers. Over the next twenty years this ratio did rise quite steadily and gently. It reached 0.49 by 1976, one transactor to every two transformers, which is an increase of 36 per cent over the two decades.

But then the ratio really takes off. From 1976 to 1996 it nearly doubles, to 0.96 — a two-decade increase of 96 per cent! The period of sharpest increase was between the censuses of 1981 and 1991, which of course covers the years of radical more-market 'reforms'. It seems indeed that free markets do not come cheap!

What actually happened? How could we get into a position where barely half the workforce is actually engaged primarily in making the goods and services that are the desired end of economic activity? It was not caused by increases in the numbers of clerks, sales workers and public servants. The big leap in unemployment is a major factor, accounting for about half the increased numbers of transaction workers. Growth in the business-services sector (for instance lawyers, accountants, data processors, guards) accounts for about one-sixth. The remaining one-third is due to the proliferation of just one occupational group — managers.

The story here is quite startling. Check out Figure 2. Back in 1956, each manager could handle about twenty frontline transformation workers — or, put another way, twenty frontline workers only needed the services of one manager to

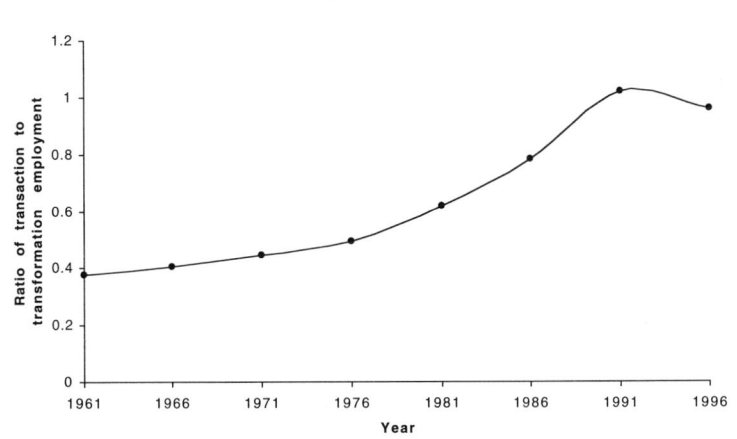

Figure 1: Ratio of transaction to transformation employment in New Zealand from 1956 to 1996

do whatever managers do. The ratio rose steadily but quite gently up to 1981, when it reached about one to nine. Then it just exploded, more than doubling over the next decade, and continuing to increase to 1996, even though the overall transaction/transformation ratio seems to have settled at a high level. Now there is nearly one manager for every *four* frontline workers — apparently, a massive decline in managerial productivity.

Surely, this is one of the most remarkable structural changes ever experienced in our economy. We must ask why it happened. One factor must be the increased complexity of life in a more open, market economy. When the exchange rate was fixed and run by the Reserve Bank, firms didn't need to hire specialist foreign-exchange managers to guide them through currency fluctuations. With centralised wage setting, you didn't need phalanxes of 'human resource' managers to negotiate one-on-one compensation packages with other employees. These changes have had their benefits (and drawbacks), but what even their most fervent fans must face is that they have not come free. A decentralised market economy is more costly to operate than one based on centralised rules and custom.

What do managers actually do? They give orders and try to make sure that these are carried out. They are therefore unnecessary to the extent that people know what they should be

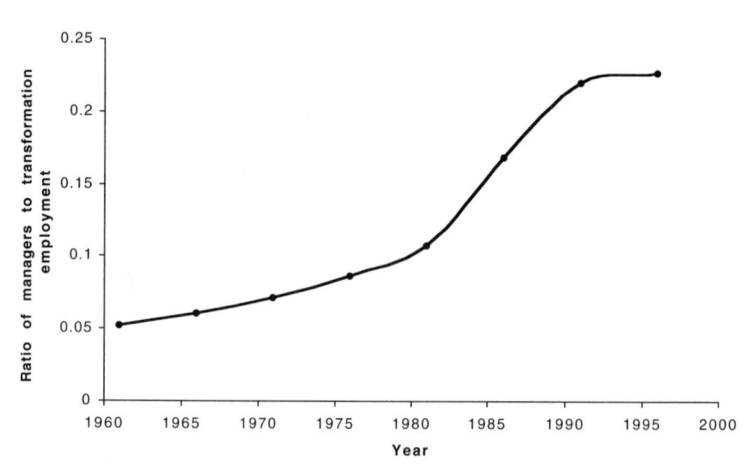

Figure 2: Ratio of managers to transformation employment in New Zealand from 1956 to 1996

doing (on which they are often better informed than their managers) and are well disposed towards doing it. This requires empathy and sympathy amongst workers — a willingness to cooperate. When we only needed one manager for every twenty transformation workers in New Zealand, we were evidently quite good at cooperating with each other and managing ourselves.

And then there is the commercialisation process that has been pushed upon us since 1984. But cooperation is the bane of commercialisation, which is based on the opportunistic model of economic behaviour in which every 'agent' focuses solely on maximising their own personal welfare. This is supposed to be more 'efficient', but it manifestly, ludicrously, is not. Take our leading example of the villagers sorting out their water-supply problem in a mighty cooperative venture fuelled by a willingness to work together for the common good. The commercialisers who have overturned New Zealand would be horrified by this. Where is the competition? they would cry. The village must make its water supply 'contestable' to outside suppliers. Proper profit targets must be set; incentive-based employment contracts negotiated to reward the strongest workers ahead of the others.

The result? Inexorably, more managers and associated support staff, to call tenders, to draw up contracts, and to monitor the efforts of workers who previously, in the cooperative setting, could be relied on to monitor themselves, but who are now being enjoined to be opportunistic and will indeed behave that way. Surely, there is something very foolish about all this.

The results of commercialisation in terms of bureaucratic bloat can be quite spectacular. Our new disclosure rules require that companies give details in their annual reports on numbers of employees paid more than $100,000 per year, broken down into $10,000 salary bands. These make for interesting reading. Fletcher Challenge Ltd's 1996 report admitted to no fewer than 2,301 members in their 100K club. If we sort these hierarchically, with each manager in charge of three or four subordinates, we get seven levels, from $100,000 to $1,000,000, the managers on each level getting a salary about 40 per cent higher than the level below them — a splendid illustration of the 'Iron Law of Hierarchy' in action.

Now there really is some serious money at stake here. Just the direct salary bill for those 2,301 Fletcher Challenge executives came to $292 million in 1996. That money would cover the entire operating budget of the University of Auckland, with enough left over to halve student fees. The comparison is valid, because in human terms the two institutions are the same size — each has about 25,000 people in total. And even more money than managers' salaries is involved. The great hierarchical pyramid of senior management is underpinned by an equally large 'shadow hierarchy' of secretaries and administrative assistants — the people who really know what is going on and who get things done as their bosses spin out the hours in endless meetings and intrigues. The shadow hierarchy is mostly made up of relatively low-paid women, but they do cost something, as do all the necessary commercial and legal advisers, not to mention air-conditioned offices for all these people.

Of course, administration is an honourable enough trade, and good managers are useful citizens. But why do we have so many of them, and why do we pay them so much? It is surely an irony of the market 'reforms' that their most outstanding consequence has been an explosion of transaction costs in general, and management costs in particular. Who would have thought that 'more market' would actually mean 'more bureaucracy'? But it has, and it is no fluke. We have found out that imposing a full-blown commercial regime basically means tossing aside as 'uncommercial' much of the trust and mutual forbearance — the social capital that enables people to manage themselves — and replacing this with an expensive system of monitors and guards, known politely as managers. And to the old question *quis custodiet custodes ipsos?* (who will guard the guards themselves) the answer is: more guards, more managers, reaching up to the million-dollar club in lofty pyramids of bureaucratic excess. All this is a great problem for the rest of us, but it is also a great opportunity: some managers are power-hungry oafs, but many are intelligent and able people, who will contribute something useful to society and the economy if we can figure out how to dismantle the hierarchies and rebuild a more moral, humane and efficient system for doing business.

Chapter 13
Deconstructing the Rich List

Four years ago at a conference in Sydney, I ran into a professor from Nashville, Tennessee, by the name of John J. Siegfried. 'So you're a Kiwi,' he said. 'Do you guys have a Rich List in New Zealand?'

'Of course we do,' I replied huffily. 'We are a modern developed economy, you know.'

'That's just fine,' said Siegfried soothingly. 'So let's you and I write a paper about it.'

And so we did, eventually. It can be found in the June 1997 issue of *New Zealand Economic Papers*, under the title 'How did the wealthiest New Zealanders get so rich?'

In collaborating with John Siegfried I was in effect becoming his franchisee, like an ideas version of setting up a McDonalds outlet in New Zealand (though you could say that McDonalds is just an idea, too). The idea — or hypothesis, as we call it in economics — that Siegfried is peddling to his local partners was tested first in his home market of the United States. It worked. So he tried it out in Britain. It worked there, too. Then he found an Australian collaborator — more success. And so on to New Zealand. What happened here?

Well, there were some interesting surprises. But before I tell you about these, just what is this idea of Prof. Siegfried's that seems to have a McDonalds-like ability to succeed across borders? It is about how, or more precisely where, people get rich — and he got it from his wife. She was doing an evening course in economics at a local college in Nashville, and she came home one night and told her husband that this economics he taught for a living was total hooey.

'Yes, dear,' said John Siegfried. 'Any part in particular?'

'You bet,' replied Mrs Siegfried. 'It's that perfect-competition stuff.'

John Siegfried was slightly shocked. The theory of perfectly competitive equilibrium, encapsulated in a marvellous diagram on which all six demand-and-cost curves miraculously cross at the same point, is the *pièce de résistance* of the modern microeconomics textbook. It 'proves' how competition knocks out all the slack and surplus from markets so that, in 'equilibrium', all entrepreneurs are earning just enough, and no more, to keep them in business (called 'normal' profit) and prices paid by customers exactly reflect the true costs of supplying the product.

Now it has long been conceded that the theoretical preconditions for perfect competition are only in reality found in one sector — farming, where we find quite small businesses (farms) selling products (wool, meat, wheat, etc.) indistinguishable from the products of thousands of similar businesses. And perhaps it should have worried the theorists that just about the most vociferous and successful group in lobbying for subsidies and protection from competition has always been farmers. It seems that earning only 'normal' profits just ain't much fun, and that those thus afflicted by their economic market have no scruples at all in switching to the political market to earn relief.

But, forgetting about farmers for the moment, economists have always believed — and certainly taught — that something called 'workable competition', being a reasonable approximation to perfect competition, holds sway across large segments of economic activity: in most of retailing, most personal and business services, construction, trucking and light manufacturing. These are industries in which the capital requirements to start a business are quite small, the technologies are well known, and the number of competitors and the similarity of their products should be sufficient to keep all of them honest, in the sense of not being able to extract excessive profits from the customers. Such large profits could be generated in monopolies (rare, outside of telecommunications and other 'network' industries), and in what we call oligopolies (few sellers) — the big consumer-product and heavy manufacturing industries in which economies of scale or branding limit the number of competitors. The idea is that you can't get rich doing what just about anybody else could do as well.

This, anyway, was what Mrs Siegfried was told by her night-class economics instructor. And it didn't make sense to her. The great fortunes that came to mind had all been won in those 'competitive' industries — food preparation (Ray Kroc), dry-goods retailing (Sam Walton), computer software (Bill Gates), real estate, clothing manufacturing, and various consumer-service activities. Even though the very success of these entrepreneurs eventually enabled them to build strong oligopolistic positions for themselves, they had started, and gone a long way, under truly competitive conditions.

John Siegfried had to concede the force of these examples, but being a good empiricist he wanted to find out whether the competitive route to riches was really all that widespread, or whether it was just that those following that route happened to be better known than the other super-rich. So he decided to analyse *all* the great fortunes of America, using published Rich Lists as his data source.

There is no shortage of material on this topic. The public has a passionate — almost prurient — interest in the lives of the rich, and compilations of the number and size of their fortunes have long been journalistic sure-fire hits. An early Rich List published in the London *Spectator* in 1870 was a huge success, selling more copies, as its editor wanly noted, than 'the best essay on politics we ever published'. In New Zealand, the *National Business Review* has put out an annual Rich List since 1986, and it is easily their most popular issue of the year. As well as estimates of the size of personal and family fortunes, most Rich Lists also give information about the current and original sources of the wealth, which can be categorised by a skilful analyst into competitive and non-competitive markets.[1]

John Siegfried was able to work his way through the Rich Lists of the United States, then Britain, and then Australia, before he got to me in New Zealand. He published his results in scholarly journals under the tantalising title: 'How did the Wealthiest Americans [or Britons, or Australians] get so Rich?' And in each of the three larger countries he found the same result: a majority (about two-thirds) of the great fortunes originated in what we would call competitive or workably competitive industries open to anyone to enter and make their mark.

So what is the story in New Zealand? How do our rich folk stack up against the millionaires and billionaires of America, Britain and Australia? Well, first of all, what do we mean by 'rich'? The entry requirement for the *National Business Review*'s Rich List is ownership of net assets worth at least $10 million, which is well below the standard set in other, larger countries. The British list kicks off at £30 million, for example, which is high enough to exclude Ringo Starr but includes George Harrison and — of course — Sir Paul McCartney. A New Zealand Rich List with this cut-off point (more than $80 million, at current exchange rates) would be a rather slim volume — barely a dozen entries. It seems we like our rich poorer in this country.

Too poor, perhaps. At what point does serious richness begin? Let us do some figuring. Define 'seriously rich' as being able to live a genuinely luxurious lifestyle without significantly eating into the capital that pays for it. First, the home base: $1 million in Parnell or Remuera will only buy you a little three- or four-bedroomed townhouse with at most a small, cramped pool. You will spend at least $2.5 or $3 million to make a splash. You will need a serious boat, well moored — and new, of course (you wouldn't buy a used car, either), with a custom interior. If you want space and pace you'll really have to shell out: more than $3 million for a 65-foot Hatteras that will pull 36 knots. It's shocking, really. You will certainly have to spend close to a million to step ashore from anything that won't make you ashamed to front up to the bar at the RNZYS.

Then there's the 'other house', which in New Zealand (or Queensland or the Islands) must include a 'compound' of buildings on at least a hectare of prime lake or ocean-front land. If you can source one of these for $1.5million, snap it up. If you have any pretensions to style at all you must have something in the northern hemisphere, ideally a well-presented first-floor flat in a good mansion block in Knightsbridge, kept for your annual visit to Royal Ascot, and for the use of the children on their OE — £400,000 absolute minimum. You may get by without a private plane, but if you do have one, it must have two engines, for style if not safety, and at least eight seats. Secondhand is okay for planes, which are hardly ever used anyway, and you should be able to find a good straight Cessna or similar for around $400,000 — surprisingly cheap. Of course, you will be stabling a suitable portfolio of vehicles: a serious Rolls or MB; Range Rover or Pajero for shopping; small Ferrari or similar plaything; Jeep Wrangler for Junior to hoon around in, and smart little Alfa or BMW soft-top for his sister.

Without buying any furniture or putting any decent pictures on the walls or hiring any servants you have already spent about $7 million, leaving only $3 million in the business to actually earn income to pay for using and maintaining all these toys. It just can't be done on this budget. As poor old Joan Collins said when her publisher unsuccessfully sued to get back an advance she had already spent for a book she hadn't written: 'People think a million pounds is a lot of money, but it really isn't.'

You will need at least $20 million unencumbered capital to be comfortable, and even then you will have to make some trade-offs and sacrifices from time to time. It is almost possible for us to start feeling sorry about the high cost of living rich these days. The expansive urban estates that in my parents' generation were accessible to the merchant and even the professional classes have long been subdivided out of existence. Now we see the houses of the Auckland rich on Paritai Drive, crowded together along the windy clifftop, oversized for sections on which there is barely room for a tennis court, staring blankly out at Rangitoto or over into their neighbours' boudoirs. There they huddle, a convenient target for the buses of rubbernecking tourists, who sometimes get out and pee in the garden. It is all rather tacky.

But most of the Kiwi rich would spurn our sympathy. They do not aspire to a 'rich and famous' lifestyle. Excepting the odd extravagance — perhaps a penchant for collecting something valuable, like old Rolls Royces, for example (well, someone has to look after them), they actually prefer, or pretend, to live almost frugally. Indeed, an ingrained frugality, which no doubt assists the wealth accumulation process, seems to be a lifelong characteristic of many rich folk. I remember from student days in Dunedin a Friday-afternoon session in the old Lager Bar of the City Hotel — now long defunct, as is the price of a jug of beer in those days: thirty-five cents. Rounds were being bought. Someone put a dollar on the bar and ordered two jugs. 'Make that three jugs,' said a future illustrious member of the Rich List, adding his five cents to the other fellow's dollar.

I can't remember if this story, which I may have started, is actually true; but the point is, *it could be true*. It has the ring of psychological truth. Another more recent story also concerns a Dunedin Rich List stalwart of that generation. He and his wife kindly lent their modest Wanaka crib to some relatives of friends of mine. These people reported privately that the mattress in the main bedroom of the cottage was the oldest, lumpiest and most uncomfortable they had ever tried to sleep on since their own student flatting days. (Apparently this mattress has since been replaced.)

Perhaps it is only in New Zealand that Hemingway's famous riposte makes any sense. Scott Fitzgerald said: 'The rich are different from us, Ernest', to which Hemingway's reply was: 'Yes, Scotty, they have more money.' In the class-ridden societies of Europe and America the rich clearly do differ in many other respects from the hoi polloi, but maybe not so much in egalitarian New Zealand, whose high achievers in all fields tend to sprout from the common stock. For example, I expect that most New Zealanders can say that they know, or were neighbours of, or at least went to school with, an All Black, or a New Zealand cricketer, or a Silver Fern. In my time at King's High School, Dunedin, we had two future All Blacks (Chris Laidlaw and Laurie Mains), one national cricketer (Warren Lees) *and* Murray Deaker, who must count for something.

It is — or has been — somewhat the same with our rich. When John Siegfried and I were planning our research into the New Zealand Rich List he was, as an American, quite amused by my explanation about how we would resolve any technical problems in identifying the origin of each fortune. 'I'll just phone up and ask them,' was how I proposed to settle any ambiguities. I didn't, as it happened, need to do this, but I could have, at least for the Southerners on the list (just as you used to be able to phone the Prime Minister at home, and he would answer your call himself).

Although I am not, of course, wealthy myself, nor from a wealthy background, probably all of the eleven or twelve Otago multimillionaires on the Rich List are known to me or to members of my immediate family. Indeed, I see that one *is* a member of my immediate family: he married one of my sisters. Another has been a personal friend for more than thirty years. One was at King's High School a couple of years behind me and is a friend of a brother. One has a house next door to my mother's, in Wanaka. One is a nephew/cousin of old family friends. Several are friends/business associates of my sister and her husband. And one I can actually claim to have given his start. When we were neighbours in Musselburgh Rise (not at all a flash street) in Dunedin in the early 1950s (me a very small boy; the budding tycoon a few years older) he persuaded me to exchange my pocket money for used spark plugs purloined from his father's toolshed. This is justly to be claimed as the foundation of the fortune, not only because it must have revealed to my erstwhile chum how easily a fool and his money are parted, but also because it gave him his financial stake, his start-up capital. Six shillings in 1953, doubled every two years, becomes $10 million in 1997.

I am quite happy to have these links, such as they are, with the Otago rich. It certainly doesn't reflect any glory on me (much less riches!), but I don't begrudge these people their wealth. It really isn't a big deal. The only potential problem is that association with the rich can be impoverishing. When I go to dinner at the house of the one who is my long-time personal friend (not the one who sold me the used spark plugs) I always bring a couple of very good bottles of wine — pricier than I would normally buy — to try and match the quality of the stuff I know he will serve from his own cellar. You have to watch that sort of thing.

But this is heartland country. Most of the Otago rich fit rather well Sam Neill's description of New Zealanders in general as 'dull, decent, phlegmatic'. With the exception of Sir Tim Wallis and Neill himself, they are notably lacking in glamour and pizzazz. But the much longer list of Auckland-based rich is quite different.[2] There is no shortage of phlegm and dullness (no Tony O'Reillys or Richard Bransons in this mob!). But I would be hesitant to certify the decency of everyone on the list, especially those with strong Business Roundtable connections, though it is true that most of the arrant rogues and scallywags who polluted the first, late-eighties, Rich Lists have been cleaned out one way or another.

What is really missing, though — with a few honourable exceptions — is that sense of connectedness with their community that the Southerners mostly have. Of the seventy very rich Aucklanders, I see the name of one person whom I shouted a couple of beers once (he didn't buy a round — not even five cents of one), and that's it as far as my personal acquaintanceship goes. Other people whom I have asked — Auckland-bred locals — have similarly skimpy linkages. These rich fellows are not men of the people, pillars of the community, friends of friends or neighbours. They are apart from us.

Which at least should give us the distance to be objective about them, to ask the big question: *are the rich any use?* The classical justification for great wealth was that it was fine as long as the people who possessed it never tried to consume it. Entrepreneurs were the 'engines of growth' of capitalism, relentlessly funnelling their profits back into their businesses, and thereby generating growth and prosperity for all. The aphorism was: the worker spends what he earns; the capitalist earns what he spends.

That's not so relevant now that we have achieved a fairly high overall level of prosperity. Now most workers are middle-class and do some savings themselves — either directly or through their pension funds — and publicly held companies routinely reinvest much (perhaps too much) of their profits. So the classical entrepreneur is no longer the sole source of investable surplus. And it is also clear that our modern-day plutocrat (and family) is quite keen to do some serious consuming of the surplus as well — even the relatively frugal Otago rich actually do live pretty well, apart from the odd lumpy mattress.

But we should certainly ask that our rich be at least, on balance, givers not takers; that their contribution to the wealth of the nation exceeds the claims they make on it; that they be not just winners in a game which the rest of us lose. And are they? What John Siegfried and I found from our the analysis of the New Zealand Rich List was this:

- Exactly two-thirds (80 of 120) of the New Zealand fortunes were founded in industries we judged to be 'competitive', with a further 12 per cent from industries by nature competitive but subject to regulation in the 1938–84 period
- The rate of accumulation of Rich List fortunes does not appear to have changed much since the deregulation of the economy beginning in 1984. Since the war, each decade has produced about twenty new fortunes that remain significant today.
- Nearly three-quarters of the fortunes were made by the person or family who owns them still. This proportion of self-made wealth is actually higher than found in other countries (though the higher cut-off point for larger countries' Rich Lists is probably a factor here).
- Unlike Australia, where first-generation immigrants are more than twice as likely to get rich than the rest of the population, New Zealand immigrants are just about exactly represented in the Rich List in the same proportion as they are in the total population (15 per cent.)
- Compared with its share of total employment, the manufacturing sector has had a relatively high propensity to produce fortunes — higher than in Australia, the United States or Britain.
- But it is the 'deal-making' industries — banking, brokerage, investment, insurance, real-estate agencies, property development — that provide the really fertile soil for growing fortunes. In particular, the property-selling/investing/developing business is wildly overrepresented, statistically, with 17 fortunes in a total workforce of just 8,000, which implies that about one person in five hundred working in this sector becomes extremely rich.

It is these deal-making fortunes that might make us a bit nervous. It was recently reported that the highest-paid person in Britain is a securities trader who earned £40 million in 1997

— more than $NZ100 million, and enough to catapult him into the top ten of the New Zealand Rich List in just one year, if he didn't blow it all on cocaine. I don't know if this fellow was worth this much to his employers, but I am pretty sure that he wasn't worth it for his country — most of those profits from his spectacular buying and selling would have been losses for others on the wrong side of the deals: a zero-sum game, at best.

And so it may be for our New Zealand deal-making wizards, to some extent at least. However, it is easier to admire the fortunes earned in goods-and-service-providing industries, wherein wealth can only be accumulated from thousands or millions of successful small transactions under market conditions in which customers are well able to judge whether they are getting their money's worth. I think most of us can feel quite appreciative of, for example, Nightingale and his (Resene) paints, Pye and her children's books, Tindall and his Warehouse, Ullrich and his aluminium products, even Hill and his jewellery shops and Levene for a decade or so of successful retailing.

With these people we can see what they have added to our lives by their energy and imagination. But even then there is no such thing as a self-made man or woman. Making money remains a social activity, a team effort. Take the richest member of the Business Roundtable and put him by himself on a desert island — please! — and see how much 'money' he can make for himself. You need people to buy your products and people to make them, and it is a legitimate enough question, in terms of the social contract, to ask whether the rewards are being reasonably shared between capital, entrepreneur, labour and consumers.

But leaving aside the social legitimacy of great wealth, let us finish with the most interesting question of all: *how do they do it?* The rich themselves aren't always very forthcoming about this: J. Paul Getty's advice was: 'Rise early, work hard, find oil.' We have seen that in New Zealand as elsewhere the majority of fortunes are founded in what economists call 'competitive' industries — basically, activities any of us could have a go at. The rich just seem to be better at it than the rest. But what does being better actually involve?

For what it is worth, my own observation is that there are three qualities found in superabundance amongst very successful people in just about all walks of life: energy, creativity and leadership — and in terms of financial success we could add another: good at getting a deal. Perhaps you don't always need all four — leadership isn't necessary for hotshot financial traders, for example — but with only two I believe you will be struggling to raise yourself from the common herd. I don't include 'luck' as one of the necessary attributes, perhaps excepting oil prospectors. I think these people make their own luck or, as the great golfer Gary Player once put it: 'Yes, I am a lucky player. And I find that the harder I practice the luckier I get!' Perhaps we can talk about the luck of being born exceptional, but even there no one who buys lottery tickets can really grumble. Is the lottery of birth any less fair than Lotto?

Let us give the last word on all this to George Bernard Shaw in *Candida*: 'We have no more right to consume happiness without producing it than to consume wealth without producing it.'

Chapter 14
The Good Things in Life

A few years ago I visited Poland, as a member of a Canadian team giving courses in market economics to Polish agriculturalists. We all — Canadians and Poles — worked hard and had some fun as well. It was for me a very interesting experience. Poland was then struggling to convert itself into a market economy, though we found that the most efficient operation was the railway system, still run on a day-to-day basis along strict Stalinist central-planning lines — i.e. rigid adherence to a fixed timetable — as good railways are everywhere, including New Zealand.

But the thing that most struck me was quite mundane. One Saturday morning we were taken by a Polish academic colleague to visit his office in a university agricultural-economics department near Warsaw. I was then teaching in an agricultural-economics department myself, at the University of British Columbia in Vancouver, and, as it happened, ours and the Polish department were about the same size in terms of staff numbers, and were similarly housed in nondescript two-storey buildings.

But as our Polish friend showed us around I realised that there was something different about his outfit. The offices were about the same size as ours, with the same things in them — desks, phones, filing cabinets, computers. There were bookshelves, though they weren't very well stocked by our standards. But something was missing: *there was nothing on the walls!* They were bare of all but a few typewritten lists and announcements.

I thought of our own building in Vancouver — Ponderosa Annex D, or 'The Pond' as we all called it. In The Pond empty wall space was practically nonexistent in the corridors. There were of course notices about jobs and studentships and lectures and courses. There was a big map of the world dotted with pins showing the present locations of our graduates. There was a board layered with photos — snapshots from departmental outings and parties, postcards sent back by our far-flung former students. There were home-made posters left over from open days depicting various staff and student research projects.

Most of this is, quite literally, kids' stuff — the sort of displays you would see on the walls of a primary-school classroom. It certainly wasn't costly — just photos pasted onto cardboard sheets, things like that. But it had taken lots of volunteered energy and spirit and camaraderie, and this seemed sadly lacking in the Polish office, which was also empty of people apart from our guide and us. This, we were told, was because it was Saturday. But The Pond back in Vancouver was busy seven days a week, and most hours of the day and night. There were always members of staff and students working on their assignments and projects, helping each other, falling in love, or just yarning. The Pond was a place of life, meaning a place of work and play.

That Saturday site visit was the second saddest thing I saw in Poland (I also visited the Lublin concentration camp). It made me realise how stultifying life must have been under the old regime, but also how relatively unimportant were differences in material standards of living to the quality of this life. My Polish colleagues' computers were a bit clunky by our standards, and their phones had old-fashioned diallers, but we had had such things in Canada only a few years before. The buildings were solid and well heated. The real difference was that the Poles didn't seem to have as much going on in their lives as did we and our students. They didn't work as well and they didn't play with as much pleasure.

Here is not a simplistic 'communism versus capitalism' issue. The spirit of productive fun that we had in The Pond does need to be underpinned by a sufficiency of material goods (though many of our students were pretty hard-pressed financially, as students tend to be), but mostly it needs what might be called 'space' — room for people to live, work, to develop in different ways and at their different paces. This space can be ground away by the imposition of any narrowly dominating ideology, but perhaps especially one based on materialism. There has been no more crudely materialist dogma than that of communist Eastern Europe, but perhaps the commercialist dogma of the new New Zealand, with its obsessive concern for narrowly defined 'outcomes' — in particular the outcome of maximisation of growth of a statistic called here gross domestic product (gross material product in the former Soviet bloc) — is running communism pretty close in this respect. What irony!

Because of its mean and inadequate perspective on what life and people are really all about, commercialisation — like communism — is poor at delivering its designated outcome of economic growth or GDP narrowly defined, but that goal itself needs close scrutiny. One quite well-known approach is to argue that GDP is inadequate because it is too narrowly measured; that it misses out important contributions to the economy. Another, rather different, point of view is that GDP measures too much, in the sense that we shouldn't be so concerned with monetary measures of wellbeing.

It is the second viewpoint that will be put forward here, but first I should acknowledge the conventional critique, as developed in what indeed may be the best book on economics written by a New Zealander — *If Women Counted*, by Marilyn Waring, goat farmer and former parliamentarian. The 'counting' is the measurement of gross domestic product which, notoriously, excludes the value of (non-marketed) household production; work that is done mostly by women.

Waring cites a survey of 75 evaluations of the uncounted economic contribution of the household sector in many countries: the range of estimates for this is between 25 per cent and 40 per cent of GDP.[1] This is a rather large number, and can be used to support arguments that women's contributions to the economy are systematically undervalued.

Yet, there are problems with monetising household 'production'. In a recent book Euston Quah replicates the analysis for Singapore and finds a figure of around only 5 per cent of GDP for household production.[2] Why is this? Are Singaporeans — so famously clean and tidy in public — lazy slatterns in their homes? No, of course they are not. There are two reasons for the low number. First, many Singaporeans employ full-time Filipino maids. Thus, much housework is actually counted in official GDP as the earnings of domestic servants. Second, the wage paid to maids is the natural rate to impute to whatever unpaid domestic production does get done, and this wage is rather low. In a country like New Zealand, which does not (yet) have a large underclass of imported domestic servants, the market value of household services is somewhat closer to (though still below) the average for wage labour in general.

Thus, measures of what women contribute are very sensitive to the structure of the male-dominated market economy. They are also rather selective in scope. The studies of household production focus on cooking, cleaning and child-minding, perhaps because these are the responsibilities most disproportionately shouldered by women. But they are rather coy about some of the other things that go on inside households, for which a market value could equally well be imputed. For example, sex. What is the value of the household production of sexual activity?

We can do some back-of-the-envelope calculations. According to the 1996 census, there are about 600,000 households in New Zealand headed by or including a cohabiting couple. Let us suppose that these couples have sex twice a week, on average (I hope this is not an exaggeration). That's about 60 million couplings a year. What are these worth, on the market? Apparently, the going rate for the services of a sex worker is $50 for a half hour, $100 for an hour.[3] How much for all night? Let us say $500. And then double this, because when a couple has sex there are two people getting pleasure, not just one, as in a commercial transaction. Add it all up, and the market value of the household-produced sex turns out to be about $60 *billion* per year — about 60 per cent of the present inadequately measured gross domestic product!

Think of the implications. If the government could persuade all the couples in New Zealand to have sex just one more time every fortnight, it would, with one stroke, have increased GDP (properly measured) by as much as all the economic policies and reforms of the past ten years put together! Of course, this would be just a once-for-all increase in GDP; in order to achieve permanently higher *growth*, the copulation rate would have to be increased further the next year, and yet again the year after that. The women could probably cope, but the men might not be up to it.

From a technical economics point of view, imputing a market value to sex is no different from putting a value on washing up the dishes. What it does do is put conventional 'work' in its place. By including and valuing all the things people do with their lovers and family and friends and communities we could easily 'prove' that non-marketed activities are more 'important' than market work, especially if we adjusted upwards the imputed market wage rate for household production to compensate for this being currently held down as 'women's work'.

But I do not think we should do this. If, as Pierre Trudeau once said, the state has no business in the bedrooms of its citizens, surely nor does the economic statistician. The crassness of commercialisation becomes unbearable in a family context. What price loyalty, trust, affection, love itself? These are forces which simply cannot be bought and sold; which, indeed, evaporate when we touch them with a price tag. Yet they are, as I continue to stress, utterly essential to human existence, in all its spheres of activity, including even the narrowly economic.

Instead, I suggest we go in the opposite direction. To those who push the primacy of the commercial or narrowly economic world we can say, first, that even playing by the commercial rules non-market activity is at least commensurate with what currently comprises GDP, and second, *that we do not want to play by those rules*; that life is too rich and varied to be measured by the rod of monetisation.

We find support for this position in surprising places. Robert Lucas, who won his Nobel Prize in 1995, is one of the coterie of Chicago economists — the intellectual masters of New Zealand's rationalist revolutionaries — who have championed the commercial or 'economic' approach to just about everything: the notion that human choices are made by 'rational' self-seekers responding only to the stimulus of individual gain or loss. But even Lucas has his limits. He has said that he doesn't 'use economic principles at home. I never pay my children to do their jobs. I try to use family loyalty or an exchange system; you help me, I'll help you.'[4] Now, it comes as a bit of a shock to learn that when the great Robert Lucas returns to the bosom of his family in the evening he casts aside the principles of rationalist economics — principles which he has been pre-eminent in disseminating and which now govern our policy approaches to issues from inflation to unemployment to managing the health system — and reverts to primitive loyalty and barter-based systems.

But in fact Lucas may be a lot smarter than his vulgar disciples.[5] As a true conservative, he may realise that a real-world society based on pure rationalism would be unworkable; it would collapse under the burden of mistrust and cheating. As I have stressed in previous chapters, a market-type system can only function efficiently if people behave well: if they are honest, reliable, and do not seek to extract the maximum personal advantage out of every unforeseen eventuality. And where do people learn to behave well? Perhaps, primarily, at home, in the family. Conservatives are very keen on the notion of the family as the training ground for the marketplace, and get quite cross about 'disfunctional' families who do not take their training responsibilities sufficiently seriously. Along with the great Adam Smith, they believe that 'It was in the family that children learned to curb their passions and accommodate their desires with those of other people.'[6]

That is, families train children to become adults, which is a very good thing, of course. But there is a lot more to this than just producing the next generation of market fodder. In the good society we have a basic unity of morality that traverses all the layers of human interaction. We do not value and trust people whose behaviour in business is at odds with their behaviour to family and friends. True, passions run higher within the family than in the (usually) more mundane world of the marketplace, amplifying the importance of honesty, loyalty and willingness to take responsibility for one's actions, but the basic game is the same. One of the paradoxes of the 'more-market' movement is that by forcing people to behave more 'economically' through commercialisation, contestability and so on, it inculcates in us what the late Bernard Nossiter called the 'ruthless egoism' of the competitive marketplace, thereby threatening not just the standards of family and social life, but the foundations of civilised and effective market behaviour itself.

There are other positions, of course. The economist Nancy Folbre contrasts neoclassical (traditional, male-dominated) and feminist views of home and economy thus: neoclassical stands for altruism within the family and self-interest outside it, whereas a feminist alternative would be self-interest within the home and group solidarity outside it.[7]

This is interesting. It is true that, with the exception of the remorseless Gary Becker (also of Chicago), to whom no aspect of human interaction is too private to be subjected to the marginal calculus, neoclassical economists have taken the basic economic unit to be 'the family', heedless of how the family reaches its decisions, or of what goes on within it (hence the exclusion of household production from the national accounts). The image is of the little lady selflessly keeping the home fires burning while the man of the house strides out to maximise profits in the competitive marketplace.

This is not a caricature of neoclassical economics, and nor, unfortunately, is it a caricature of the real world: it is something to be changed. But is Folbre's version of a feminist alternative appealing? It conjures up visions of an Amazonian sisterhood running the economy in collective solidarity, while at home the battle of the sexes rages unfettered.

This seems to me like replacing one unpleasant dualism with another. My point is that we should be struggling to achieve some unity in how we cope with our personal, social and economic lives. I do expect that, to achieve this, men will have to change more than women (and we are, aren't we?). I admire and value feminism both for its struggle against sexual discrimination and as a humanising force; for proposing not just that women should have more economic power, but that an economy with women more equally involved would be a fundamentally *different* economy: less dualistic, more integrative, relying on cooperation rather than competition; focused on means rather than ends.

That is why I find disturbing Nancy Folbre's representation of children as a 'positive externality in fiscal terms' (because they will eventually pay our pensions), thereby justifying tax credits for parents. To put it bluntly: this is the state buying babies — the ultimate act of commercialisation. I hope nobody is misguided enough to have a baby as an act of civic duty, and we should not encourage them to do so with financial incentives. We should put the market economy in its place: essential, of course, and something in which every able-bodied household should participate, to bring in the commodities they need to survive and flourish; but its scope is properly limited to the mundane provision of goods and services, and market life cannot be the sole focus of a healthy person's existence. We should resist the process of commercialisation that imposes the primacy of the growth in marketed GDP above all else.

After all, what do you need for a good night's sleep? Peace of mind, mattress hard or soft according to taste, and perhaps the comfort of an accustomed warm body beside you. None of that is expensive in material terms. The waking hours are more demanding, but here too if someone in the household can bring home a fairly earned income capable of supporting a decent material standard of living, then most people will be content to get on with the other important things in their lives.

If figures are needed, there is plenty of evidence of the lack of congruity between 'economic' performance and basic well-being. One international survey conducted in the mid-1980s simply asked people how happy they were.[8] At the top of the 'World Happiness League' (which did not include New Zealand or Australia) were the Republic of Ireland, Northern Ireland and Great Britain. In each of these economically laggardly countries nearly 40 per cent of the people stated they were 'very happy'. At the bottom of the table were the Japanese (about 15 per cent very happy) and the West Germans (10 per cent), despite the evidently superior economic performance of those nations.

A recent New Zealand survey found 83 per cent agreement with the proposition that life is better here than elsewhere.[9] Only 7 per cent said that work was more important to them than anything else in their life, but 73 per cent enjoyed their work and 74 per cent admitted to sometimes getting passionate about it — the same proportion of respondents who got passionate about watching sport or at a performance of a play, concert or show. People got most passionate about — well, passion itself: 95 per cent feeling that way 'sometimes or often' about their spouse or partner. For 83 per cent, family was the most important thing of all. And 86 per cent of New Zealanders (as surveyed here) get passionate about their country's natural environment.

We may not be particularly surprised by numbers like these, but do we take them seriously enough? Is the path that New Zealand is currently pursuing likely to lead to a future in which work and play, family and colleagues, love and duty are integrated in the way we seem to need and wish? An indicator of the way things have been changing is that while the respondents to the survey tended quite strongly to see an improvement in private goods and services (telephones, cars, airlines, home appliances, restaurants), they were just as firm in the opinion that public goods — public transport, television programmes, schools, hospitals — have deteriorated. Seventy-seven per cent believed that moral standards are declining (but doesn't every generation believe this?), and 80 per cent believed the best way to reduce crime is to reduce unemployment — a sound insight.

The figures on changes in the quality of private and public goods raise an important question.[10] Is there an unavoidable trade-off between private consumption and the provision of social services? The economic rationalists argue that there is not: just apply to the public sector the same commercialised, consumer-driven principles that have been successful in improving the range and price of consumer goods available to New Zealanders and the same 'miracle' will be seen in our schools, hospitals and other public services.

But have we taken consumerism too far? I don't just mean the possibility of catching 'consumeritis', an affliction whose symptom is an insatiable obsession with material goods. What is worrying is the lack of balance: another dualism. We glorify consumption; what about production? At the individual level there is a natural unity between the two activities. I produce goods or services for others: in exchange I am able to consume my fair share of what they produce. That unity was almost universal in the old New Zealand. Every household sent someone out into the economy (usually a man) to produce a cash income that could be traded for goods and services.

It's different now. More women work, but hundreds of

thousands of able-bodied adults do not: the unemployed, beneficiaries, 'discouraged' workers, the involuntary early retirements and redundancies. Of course they and their young children must consume, which imposes an additional burden on the remaining producers, a burden which is unfair and ultimately unsustainable. I do not believe that our society can flourish under the dualism of an arbitrary division of the population into workers and drones.

How did this happen? In the bad old days, with stringent import controls, the production/consumption loop was closed — we really did produce for each other's consumption and as a result we had extraordinarily low unemployment rates: every household really did reap what it had sown, even if what we reaped was (in many but not all instances) limited in quality and high in price.

Now, in our smart modern 'open' economy, we are encouraged to scour the world for the best deals, no matter what the implications of this behaviour for production back home in New Zealand (nor with a care about the conditions under which our imported goods are produced). There may be a trade-off here that we should face up to. In the next chapter I will suggest means of 'closing the loop' again without turning back the clock to import controls, and will discuss how much this might 'cost' us as consumers. Not a lot, I believe.

The good things in life are not free, but nor — as Mae West once said — are they 'very, very expensive'.[11] A decent day's pay for a decent day's work; freedom from fear; hope for the future; a sense of living in a just society; civic pride; an environment that is not abused; opportunities for doing interesting things and having some fun before you die. These are all, I believe, within our grasp as a nation. To get there, we need to change how we look at ourselves: specifically, to cease our grotesque obsession with economic 'growth', narrowly measured as changes in gross domestic product. And, more fundamentally, we really have to believe that there *is* a viable alternative.

Means

Chapter 15
Doing Our Own Thing in a Sovereign Economy

Could it turn out to be that the most significant act of a New Zealand government over the past two decades was not any or all of the hundred or so major economic reforms, but the banning of nuclear warships from New Zealand ports? This was a bold, even stylish act of principled political sovereignty by the David Lange administration, maintained, by popular demand, by the National government that succeeded him. It annoyed our great patron the United States, and embarrassed our neighbours the Australians, who didn't have the nerve to do it themselves. We were made to suffer various sanctions, such as exclusion from military alliances, and some stiffness on trade access matters. But we stuck to our guns — so to speak — and the policy stands, with no lasting damage done to our international relationships, and probably some good.

But why are we such patsies in matters of economic sovereignty? Why have we allowed the American-franchised 'McModel' — the paradigm of universal 'free' markets — to invade and conquer our economic and social institutions almost without putting up a fight? Instead of pathetically lying down in front of the Washington Consensus and its local agents, such as the New Zealand Business Roundtable, why could we not show the nerve and resolution in economic affairs that we showed over those nuclear warships?

Well, we could and we should. We should be inspired by the success of our acts of political independence to take charge of our economic destiny too. And in so doing we may find we are in the vanguard of history, not struggling against it. The tide of globalisation, of international economic integration, has flooded far, but it may be about to ebb. There is increasingly stubborn resistance — particularly on the Asian side of the Pacific rim — to sacrificing local and national cultures as grist to the mill of the American homogenising machine. Such resistance is based not just on a desire to preserve independent cultures and institutions for their own sake — which is understandable enough — but also on a growing realisation of their *economic* validity, which is of course a major theme of this book.

People are saying to the Americans, no, we are different from you. We take that seriously; we want to retain our differences with our own space in which to foster the institutions that are appropriate to our culture and environment. And we are not being economically irrational in so doing: it works for us, even if it might not work for you. Now, this is easy enough to say, but to establish or re-establish our national economic autonomy will not be easy, as powerful forces will be aligned against us. But if we want to do it, we can — really!

In this chapter I will approach the matter of sovereignty from an economic perspective, dealing in turn with the financial (flows of money or capital) and 'real' (flows of goods and services) sectors. The perspective is that of a nation — in our case New Zealand — coping with pressures from abroad. How do we handle these? How much autonomy do we have?

International capital itself divides into two great forces: the 'short-term' flows on money markets; and the 'long-term', lumpy investments of multinational enterprise, of firms building and buying firms in other countries. Short-term flows have been hugely stimulated over the past two decades (since the move to floating rather than fixed exchange rates) by better communications technologies and the opportunities for arbitrage and speculation generated by volatile fluctuations in exchange and interest rates. Daily turnover on foreign-exchange markets now exceeds one *trillion* US dollars in value.[1]

These are frightening magnitudes. There is plenty of evidence of the harm that can be caused, especially to small economies for whose currency the market is necessarily rather 'thin', meaning that relatively small (by world standards) transactions can have a big effect on the price. The problem is that the prices affected by international speculation — a country's exchange rate and its domestic interest rates — are also key prices for the basic goods-and-service-producing activities that really do create wealth, and which can be distorted by the unpredictable whims of world financial markets.

We have been sorely tried in New Zealand by the effects of such distortions: in the name of a fanatical obsession with zero inflation, both our exchange rate and our interest rates have periodically been pushed up to levels quite harmful to domestic production, especially in the exporting and import competing sectors, with the link between exchange and interest rates being the inflows of foreign capital seeking the generous premiums offered in our money markets.

The sensible goal for a small economy is to be ignored by the money markets; to be 'not in play'. Then exchange rates and interest rates can be set (by markets) to reflect the fundamentals of demand and supply for real goods and services, instead of as the aggregation of ill-informed hunches and gambles by the likes of thousands of callow 'traders' hunched in front of computer screens in windowless rooms in Wall Street and Wellington.

But how to achieve this? The problem is that it is hard to separate the money market from the goods market, because they both deal in the same means of exchange — national currencies. The eminent Yale economist James Tobin has given his name to the proposal for a 'Tobin Tax', a very small tax levied on each transaction in foreign-exchange markets.[2] A tax of, say, half a per cent on the value of the transaction would not deter a genuine long-term investment, but it would suck the profitability out of short-term, in-and-out, speculative deals. On three-monthly 'round trips', for example, such a tax would add up to 4 per cent annually, which would exceed the returns available from arbitrage and most other speculative transactions, and thereby discourage them from happening.

There is debate about whether a country could impose a Tobin Tax unilaterally, or whether it would have to be done multilaterally, by all countries. If it weren't done in concerted action, then the market in whatever currency was subjected domestically to a Tobin Tax could move offshore, beyond the reach of the national tax-collection authorities. Such concerns are obviously warranted in the cases of the great international currencies like the greenback and the mark and the yen, for which well-developed offshore markets already exist. But might not the Kiwi dollar be too small a fish to fry on its own, away from its domestic-market base? It is an idea worth following up.

What about those long-term investments, which have resulted in about half of New Zealand company shares now being held overseas, including all or most of the ownership of our largest corporations?[3] Multinational enterprises (MNEs) are now one of the most dominating facts of international economic life. It is estimated that they control about 70 per cent of world trade, of which about one half consists of transactions between the subsidiaries of individual MNEs.

It is interesting to examine the economic logic that drives the activities of MNEs. In the old days, international enterprises like the East India Company and the Hudson Bay Company roamed the world looking for raw resources to exploit. This motive still exists — for example, we have a multinational aluminium company based in Bluff, mining our hydroelectric power at a subsidised price. But, more often now, the resources that are being 'mined' are not raw materials but cheap labour and favourable tax regimes.[4] Much of those huge trade flows between and within multinationals is not based on any fundamentals of comparative advantage (such as climate or mineral reserves) but on artificial opportunities for arbitraging cheap labour for dear, and favourable tax treatment against a more demanding system. Raw materials are sent to Indonesia, processed, assembled further in Malaysia with the addition of sophisticated components shipped in from Korea or Japan or the United States, then sent to Singapore for distribution to world markets, including the markets in which some of the value was added.

From a global point of view, a lot of this trade and investment activity is seriously inefficient, given the very substantial costs of storage, distribution, transport and so on — costs which are probably significantly larger than those actually born by the multinationals because of environmental impacts which are not factored into the decision.

There is much good to be had from multinational enterprise, of course, just as there is from trade itself. We get to open a Pandora's box of products and ideas that bubble up through the seething mass of six billion souls with whom we share this planet. But there are many ways of mediating the exchanges between ourselves and the rest of the world that stop short of the extreme 'take us . . . *please*' attitude that typifies current New Zealand policy towards both foreign investment and trade. From a social-capital perspective, it is disturbing to have major investment and employment decisions that affect New Zealanders being made by foreigners and foreign-owned firms, because they do not — *cannot* — have our interests at heart. That empathy and goodwill which appears to be the key to a successfully integrated society and economy is lacking. This is not saying foreigners are wicked or malevolent; just that their hearts and minds are somewhere else.

People — politicians in particular — say the most extraordinary things about foreign investment. It is responsible for one job in three; it will raise our growth rate to 5 per cent per annum forever; and even though it is so manifestly wonderful, we have to sign a contract (the Multilateral Agreement on Investment) which will prevent us from ever changing our minds and interfering with the sovereign rights of foreigners on our soil. None of these wild claims are ever supported with evidence and I do not believe they can be. On the contrary, I argue that an economy with more of the decisions made by and for New Zealanders can achieve a much lower unemployment rate than we suffer now (as it did a generation ago); that the growth obsession is fundamentally misconceived, but in any case the true development path is only to be found for ourselves by ourselves; and that it is wrong to the point of wickedness to sign (without due process, including parliamentary debate) a treaty which is expressly designed to limit the sovereignty of all future New Zealand governments in matters of foreign investment and the treatment of foreign-owned firms operating in our country.

Trade in goods and services has also expanded over the past two decades, though not nearly so much as international financial flows. But there is nothing new about trade, of course. Paul Krugman reports that the world ratio of merchandise exports to GDP in 1913 was 11.9 per cent — a couple of points higher than in 1973. By 1993 the ratio had risen to 17.3 per cent. New Zealand is in the low twenties — not a high ratio for a small economy (Ireland's trade ratio is over 70 per cent), which reflects the fact that trade does not come easy to us, on account of our isolation from markets and supplies. Nevertheless, trade is very important and we want to do it well. But trade being basically a 'good thing' doesn't mean you can't have too much of it, nor that it should be pursued at any price. And New Zealand has shown such enthusiasm for 'free' trade that it has gone beyond its signed GATT obligations in cutting tariffs unilaterally.

Yet there is a sensible case to be made for keeping a structure of import tariffs on the books: it gives a sovereign country something to bargain with. A marvellous example of shrewd government use of tariffs as a bargaining tool is the Canada/United States autopact, signed in 1965. Indeed, this is perhaps the most successful single economic policy in modern history, even though (or perhaps because) it cost just a few hundred thousand dollars to negotiate and costs nothing to operate.

The autopact has, for more than thirty years, been responsible for trade flows in excess of twice New Zealand's entire annual gross national product. It provides for duty-free movement of assembled automobiles and parts across the Canada/US border, provided that total sales in Canada of North American made cars do not exceed the value of production in Canadian-based assembly plants, and provided that value added in Canada is above a base level.

Some background to this. Canada had, since the Depression, imposed quite high tariffs (25–30 per cent) on imports of automobiles from the United States. To jump this tariff wall, the American manufacturers — General Motors, Ford, Chrysler and a few others (now defunct) — had set up 'miniature replicas' of their Detroit plants in Canada (mostly in southern Ontario), producing a full range of products for the Canadian market only (along with a few specialty items, such as right-hand-drive cars for the British Empire market).[5]

This was fine, but the Canadian government saw a couple of problems looming on the horizon. The first problem stemmed from the limited Canadian market size, which meant that production runs were rather short, and thus unit costs high. The second problem was that tariff duties were steadily being reduced under rounds of the GATT[6]. The first problem meant that it would be more efficient, from a production-cost point of view, to specialise the production of each car model in one or two giant plants, producing for the entire North American market. The second problem meant it would eventually be efficient from a marketing-cost perspective to do this, as the tariff wall protecting Canada was chipped away by the GATT. And why were there these problems? Because the Canadians anticipated the most likely route the American auto firms would follow to realise these efficiencies would simply be to close their costly Canadian plants and centralise all production in Detroit.

So the Canadians acted quickly, while they still had some tariffs to bargain with. The 'autopact' was negotiated and signed with very little fuss, and the United States car companies quickly rearranged their production to take advantage of it, basically by giving their Canadian subsidiaries responsibilities for producing a few models for the entire North American market. For example, all of Chrysler's highly successful minivans are built in Windsor, Ontario.

The autopact has been a great success. The proof of this is that now, with all tariffs between the two countries eliminated as a result of the Canada/US free-trade agreement, the Canadian automobile industry remains firmly in place, productive and profitable. It is truly an example of an 'infant industry', conceived under a protective regime, and growing up to stand on its own feet in an open-trading environment. Note that it is an example not of free trade, but of *managed* trade. It certainly explodes the myth of 'comparative advantage', the notion that countries should restrict themselves to producing and exporting commodities for which their natural resource endowments particularly suit them; to be, in the Canadian phrase, 'hewers of wood and drawers of water' (and reapers of wheat). Canada has no 'natural' advantage in producing motor vehicles (no-one does), but its exports of vehicles and parts are several times its exports of timber, hydroelectricity and wheat put together!

The insight that competitiveness is created, not given, is now becoming widespread. As someone (probably Paul

Krugman) said: 'The success of Silicon Valley is not because it sits on rich reserves of silicon!' In fact, all the smaller, late-industrialising economies — Canada, Korea, Taiwan, Australia and New Zealand — built up their processing and manufacturing industries behind high protective tariff walls and other barriers. Korea developed its now huge auto industry under the shelter of a total ban on imports from Japan (which instead was permitted to supply technology and know-how to the Korean firms). That is too extreme for us, but so too is the current policy of allowing our own auto assembly and parts industries — the productive products of decades of development — to go to the wall in the name of 'free' trade (in a world, of course, where no one else behaves like this).

New Zealand began its industrial development programme in earnest in 1938, and it is just as well it did, because it gave us the makings of a broad-based industrial and commercial economic structure when the collapse in wool prices in the mid-1960s forced us into a crash programme of diversification of exports. This programme was well advanced by about 1980,[7] though it then suffered the major setback of the devastation of manufacturing in the first six years of the 'reform' process, when one job in three was lost and our productive capacity severely truncated.

But is exporting the answer to every problem? All the political parties think so — or, really, *assume* so, since they haven't given it much thought. Actually, there are some political differences: those on the right tend to be free traders, which means importing more, and those on the left mercantilists, which means exporting more, but since more of one means more of the other (because all export income is spent eventually on imports, or all imports have to be paid for eventually by exports), they really are on the same track: *trade more!*

And I think they are all wrong, as people usually turn out to be when they accept a long-unchallenged orthodoxy. The standard response to setbacks in international markets, such as the 1997/98 Asian crisis, has been 'we must trade our way out of it!' But does this really make sense? Suppose you are playing tennis and losing every game despite trying very hard. Should you respond by playing even more tennis, or should you see if your swing is better suited to something else — say, golf? When you are engaged in an activity which is causing you problems, perhaps the smart thing is to do *less* of it, not more, if there is something else you can do instead.

There is something very sensible that we could do instead of exporting more, which is to produce more for our own domestic market. We could *trade less*, meaning export and import less, and do more for ourselves. Of course this goes right against the ruling 'free trade' dogma, but what has free trade done for us lately? In the next chapter I argue that production for the home market is conducive to high-wage full employment, because it 'closes the loop' between supply and demand, and I suggest a number of specific policies to help us redirect our efforts towards getting the home fires to burn more brightly.

But focus now on exports. In aggregate, exporting does not appear to be particularly profitable for New Zealand, and it is certainly, at the margin, difficult. We really do need to re-evaluate our approach to all this. Take the great sacred cow, dairy products, which account for about 10 per cent of our total foreign-exchange earnings (including tourism). Most of the countries we sell to have their own dairy industries, which they protect in various ways. This protection gets us very upset and self-righteous, and we dream that if the nasty Americans, Europeans and so on could only be persuaded to play fair we could supply them with wonderfully cheap butter and cheddar and the world would be a better place for everyone.

But we really are dreaming if we think these countries are going to stop protecting their small-farm sectors, including dairying. We are just beating our head against the EC's butter mountain. And if they did open up, it would not necessarily be to our benefit in the end. Policies that protect inefficient small farms in, say, Holland, also make it difficult for larger, efficient Dutch dairy operators to expand. Without such impediments New Zealand farmers have become great virtuosos of large-herd dairying, but the Dutch are quite smart enough to learn these techniques too (after all, many New Zealand dairy farmers are from Dutch immigrant families). We do have a good climate for pastoral farming (though not particularly good soil) but against this is the cost of getting the bulky, low-value commodity to the northern hemisphere, and the impossibility of ever economically supplying these markets with the most important dairy product of all — fresh milk. On balance, perhaps we do not actually have a strong natural comparative advantage in dairying.

Similar arguments can be made about other bulk commodity exports — meat, wool, logs — which together with dairying and tourism account for most of New Zealand's exporting effort. I am not, of course, suggesting that we shut up the trade shop in these or other markets, but that we scale it back (or stop trying so hard to expand it beyond its naturally profitable limits). If we exported (and imported) less, we would enjoy it more — get a better price and be not so vulnerable to other economies' ups and downs. Just one big macroeconomic shock, such as that threatened by the downturn in East Asia, can wipe out years of trade-efficiency gains.

This criticism is not aimed at individual firms and exporters. Selling to foreigners is in itself a specialty, niche business, which most people are not good at, for various reasons; but there are some who excel, and this of course is what they should do. I happen to have two close family members — a brother and a brother-in-law — who are formidably successful exporters, one of shellfish, the other of venison. I haven't a clue how they manage it, but I think it is marvellous, and I certainly wouldn't want them to do anything else. But overall, as a nation, we may be putting too much effort into trade. We still subsidise two of our largest exports (tourism and aluminium), and we tend to glorify exporting — 'They're drinking our beer here!' (but we aren't making much profit from it) — perhaps because of a residual national inferiority complex.

Why not glorify selling to New Zealanders, especially when this involves beating import competition? Why give away all the good stuff to foreigners? The only macroeconomic justification for trading our goods for pieces of paper (foreign currency) that can't be spent in New Zealand is to pay for imports, for which the justification is that we don't make them ourselves (or don't make them well enough or cheap enough). So, instead of 'The Exporter as Hero', I give you 'The Import Substitutor as Hero'. As a slogan, it doesn't quite have the same ring to it, but it may make more economic sense.

Chapter 16

A Decent Day's Pay for a Day's Decent Work

I don't believe in the existence of a complete, foolproof blueprint for reclaiming high-wage full employment. The 'solution' will not come as the neat application of some smartly packaged manifesto from a single economist (or politician), but as the result of a process to which just about everyone contributes, in ways which no one can possibly predict in detail. Need I stress how different this essentially bottom-up approach to economic policy is from the top-down, know-it-all dirigisme of Muldoon, Douglas, Richardson and Treasury that has knocked us around for the past two decades?

What I think I know something about is the *framework* within which such a process would flourish: it is a secure, protective framework that gives us some space or sovereignty to sort things out for ourselves. And I do have my own economist's ideas on how to flesh out that framework with specific policies and programmes — ideas developed through this book. I like the concept of an 'attractor' — specifically, of high-wage full employment as the norm to which behaviour is strongly attracted, so that when an employer is confronted with someone looking for a job, their natural response is to look for an answer to 'How can I make productive use of this person in my organisation?', not — as is encouraged in New Zealand now — to say 'Ha! Here is an unemployed person whom I can use as a bargaining pawn to push down the wages of my present employees.'

On the worker's side, the attractor should be such that a person out of a job is encouraged to think 'I won't work for peanuts but I will work, and soon!', rather than 'Now's my chance to have a bit of a spell and go on the benefit.' Once established, these norms are self-reinforcing, both at the micro-level, where each person's behaviour is strongly influenced by how others behave or are expected to behave, and at the macro-level, where the wages earned by a new worker end up back in the economy as extra spending on goods and services which justify, in aggregate, the employment of an additional person.

What about 'efficiency' — the buzz word of our age? What will the workers do? The good news is that within reasonable limits *it doesn't really matter a lot what the jobs are producing!* This startling assertion needs some justification. It depends on us being willing to go beyond the narrowly economic dimensions of work and jobs to appreciate properly their social, psychological, even moral significance to our lives. If every able-bodied adult who is not involved full time in looking after their small children gets up in the morning and goes off to a decent job which pays enough to bring up a family in some decency, then we will be living in a pretty satisfactory country. Worrying about whether the particular mix of goods and services produced under these circumstances is 'optimal' is not just unnecessary; it is actually counterproductive, because the sort of flexibility required — willingness to chop off some activity here and graft on something different somewhere else — weakens the bonds of empathy and sympathy that are needed to reinforce the attractor of high-wage full-employment behaviour.

I will illustrate the point with an example: the Toyota assembly plant in the town of Thames, at the base of the Coromandel peninsula. This showpiece operation has (I am told by a union official) achieved rates of productivity better than those in some of Toyota's Japanese plants. It is a model for other firms, and a training ground for workers and managers. It is, of course, a crucially important employer to the Thames region. It turns out well-designed, well-made cars tuned to New Zealand roads and conditions. Yet all this is about to become past tense. The assembly line is about to shut down, with the elimination of its remaining tariff protection.

Now, there have been manufacturing activities in New Zealand which really were silly. We hear about them all the time — the same few stories over and over — such as the particular

Japanese car model which, having been fully assembled in Japan, was then taken apart and put in pieces into a crate, shipped to New Zealand and here solemnly reassembled. Such foolishness — though not the norm (and beware of accepting these yarns as gospel truth) — could happen in the old system of import licensing and very high tariffs.

But that is not the system now. Import licensing was being phased out before Rogernomics came into vogue, and tariffs are not at frightening levels. It was not silly to assemble Toyotas in Thames — Toyotas made in New Zealand, 'tuned' as they were by Kiwi Grand Prix ace Chris Amon to suit our driving and living conditions, which differ a lot from those in Japan. It is in fact very sensible to have people earning good wages in good jobs, for all those social, psychological, moral reasons the *economic* importance of which (in building and sustaining social capital) I have stressed throughout this book, and much less important to get the 'optimal' mix of goods and services being produced. This doesn't mean that prices don't matter as signals about where resources should be allocated, but it puts them in their place: prices aren't everything. In the simplistic rationalist McModel paradigm, prices are the *only* thing that matters. In the richer and more realistic view of how economy and society function that I have been supporting in this book, short-term price signals are part of the picture, but they do not predominate. If we have a smart, efficient, high-quality operation in Thames (and Porirua and South Auckland and Nelson, where the other assembly plants were), then the social benefits and long-term economic spillovers from this should override the short-term calculus of relative prices in world markets. I think we all instinctively *know* this, but we have been bamboozled by the McModel propagandists into thinking that it is economically incorrect to say so. Well, it ain't! Can you picture the people of Thames dancing in the main street to celebrate being liberated from inefficient vehicle assembly so that their 'resources' — they themselves — can be redeployed in more 'efficient' activities?

This perspective makes things a bit easier for achieving full employment. We need jobs — good jobs — but we have some leeway over just where the jobs are and what they are producing. But where will they come from? Start with a question: New Zealand winemakers earned around $40 million in 1997 selling their delicious sauvignon blancs and chardonnays to the British, our biggest customers — what was all that foreign exchange spent on? About half of it — the first six months' earnings — was used to import LPG cylinders for gas barbecues. So why don't we make our own LPG cylinders? It isn't a matter of inaccessible technology, given that a large fraction of the cylinders are sourced from Thailand, which is still not an advanced manufacturing economy (and, anyway, Kiwis are highly capable technologists). Nor can labour costs be crucial — the two other largest suppliers to us are Australia and the United States. Indeed LPG cylinders are an excellent example of a manufactured product which is perfectly suited to domestic production. The market (around 150,000 units annually) is big enough to support efficient-scale local plants, and the cylinders are too bulky and heavy to make air freight economical, so that local suppliers have the classic advantage of being closer to their customers, with the ability to respond quickly to fluctuations in demand, using 'Just-In-Time' inventory- and production-management techniques.

In fact there was until recently a New Zealand supplier of LPG cylinders, and the difficulties faced and eventually succumbed to by that small firm are quite instructive. The story begins with a young couple — he an engineer — doing their OE in Asia in the classic Kiwi style in the 1970s. They were impressed by woks as a means of cooking fast and tasty food. They said: 'That's what New Zealanders are going to want. Let's go home and start making woks for them.' And they did, quite successfully, having built a suitable metal-spinning lathe for the job. Then, in the 1980s came the use of LPG as a fuel, in particular as a replacement for the traditional driftwood or charcoal in household barbecues. The engineer thought: 'What is an LPG cylinder? It is just two woks, bent a bit more, made of heavier steel, welded together and with a few bells and whistles such as a valve and handle added on. We can make those!'

And so they could, and did. But then life wasn't so simple. Whereas the marketing as well as the production of woks might be a 'cottage' industry — an activity carried out efficiently by small-scale traders operating in a network of informal business linkages — our husband-and-wife team now found themselves playing in a bigger, more demanding league. Though LPG cylinders are about as close as it gets to being a pure 'commodity' item, they are predominantly sold in conjunction with gas barbecue sets, which are much more of a differentiated, branded, high-value consumer good. As a result, the market in New Zealand had become dominated by four big nationally operating importer–retailers: The Warehouse, The BBQ Factory, Mitre 10 and BP Link Centres.

So, to break into the market on anything like a viable scale of operations, husband-and-wife needed to secure a supply contract with at least one of the big four. This threw them into a catch-22. For a major retailer, security of supply is crucial. 'Stock-outs' resulting in empty shelves are anathema. So the buyers would say: 'How can we be sure that you can supply us regularly with good-quality merchandise? Where is your track record?' To which husband-and-wife would respond: 'But how can we *establish* a track record unless you give us an order?'

There is no real answer to this, unless the buyer is willing to take a punt. And, after much effort (which might better have been spent in actually making LPG cylinders), one of the big four retailers was persuaded to put in a moderate-sized order. But then there was the issue of price: the retailer naturally didn't want to pay more than they were paying for imported cylinders — about $40 each, landed — which was just manageable for the local firm, though not very profitable until volume could be increased. There was a 16 per cent customs tariff on the books, but this had been waived at the request of the retailers because there had been no domestic producers to protect. The new manufacturer could apply to have the tariff reinstated once it achieved a significant level of output, but there is another catch-22 — it is tough without the tariff to achieve the output levels that will persuade the Minister of Commerce to reinstate it.

Husband-and-wife (now with sixteen hard-working employees) did manage to crank up production to a quite efficient level of 900 units/week, and the tariff was reinstated by the minister. Understandably, their major customer had somewhat mixed feelings about this, since it was still importing some of its requirements. Indeed, you might imagine that it would be quite cross with its fledgling supplier for sneaking off to the ministry to have the tariff restored. But things are a bit more subtle than that, since with the tariff applied on imports, this retailer with its supplies sourced domestically could hope to get a competitive edge on its rivals, who would need to increase their prices by about 8 per cent or absorb the tariff in lower profit margins.[1]

These are tricky games for a small business to be involved in. The situation with respect to the tariff was never very easy, and they had other problems. If dealing with a downstream oligopoly of four big potential customers is hard enough, it is not much fun facing the upstream monopoly supplier of the major input, New Zealand Steel, who had fairly stringent advance-payment requirements that were difficult to meet in a cash-flow-scarce environment.

The difficulties do not end here. It is a definite no-no for LPG cylinders to explode in their customers' faces, which means quality control (especially of the welds) has to be very stringent. However, even in the chronically litigious USA the manufacturers are allowed to self-inspect. But for some reason the New Zealand authorities weren't happy to permit this, and our husband-and-wife had to employ a full-time independent inspector, generating a very substantial fixed cost. There was also a problem about the steel, resulting from a technical difference between standards in Australia and New Zealand, which resulted in a (ultimately found to be unnecessary) close-down of the production line for some months.

With all this, you may not be surprised that the venture eventually failed, which is why we now import 100 per cent of our LPG cylinders from places such as Australia, Thailand and the United States. This is rather sad, but let us take from it some positive lessons in the cause of homespun enterprise. Of course no one is going to wave a magic wand and eliminate all the inherent problems of small businesses trying to get started. Many of these come with the territory (especially the chronic mistake of undercapitalisation), and in a healthy, risk-taking economy business failure is the inseparable companion of business success. But consider the following points:

- There are hundreds — thousands — of products like LPG cylinders which could be economically produced in New Zealand. Many are already, and some are even exported. The smallish scale of the local market is often (though not always) a disadvantage, but on the positive side of the ledger are lower transport costs, better infrastructure links (such as financing), the facility to adapt to local conditions and special needs, and the ability to draw on the social capital — the common store of empathy and goodwill that reduces the transaction costs of doing business with people you 'know'.
- This means that, within quite wide bounds, *it is up to us* to decide what we produce in New Zealand.
- Tariffs (at a moderate level) are clearly quite useful. But allowing importers to petition to have the tariff lifted if there is *currently* no local supplier acts as a barrier to new local manufacturers starting up, as they have to go through the usually lengthy and expensive business of applying to have the tariff reinstated (which also naturally annoys the downstream retailers they are trying to sell to). It would facilitate small-firm entry and reduce transaction and lobbying costs on all sides if tariffs were applied as a matter of routine, without question or fuss, perhaps excepting (as is done now) on items like large commercial jet airliners, which are never going to be made here.[2]
- Manufacturers and suppliers, especially when new and small, often need help in meeting the technical and commercial standards set by their customers, when these are large national and international operations. The best source of such help can be the customers themselves. Famous examples of this include the upstream linkages of the Japanese car makers and the stringent and proactive quality control exercised by the great British clothing retailer Marks & Spencer over its network of all-British suppliers. In New Zealand, The Warehouse has had a policy of encouraging local suppliers, but this may have faded away somewhat — their fliers now rarely have the kiwi-in-a-triangle logo that denotes made in New Zealand.
- Large manufacturers and retailers should be encouraged

to foster local suppliers. There is a legitimate role to be played here by a government-backed agency 'coming to the party' with lines of credit for working capital to reduce the risk faced by a big firm putting its reputation on the line by dealing with an unknown new supplier: we need to cut through the catch-22 that makes it so hard to get a reputation for reliable supply until you already have a reputation.
- There is a bigger role for government in the whole area of fostering import substitution and local production. We already have TRADENZ — a government agency that boosts New Zealand exports. Its annual budget was $55 million last time I looked. Why not have a MADENZ, boosting production for the local market? Around $55 million a year could exert a lot of leverage in the domestic market, through network building, guarantees and modest injections of loan funding. This does not mean socialism or central planning or Think Big or even breaking GATT rules. It just means doing for our import-substitutors what we — and just about every other country — does for its exporters. Why do we seem to think that selling something to a foreigner is more noble than selling to ourselves? It truly isn't! Indeed, I suggest a basic shift in our point of view. Instead of thinking of local production as import replacement, we should think of imports as production replacement. Local production is the true norm, not imports.
- Government is itself a major purchaser of goods and services and should operate its own vigorous buy-New-Zealand-first policy. To that end there is already something called the 'Industry Supplies Office', eking out an annual budget of $380,000, which is less than one-hundredth of the TRADENZ annual spend. This is pathetic!

According to conventional macroeconomic theory, import substitution could not in itself solve the unemployment problem. A reduced propensity to import would raise the Keynesian 'multiplier', which would give a short-term boost to job creation, but in the long run resources diverted into import substitution would have to come from other uses — existing domestic production and production for exports. Importing less means less exporting is needed to earn the foreign exchange to pay for the imports; and various adjustment mechanisms, such as the exchange rate, would operate to effect this change.

But the point of view expressed in this book is quite different. We are not operating within the confines of the conventional model (which, within its limits, has some merit). My concern, throughout, has been to query the system within which the economic model functions: *why do we now apparently need a massive reserve of unemployed (and another small army of underpaid employees) to keep the economy functioning, when once we didn't?* The answer is that we don't, unless we are content to continue treating labour as just another commodity, to be bought and sold like fillets of frozen fish in markets that require inventories of unused commodities to act as a buffer between the independent fluctuations of supply and demand.

The better way is to bring supply and demand together; we do not need those 'inventories' of idle and often wretched people. To see how this can work, let us try and track down the source of unemployment through a thought experiment that builds up the economic system from its most basic level. Start with the archetypical 'Robinson Crusoe' economy — a one-man operation. Then demand and supply are located in the same person, and, unless Crusoe is schizophrenic, a mismatch between them is unimaginable. Nor will income distribution be a problem, for the same reason: Crusoe pays Crusoe. As for the investment decision, if Crusoe succumbs to the temptation to lie in the sun instead of gathering coconuts, and goes hungry in the winter as a result, he has no one to blame but himself — the 'intertemporal consumption allocation decision' is fully internalised.

Now move up to the next level of societal complexity: the family. Consider the case of a large family farm, operated by a group of adult brothers and sisters who share the work and the decision making. Again, 'unemployment' is not a meaningful concept. The demand for labour will probably vary quite a lot, if only because of the seasonal swings in farm activity, but if it drops, say, by 20 per cent, and there are five family members, it is hardly likely that four of them will carry on working as hard as before while a fifth wanders around saying 'give me a job'. All five will cut back their work effort, or labour will be diverted into investment activities, such as repairing fences, or perhaps one person will volunteer to take some of their annual vacation then. There will not be the waste of someone wanting to work but having nothing to do.

Income distribution (which must be considered together with employment and unemployment) could be a bit trickier, because the brothers and sisters will probably differ somewhat in ability and strength. How to reward Big Jake, who can toss hay bales to the top of the stack with ease and accuracy? Should he be paid less than his weaker siblings because labour is so easy for him, or more for the extra work he gets through? Experience suggests that a family in this situation will most likely adopt the classic equal-shares formula for dividing up the farm income. This will economise on the transaction costs (and potential for divisiveness and bitterness) of working out who did what, and be efficient in encouraging the cooperation essential in a team-production situation. Of course this will not prevent informal adjustments being made — on the day after Big Jake's prodigious labours in the field, the smallest member of the family might bring him his breakfast in bed as a treat.

So no sign yet of the unemployment problem. And we have actually covered quite a lot of ground. A sizeable minority of formal or measured economic activity, and probably the great majority of noneconomic (i.e. not measured in GDP) activity is carried out by people making their own supply/demand decisions (things we do by and for ourselves) or dealing with close family or friends. And while every parent is probably familiar with the teenage whine *'I'm bored!'*, few would consider that this 'unemployment' is other than a problem to be dealt with as best as possible within the family confines.

It is when we crank up the level of organisational complexity another notch that unemployment can sprout — in the gaps between supply and demand when the glue that binds those in self/family/friends situations is weakened with the division of labour, so that suppliers and demanders become separate, specialist occupations. But does this mean that unemployment is a necessary evil if we are to enjoy the fruits of modern economic organisation? Not if we take seriously the lessons of the old New Zealand of full employment. This was not — as popular myth has it — the result of overmanning in the railways and other public-works departments. The labour shed in these industries since corporatisation and privatisation can account for only a small fraction of the current unemployment, and in any case the key point is not where and how 'productively' the workers were working but that the economy could function without that buffer stock of unemployment we have since been burdened with.

The point I am making is that full employment in the 1950s and 1960s was essentially a private-sector phenomenon, best seen as a sort of macro-manifestation of those 'family' linkages that keep supply and demand for labour in balance down on the farm. I do not want to romanticise the economy-as-family concept — nor romanticise families themselves, for that matter — but I think we need it to understand the Kiwi full-employment miracle. It was, and still is to a large extent, a matter of empathy in the sense of a shared understanding of how to behave and what behaviour to expect from others, along with a willingness to share reasonably the fruits of cooperative endeavour. Thus the worker expected to find work and the employer expected to be able to offer it: supply and demand moved towards each other.

This is why I have stressed the advantages of production for the domestic market. Though exporters and importers may develop quite strong relationships with their foreign customers and suppliers, we just cannot expect these bonds to have the strength built by commerce amongst one's own kind. Here we can claim the authority of the great Adam Smith himself, who, in one of his three references to the 'invisible hand' wrote that if there were no import restrictions, the domestic merchant would still prefer to support 'homespun' domestic industry for 'his own security . . . led by an invisible hand to promote an end which is no part of his intention'.[3]

So that is what the invisible hand is about! It is when people are producing with and for other people with whom they have a sense of kinship and empathy that we see the integration of supply and demand needed to strengthen the attractor of genuine full employment.

What about wages? We cannot extend literally the family-farm equal-shares distribution of income into the larger economy, and there are plenty of good reasons why some people doing some jobs will be paid more than others. But if we don't get a tolerable income distribution at source — in the pay packets — we will never get it. So if not equal pay, we must insist on fair shares. This means reversing the past decade's trend towards a hollowing out of the income distribution in the name of 'international competitiveness': top people paying themselves more and paying those at the bottom less (and under less secure and humane working conditions). In the increasingly brutalised — even primitive — 'free' market economy of the new New Zealand, lessons from seriously poor economies become more relevant. The economist and philosopher Amartya Sen has made a major study of famines. He finds that the problem is never a shortage of food. It is a shortage of money to pay for the food: a shortage of incomes.[4]

That is, poverty is not a physical problem of not enough food or whatever; it is the social, economic and political problem of a distorted distribution of income. There is no real question about whether a relatively rich country like New Zealand can 'afford' to pay everybody a decent living wage. Indeed, can we afford not to, in the long run? And how do we do it? It is the same issue as reclaiming full employment — indeed, they must go hand in hand. In an economy with strong bonds of empathy and goodwill, it is a generally accepted norm that a steady adult worker should earn enough to bring up a family in decency, and that those with control over the purse strings will not abuse their position to pocket large multiples of the average wage.

As with full employment, we cannot expect government to deliver us a decent income distribution on a plate, but there are key collective 'goods' that only the body politic can provide on our behalf: a respectable minimum wage; humane and sensible labour legislation (including safeguards for collective bargaining); possibly some controls on top rates of pay; a strongly proactive policy against abuses of market power and monopoly (including regulation of 'network' industries, such as telecommunications); a revitalised welfare state (on which more in chapter 18). Perhaps paramount in terms of public policy would be the set of initiatives directed at building up our social capital. Some of these I have suggested above; some remain to be invented or suggested by other people. Such initiatives would foster the internal economic linkages between New Zealanders by giving us the *space* within which we can sort out our economic problems for ourselves. More than anything, this would require a change in the mind-set of our policy makers: a massive shift in our point of view from looking outwards to trade, competitiveness and the world economy as our salvation to looking inwards to ourselves as the only holders of the keys to our destiny; to celebrating the mundane business of homespun production; to ordinary New Zealand people dealing with each other with self-respect and decency.

This emphasis on New Zealanders doing business with New Zealanders has nothing to do with foreign capitalists being wicked, or other countries being unreliable partners in trading goods and services. It stems from the simple fact that they cannot be expected to have our interests at heart and they cannot be expected to act as we do or even to understand how we behave. Because of this, when we deal with foreigners there is a split between the supply and demand sides of the market, which can be joined only by incurring expensive transaction costs, of which the most expensive and tragic is mass unemployment.

Not that it is just foreigners who are 'foreign'. Perhaps the most fundamentally worrying trend of the past decade or so is the extent to which New Zealanders have become strangers to each other in their own country. This is a *deliberate* result of the more-market revolution, which has relentlessly promoted attitudinal as well as institutional changes in the direction of self-seeking and opportunistic economic behaviour (commercialisation), telling people and businesses that they should just look after their own narrow self-interest on whatever side of the market they happen to be and not worry about anyone else.

I have argued that the competitive-market model that underpins commercialisation is simplistic. It misses too much of what is really important, in particular the social dimension to economic life. That is why the fruits of the New Zealand economic revolution have been so meagre and, for far too many, so bitter. Full employment and decent incomes for all requires a high-trust, high-empathy society in which supply and demand are not held apart in the name of commercial accountability or individual profit-maximisation or whatever.

This is not some touchy-feely, warm-fuzzy, everyone-give-everybody-a-big-hug self-help manual of the sort that clots the best-seller lists. Empathy means *understanding* how others will respond, not necessarily approving of it. Trust means relying on others (and them on you) to behave with some forbearance and honour, whether or not you always feel like doing so. Of course all this must rest on some basic mutual goodwill, though it does not rule out conflicts and tears. It is about 'family' — the nation as family — but in an everyday, ups-and-downs sense.

My specific focus here has been on reversing the trend towards 'integration' of New Zealand into the international economy by having some restrictions on foreign investment, and by fostering and celebrating home production for the home market. This reflects my own specialist area of interest in economics, and should not preclude other ideas. There are, for example, public and community initiatives such as local development trusts which already operate with some success. And I hope there are many more great ideas out there, waiting for a chance to germinate in a congenial economic environment. *Floreant.*

Chapter 17

Susan of Parnell: a Story of Work and Family

The book *False Economy* by Anne Else[1] has interviews with nine mothers and two fathers, who give mostly depressing accounts of their lives and their difficulties in mixing market, house and childcare work. Here is another mother's story:

Susan's story (*We spoke to Susan in the pleasant sunroom of her villa in an Auckland inner suburb.*)

'I'm thirty-seven years old, married to Rob, with three kids — Julius, who's eight now, and the twins, Barbara and Robert, who are just six. Rob wanted to give our first son his name, but I wouldn't have it — so corny, don't you think? Men are funny about that sort of thing — want to start a dynasty. So we named him after my maternal great-grandfather, who is a bit of a hero in my mother's family. But I relented with the twins, on the condition that he — young Robert, that is — not be known as Rob. So Bobs it is. Babs and Bobs — they're a hoot, those two!

'Rob and I met at university, at Otago. We were both freshers, living in hostels and both in the inter-hostel debating competition. We debated against each other in the finals, and I won! Rob was a bit sulky about this but so sweet that at the party afterwards I offered him a consolation prize: me! I'd actually had my eye on him for a while. He was a cute guy then (and he still is!).

'Anyway, it didn't take Rob long to accept second prize, so to speak, and we didn't stay long at that party. And we've been a steady number ever since. Had our ups and downs — who hasn't! — but we've survived and we still love each other.

'We got married the day after we both graduated. We'd

actually finished our courses at the end of the previous year, and we were both back in Auckland by then, working. We had The Plan, and we stuck to it, more or less. We were both going to work as hard as we could, and save as much as we could, until we were thirty. And we were going to have a nice house by then, mortgage-free, to start our family in. We got into the property market right away, with a *huge* mortgage initially — servicing it consumed all of one of our incomes — buying right on the limit of what the bank manager would lend us.

'We had a simple enough strategy. We focused on rather seedy neighbourhoods with good prospects. Then we studied them closely, driving around at different times of the day and weekend, to sort out just where the best streets were — you know, good aspects, shops handy, a school close but not too close — simple things that a lot of people don't really bother researching properly. Then we'd pick the crummiest, most run-down villa in the best street and buy it, cheaply. And do it up. *That* was the hard part. We did everything ourselves; plumbing, wiring, the lot. We simply couldn't afford to hire anyone. We slaved all weekends. Believe me, we were so tired on Sunday nights that going to work on Monday would just be like going on holiday.

'But it was fun, and it worked. We were too late to get into Ponsonby, but we did well in Westmere and Grey Lynn. We built up equity — sweat equity, it's called — sold out, and took our profit to move upmarket to a bigger house in a better street. We did this three times in eight years, and then we were able to buy the house we really wanted to live in ourselves. This place, in Parnell. We wanted to be close to downtown so that commuting wouldn't be a hassle for Rob; good schools, and shops and things within walking reach.

'So here we are, and it's great. We ended up with a small mortgage after all, but it's manageable. Julius was conceived the night we signed the contract on this house — quite an achievement that, considering how much champagne Rob had drunk (and me, but you know what I mean). Then, two years later, out popped the twins. We were thrilled — we always wanted to have at least three children. Then they can become a little tribe of their own; look after each other. My family was like that — I have three siblings — and Rob had been an only child, so we knew the difference.

'I gave up my job in my eighth month of pregnancy with Julius, and I haven't worked since. I've been a full-time houseperson and momma, and I've loved it. Having kids is such a kick! Especially when they are little and growing and learning so fast. Now they're at school it's a bit different. They all go to the same place, just over the hill. Julius started there two-and-a-half years ago, and he's been walking there by himself for nearly a year. His idea, not mine, but it's worked out fine. He's very independent; quite the little man. I used to send Peg along with him. (*Peg is a big black standard poodle, stretched out on the window seat in the sun. An ear twitches at the sound of her name, but she doesn't stir.*) She would come straight back home afterwards, so I knew he'd got there okay. It's not very far, and there's just one big street to cross.

'Six months ago it was the twins' turn to start. Of course I wanted to take them on their first day, but they wouldn't hear of it. Their big bro was going to take them to school and that was that. Tears and much stomping of tiny feet, and I gave in. It was one of the hardest things I have ever done: just standing there at the gate watching the three of them marching off up the street, with their little knapsacks, hand in hand, with Peg trotting proudly in front, tail up. I went back inside and bawled my eyes out. My babies, gone!

'I admit that I'd primed John Tuwhare, their teacher, to keep an eye out for them and to slip off and phone me when they arrived. It's just as well he did, because Peg didn't come back! Apparently she spent the entire day at the school gate, waiting for the twins to reappear. Then they all skipped home together, very pleased with themselves indeed.

'Now we've changed the routine with Peg. I just let her out at five to three, and she races up the hill to meet them. That's good, because I feel I can let them dawdle a bit on the way home; play with friends, explore. But they know that if they aren't back here by four o'clock — Julius has a watch — there'll be *big trouble*. And Peg gets fed sharp at four, so she's pretty keen to keep them on schedule.

'So what do I do during the day? Well, Rob's out of the house first, then the kids, then I clean up the kitchen and wave a broom around the place. I do the cryptic crossword over a cup of coffee — I'm that quick now! Then I'll probably do some food shopping and perhaps meet a friend for a natter. Or, three days a week, I go to KeepFit.

'Some days, Rob comes home for lunch, which is nice. Sometimes I'm really *ready* for him, if you know what I mean. There's something about doing aerobics that gets one horny, don't you find? One of the instructors in particular is a *hunk*; a real turn-on. Naturally I don't tell Rob about this, but he knows when I'm feeling *ready* because I wear my sexy leotard from the gym. Actually I squeeze into another one — a seriously sexy little item that I don't dare wear in public! Rob loves it. On my ready days he gets back late to the office and he hasn't even had any lunch! He sneaks out at afternoon tea time to get a sandwich or something, hoping his secretary doesn't notice. I'll bet she does! (*Susan laughs and is pensive for a moment.*)

'Where was I? Afternoons. Yes, afternoons are "MP" time. No, not listening to parliament but MP — Mum's Project. I'm converting the attic into a big playroom/partyroom for the children. It's going quite slowly because I'm a bit of a perfectionist — unlike Rob. That used to cause problems sometimes when we were doing our renovations. I'd be lovingly sanding down some tricky little cornice and Rob would come over, all sweaty from some mighty labour with his beloved chainsaw dangling from his hand and say: "Jesus, Sue, we're not building a bloody grand piano here!" And I'd just turn on him and say: "Piss off you wood-butcher!" (*Laughs.*)

'Anyway, I get two or three hours of MP — it just flies by — then the dog and the children get home and it's the usual total chaos until tea time — five-thirty, sharp. I get them fed, then we pretend they are helping me do the dishes, then Rob gets home, as close to six-thirty as he can make it.

'He's very good about this, even though his work days are pretty action-packed. Once or twice in the early days he was quite often staying later at the office, and I didn't like it. Nor did Rob. So one day, in the middle of a very important meeting, at quarter-past six he just stood up and said: "I'm sorry, I have to leave now. I have an important date with my wife and children."

It was a bit tense for a moment, then his boss — who's a woman — said: 'I wish I'd done that ten years ago when I had young children', and that's the way it's been ever since.

'Of course we let him out occasionally — for instance when there's a big overseas client to be entertained. But he has to bribe us! Home early the next day to take the kids to McDonalds, and champagne and flowers for me.

'But normally Rob's here by half past six and takes over. The children just adore him! They're all over him the moment he's in the door: 'Daddy look at this and Daddy I did that!' If it's dark, he does computer stuff with them. Or, in the summer, they all pile off down to the park and play cricket. Peg patrols the outfield, for the rare occasion when someone hits the ball that far. Anyway, it's my Quiet Time. I pour myself a big glass of white wine, come out to this sunroom, put on a CD — jazz usually — and smoke my daily cheroot (they won't let me have it anywhere else in the house, which is fair enough).

'Rob bathes the kids and puts them to bed, and I start cooking our dinner — often something quick like a stir-fry if we are going out to a movie or concert with friends, or if I have a school board-of-trustees meeting or Rob is coaching his basketball team in Western Springs. If we are staying in Rob comes down and sits on the stool at the counter while I cook, and offers helpful advice. We just talk about things, drink some wine and eat our food. It's nice. By the time we've cleaned up it's around ten o'clock. We might watch the late news, or just go to bed and read for a while. Not for long . . .

Do you expect to return to the labour force some time?
'Of course I think about that. My brain cells start to feel a bit irritable at times, and I think I should give them some exercise again. I was a bright girl, academically. I could go back to university and do something like law, but really, does the world need yet another smart female lawyer? Perhaps a graduate programme in arts — not very vocational, though, is it? But does that matter? We don't really need extra income at the moment — Rob is doing well, and we'll have the mortgage on this place paid off in two years. I ran into an old schoolchum the other day at 277. She's one of those smart female lawyers. She's a judge

now, actually — good for her! We'd always been rivals for top-of-the-class at school, and she sort of berated me for not going on and doing something with my brain. I just took her home here to meet the family, and she didn't say it any more.

'I've loved doing what I've been doing for the past fifteen years, but I know that the next fifteen will be different. We'll just have to see.'

What's wrong with this story? Statistically, it is slightly unusual, but not odd — Anne Else reports that 27 per cent of children under fifteen lived in a household with a full-time employed father and a full-time at-home mother in 1991 (more than 30 per cent of partnered women with babies under one year old were in the labour force). But it is certainly nothing like any of the stories in Anne Else's book — a smart, spirited woman happy (for the time being, anyway) and doing well as a full-time wife, child-raiser and house-tender. The unsympathetic reader (which I am not) might wish to subtitle *False Economy*: 'Middle-class mothers moan about their lives'. Of the nine interview subjects, only the two well-off ones — Kim Hill and Suzanne Snively — express joy in and love for their children. It's a bit depressing really — do you have to have an income of more than $100,000 a year before you can afford to enjoy being a parent?

Susan's husband Rob, aged about thirty-seven, and 'doing well in his job', which is probably in a law or accounting firm or merchant bank, must be bringing home close to a 100K pay cheque, which is certainly enough to bring up a family on in comfort, though they evidently do not live extravagantly, sending their children to the local state school. Susan's airy 'waving a broom around the place' suggests that she spends $50 each week having someone come in for a morning to do the heavy cleaning. And why not?

Not all couples have the energy and skills displayed by Susan and Rob to work their way up through the housing market so successfully before they are thirty. But not everyone needs to live in what, from its description, must be at least a $500,000 villa in Parnell. Even in Auckland, you can find a decent dwelling in a nice suburb for a lot less than this. The key, of course, is for a couple to delay having babies until they are emotionally and financially secure enough to handle the change in their lives without undue stress. For various reasons, most of the women in *False Economy* have not done this. Perhaps people just don't realise the power of compounding. *Every year that a young couple delay starting a family can add $50,000 to $100,000 to their net wealth ten years later.*[2]

They are also performing a service to society at large by delaying pregnancy. It is hard to think of a major problem — economic, social, political — which is not at root derived from the pressure of expanding population on finite resources. Children born in a rich country like New Zealand will be particularly greedy plunderers of those resources through their lives. Even if the number of children in a household ends up the same, by having them later rather than earlier the parents will contribute to a lower population growth rate through lengthening the generation span. And to anyone who thinks they are performing some sort of social service in having children, I would just say: *Please don't do it! Spare us and yourselves.*

But we cannot attribute all the problems of households under stress to bad family planning. Once upon a time it was the law in New Zealand that wages had to be high enough to support a single-income family. From 1936 to 1954 the Arbitration Court was obliged to determine a basic wage for adult males that 'should be sufficient to maintain a man, his wife and three children in a fair and reasonable standard of comfort'.[3]

Since then, many things have changed, some for the good. Since the signing of the Equal Pay Act of 1972 women cannot be (legally) discriminated against in the labour market, at least in terms of receiving different pay for doing the same job as a man. In response to this and other social and cultural shifts the participation in paid work of women has risen steadily to about 55 per cent of the working-age female population (and that of men fallen somewhat to 74 per cent, due to higher enrolments in tertiary education and demographic factors).[4] Much of this increase has been genuinely liberating for the women, and it hasn't done the men any harm, either. As far as I am concerned, as a male worker, the more women the merrier — an all-male workplace is a pretty ghastly set-up.

But I can also see the costs that the women bear. As Anne Else and many others point out, women do the bulk of the household work and management whether or not they have a paid job, and whether or not there is a man (or supposedly able-bodied teenage and young adult children) around the place. And it seems that events over the last decade in particular have simply forced many families with young children to send two people out into the workforce.

Let's take another example, this time of how what seems to be a marginal amount of economic pressure can force a full-scale shift in regime, causing a flip-over to a radically different type of lifestyle. Here is an illustrative case. We have a man working, say, as a telecommunications technician for the old Post Office in the days when it ran the telephone system. He earns $40,000 a year gross — somewhat above the average annual earnings — and brings home after tax a bit more than $600 each week. This is enough, with careful budgeting and supplementary 'household production', to support his household of himself, his young wife, and their two preschool children, whom the woman looks after full time.

Then, with a wave of the privatisation wand, the telephone system is sold and soon our fellow is laid off by the new Telecom, and rehired as an independent contractor on a lower earning scale — worth $34,000 a year with extra unpaid overtime hours and no benefits. This knocks the after-tax income down to $500 a week, which is not quite enough to get by on. Rent alone soaks up $200.

The wife will have to get a paid job. But here's the rub. The hours she will need to put in will not be proportional to the loss in her mate's pay — say, about one day per week. *She will most likely need to find a full-time job* to close that 20 per cent income gap.[5] Why? First, having spent most of her adulthood having children she has not built up the 'human capital' that will command a high rate of pay in the labour market. If she is quite lucky she will get a data-processing job at $10 or $11 per hour (and this is well above the minimum wage many people work at or near). After tax, this brings in $300 a week. But it doesn't, actually. There will be employment costs — transport (another car needed?), work clothing, cafeteria — which can easily gobble up $100 each week.[6] Then there is childcare. Let us hope that the children at least go to kindergarten, but there will still be those before and after hours when Mum is at work. Friends and extended family may be able to help, but it would not be surprising if babysitting expenses totalled $100/week. Then there will be the costs of lost home production — clothes that aren't mended and have to be replaced; meals that aren't cooked and are substituted for with takeaway food, and so on. Would $50 a week cover this? Even if it does, the net contribution from the full-time job is down to a measly $50/week — not enough to cover the financial deficit. She will probably have to work overtime.

On top of all this are the likely effects on the relationships between parents and between them and their children, and on the emotional and physical health of the mother. It can be a rather dismal scenario.

What can be done? Central, crucial, is restoring the well-paid, secure job as the centrepiece of the family's economic existence. A responsible adult must be able to earn enough to support a family in decency again, with a full-time home producer/caregiver if that is what the couple want. It would be nice if it were the man who took on that role more than happens now, but if it is the woman, then so be it. Men and women have to sort these things out for themselves. It is simply unacceptable to assert that we 'can't afford' to pay a family wage nowadays, when real per capita GDP is supposedly about double what it was in the 1950s and 1960s, when somehow we could afford it. We must challenge and change this unsustainable situation.

Chapter 18
The Welfare State: a Modest Proposal

It is said that the prospect of being hanged in the morning concentrates the mind wonderfully. Fortunately no one has to live through that experience in New Zealand. But suppose we decided as a nation that, exactly one year from now, all benefits — unemployment, domestic purposes, sickness — would be eliminated or sharply curtailed in their coverage. That prospect would certainly concentrate many minds.

Not just cut back benefits, as has been done in New Zealand since 1990, but cut them out completely, which is a quite different thing. Cutting back just screws down even further into poverty the people who depend on benefits to live at what must be a pretty miserable standard (around $10,000 per year). I'd much rather increase the benefits, on humanitarian grounds, than cut them further.

So given that I feel this way, why would I suggest sweeping aside benefits more or less completely? It would of course mean intolerable hardship to tens of thousands of people who rely on these payments. Intolerable unless we concentrated our minds to do something about it; to replace benefits with something better.

What that something better would be is not too hard to imagine. We've had it before in New Zealand, and it worked well: the 'wage earners' welfare state',[1] based on well-paid jobs available to all, so that each household could send someone out into the market economy and have them bring back to the family hearth a sufficiency to sustain a decent and dignified existence. This is an economy in which a couple who don't have the unusual get-up-and-go of Susan and Rob of Parnell can still save enough to start a family eventually under decent and comfortable conditions, with just one of them in the labour force after the babies arrive. If they both want to carry on working, or if the household only has one parent, there must be good childcare available, at minimal cost. If young people need training or tertiary education, these should be available too, without forcing them into crushing debt-repayment obligations.

So why not get these good things without disturbing the present benefit structure? We could let it just wither away from disuse, until we get to the point we did in the 1950s and 1960s, where unemployment benefits, though available and quite generous, were literally *never* taken up (and there was no DPB and much less 'sickness').[2] Well, perhaps this is the best way. But there are at least two reasons for taking seriously the zero-benefit option. First, it makes budgeting for the new era manageable without risking a big deficit blow-out. Any new money being spent will come from the old programmes being cut out. Second, it follows from a more holistic, integrated point of view than the standard model (on both left and right of the political spectrum) of the economy as a machine, to be tinkered with mechanistically, bits being added and cut off as desired. Instead, the economy is seen as a living system, in which the health of each organ depends on the health of everything else. The appropriate discipline for the study of such a system may actually be epidemiology rather than orthodox economics. In epidemics, small causes can have massive, systemic effects. In orthodox economics, small causes never have more than small, localised effects.

Here is how the logic of epidemics plays out.[3] Suppose one thousand people turn up in Auckland with an untreatable strain of twenty-four-hour flu. Perhaps they all caught it in Australia. Suppose the infection rate of the virus is 2 per cent, meaning that out of every fifty people coming into close contact with an infected person, one catches the virus. As long as the contact rate is less than fifty people a day, the virus will die out: the first thousand people will recover from their bout after twenty-four hours, leaving fewer than one thousand newly infected folk to pass on the virus the next day, and so on until everyone is healthy again or another plane load of infected people arrive.

But what if — say because it is near Christmas and people are out and about more than usual — the contact rate rises above fifty people per day? The virus will spread exponentially, becoming an epidemic by Christmas Day (whereafter it will suddenly die out, as the contact rate collapses over the Christmas holidays). Fifty is what is called the 'tipping point' in this particular epidemic, because small changes in behaviour near this number of daily contacts can result in large (or 'nonlinear') changes in outcomes — the system can 'tip' over into a quite different mode.

Epidemic theory has been used by social scientists to explain puzzling events such as the halving of the crime rate in a few years in the tough New York area of Brooklyn North:

> In the Seven-Five [the 75th Precinct, which covers Brooklyn North], there are now slightly more [police] officers than before. They stop more cars. They confiscate more guns. They chase away more street-corner loiterers. They shut down more drug markets. They have made a series of what seem, when measured against the extraordinary decline in murders, to be small changes. But it is the nature of non-linear phenomena that sometimes the most modest of changes can bring about enormous effects. What happened to the murder rate may not be such a mystery in the end. Perhaps . . . Brooklyn — and with it New York City — has tipped.[4]

Here's a simplified example of how the tipping model could apply to our economic and social problems in New Zealand. When someone suddenly loses their job, they can do one of two things: go right out the next morning and search for another job or stay in bed. These modes of behaviour are the two 'attractors' vying for popularity in the population. Suppose that the choice of which attractor to gravitate towards, for a young male in a city suburb, depends on what other people like him are doing. If, let us say, at least 90 per cent of the others are getting up in the morning and going to work or searching for a job until they find one, then that is what our suddenly unemployed young man will do, pressured by social norms and by the high probability of finding a job quickly. But if the employment rate is currently less than 90 per cent, then those norms etc. are sufficiently weakened for the stay-in-bed attractor to dominate.

Now, the neighbourhood is periodically subject to 'shocks' (like a sudden outbreak of a flu virus) when a plant closes and throws its employees out of work. So long as these shocks aren't big enough to push the employment rate below 90 per cent, the local economy will recover as all the unemployed set out to find new jobs. But if there is a large shock or bunching of smaller shocks (as happened in many areas during our deindustrialisation phase from 1986 to 1992, when about one manufacturing job in three disappeared), the employment rate may tip below 90 per cent, and the stay-in-bed attractor will exert its hold: the economy will not recover.

In fact, just as not everybody catches the flu during an epidemic, not everyone will stay out of work, but the neighbourhood could settle into a self-reinforcing high-unemployment regime, resistant to 'medicines' like punitive cuts in benefit levels designed to spur people into getting out and getting a job. We should perhaps not be squeamish about recognising the precariousness of the getting-up-in-the-morning mode of behaviour: a lot can be done to ensure that jobs are decent; we can do a lot to ensure that they are well paid; better than now, anyway. But we can't make every job fun, fulfilling, interesting, creative. Even jobs that have these lucky features, such as my own, have their tough bits. Try taking on a lecture theatre of four hundred first-year economics students at five o'clock in the afternoon, when nearly all of them would rather be doing something else. Or the moral effort to keep one's research up to the mark; to stomach the rejection letters and fight to improve your work to publishable standards.

Most people in the labour force are going to be doing work that is frequently boring or tiring or both. Work is what you do to get a taste for leisure. So why not just take the leisure? That attractor is too strong in New Zealand now, and although most of the solution is to strengthen the 'carrot' of more and better paid jobs, we may need too the stick of removing the temptation for people to say: 'Aw, stuff it! My head hurts,' and roll over and stay in bed in the morning.

We don't want a large group of healthy adult males

concocting a mixture of idleness, informal work and crime to pass their daytime hours. But the full-time work attractor is just not powerful enough to win out unless it is already dominant. And the resentment against paying off a class of healthy male beneficiaries will not come so much from the rich as from other poor and lower-income people — those who struggle hard to earn their keep. A substantial degree of horizontal inequity is surely not sustainable in the long run.

The same problem is not so acute with respect to healthy adult women, who always have two possible acceptable roles — paid worker and unpaid parent — and must often combine the two, whether they want to or not. But most men aren't good for much else other than paid work in the day time. If they aren't working for a wage they don't, in general, switch to housework or childcare or community work like women do. They tend, at worse, to hang out with other idle characters and cause mischief; at best, they are parasitic drones.

Of course we couldn't really abolish *all* benefits, even with a year's notice. There would have to be money available for emergencies — a town devastated by the sudden closing of its largest employer; a mother fleeing an abusive relationship. But we shouldn't be afraid to look at the process whereby these terrible things happen. Why do women get into binding relationships with men who turn out to be complete jerks? Why *are* men such jerks, so often? Why do women, with or without supportive partners, get pregnant before they are emotionally and economically able to cope with bringing up a family? It doesn't mean 'blame the victim' to want fewer victims in the first place. Fundamental are good education and job prospects, for women and for men, to give them some sense of a future worth planning for, of returns to restraint, of the value of participating fully in a society in which decent, responsible behaviour is expected and rewarded.

So if we disposed of benefits, what would we do with the money saved? How much is there? At first glance the numbers may seem a bit disappointing: out of a 1995 GNP of about $86 billion, government spent $30 billion, of which just $1.3 billion went out as unemployment benefits, about the same for the DPB, and another $3 billion for other social-assistance transfers. Administration of all this cost $1.4 billion.[5] But, as the late Senator Dirksen once said: 'A billion saved here, and a billion there, and pretty soon you're talking about some *real* money.'

So suppose we got back $5 billion of the $7 billion listed above. That is about 6 per cent of GNP, which really would be quite a useful sum. Just a tenth of that — $500 million — would go a long way to support the crèche and childcare sector. I'd like to see more resources devoted to ensuring that young people — in particular young women and Maori — have the training and education available to give them something to plan for, to make it worthwhile to defer some pleasures now for the greater gain in the future. There are quite a lot of proactive schemes aimed at creating jobs and helping people fill them that could benefit from judicious injections of funding. But this isn't, and shouldn't be, mega-spending territory. Throwing large sums of money at it won't solve unemployment or any other major problem.

Some of the money could be given back, in tax cuts. It would take about $1.4 billion, for example, to cut the GST back from 12.5 per cent to 10 per cent. That would be nice. Perhaps it should all be given back: there's nothing actually *wrong* about lower taxes.

But there is another possible fate for the liberated billions, which is to distribute them directly as some sort of universal benefit. This would differ in some key respects from the present benefit system. First, it would not be means-tested, and thus would not create the 'poverty traps' which are perhaps the most crippling disability of the way we do things now. These are the unavoidable by-product of targeting benefits to those who need them, meaning you lose the benefit when you don't need it, which amounts to imposing a huge tax — estimated to be as much as 100 per cent or even more at the margin— on the transition from benefit dependency to paid employment.[6] In New Zealand, rich persons' lobby groups such as the Business Roundtable whine endlessly about the alleged 'disincentive' effects of marginal tax rates at 33 per cent. In fact there is no real evidence that taxes at this level do have any effect on work effort, but taxes of 100% are a different story.

But then, if we avoid the Scylla of poverty traps by having a universal benefit, we immediately bump into the Charybdis of affordability. There are about two-and-a-half million adults (aged twenty years or over) in New Zealand. To give each an annual benefit income of just $20,000 would cost $50 billion — more than half the total GNP produced each year! Even much lower benefit levels would require swingeing increases in marginal taxes on earned incomes. Now some enthusiasts for a universal basic income (as it is known) are happy about this, but they are not going to win any elections. Others have a dreamy concept of the economy as a sort of shiny machine, which ever more efficiently churns out goods and services requiring less and less labour input, so that there won't be the need or even possibility of everybody having a full-time paid job.

Anyone who has read this far will know by now that I consider such views to be hopelessly unrealistic, even immoral. Work as I see it (that is, paid work) is a fundamental social activity, a duty, an act of participation in one's wider community. To put it at its bluntest, outside of periods of crisis, earning taxpayers like me just won't tolerate having large lumps of our incomes diverted to support folk who make a lifestyle decision not to work. This doesn't mean that every household should be forced to send someone out into the labour market, but it does mean that, if they don't, it is because they are living off the proceeds of previous work — their savings — or are on the pension, which the state should cheerfully dispense on society's behalf to all who have honourably survived serving out time in the home or workplace.

It is the pension which suggests an idea for a benefit that might be shared out to all citizens of good standing — say, on their birthday to every registered voter with no criminal conviction over the previous twelve months. The justification for this comes from the 'social capital' perspective — the idea that we are all in this thing together, that behaving well is not just its own reward but also a reward for others. Every time someone behaves honourably in a social or economic transaction, they benefit not just the person they are dealing with at the time, but everyone else, because each additional honourable act raises the future likelihood of such acts — makes them a more powerful 'attractor' for other persons' behavioural choices.

Since such behaviour is critical to the production of goods and services, it seems fair enough to give us all some direct remuneration for contributing to the social capital — a 'social dividend' on it, if you will. How much could that be? Not a huge amount. Just $2,000 paid to each of the 2.5 million adults would cost $5 billion a year, which could be about 50:50 funded by benefit savings and by increased tax revenues from higher employment levels.[7]

Now, a lump-sum, tax-free birthday present of $2,000 from the people of New Zealand as thanks for having been a good citizen for the previous twelve months would be quite useful to most of us. It could be used to pay for house improvements, or to pay off credit-card debt, or to finance an escape from a bad relationship, or just to take the family to Fiji for a bit of a break. It would not be enough to live on permanently, but nor should it be — that is the point.

We are not going to let people who don't earn a living starve to death, but the country cannot afford to keep them in comfort either. We need people to be participating in the economy, to be putting in as much or more than they take out, for their own sakes and for their children's sakes, as well as for the rest of us. Not everybody has to be a sharp-as-a-tack world-beater, which is just as well, because not all of us can be. What matters for the economic and the social health of a nation is that everyone is contributing in some way, and getting decently rewarded for doing so. The whole of such a system is greater than the sum of its parts.

I will illustrate the point with a story. There is a New Zealand politician who is very fond of — really, addicted to — telling anecdotes about overmanning and waste in the old government departments, especially the railways. Well, I heard an anecdote about the railways which imparts a rather different spin to the story. Like all such tales (including those of our politician), I have it at third or fourth hand, and so I've probably got it a bit wrong (though I tell it in good faith). But it makes a point.

Once upon a time there were two young men — brothers — who lived on Waiheke Island near Auckland, but who worked on a railway gang based in the Waikato. Every Sunday evening they would take the ferry to Auckland and catch the bus to Hamilton, where they lived in lodgings. On Monday morning they would turn up for work and potter around the railways, doing the jobs assigned to them by the foreman. Thursday was pay day, and that night they would go out with their mates and drink a lot of beer. On Friday morning they probably didn't get a lot of work done, and in the afternoon they would sneak off early to catch the bus so they could get home to their family on the island in time for late supper.

Neither brother was very bright, and indeed they were on the margin of being unemployable for this reason. But they were steady enough hands, and their workmates kept an eye on them, and made sure that they didn't get out of their depth. The point was that they worked and they got paid — not a lot, of course, but enough to pay for their lodging, buy their round in the pub, and contribute something to the family on Waiheke. Of course, their work was 'inefficient', and when the waves of corporatisation and privatisation swept through the railways, the brothers were amongst the first to be fired (followed by thousands of other workers, including many excellent supervisors and skilled tradespeople). They went back to live on Waiheke, and haven't had a job since. Now they truly are unemployable, though of course they still have to be supported, by the dole and perhaps the proceeds of petty crime, into which many in their situation have slipped away from the steadying influence of their former workmates. Now I ask, which way makes more sense?

Chapter 19
Schools, Health, Housing, Crime ... It's the Economy, Stupid!

Opinion polls before the 1996 general election in New Zealand were headed by health and education as the big issues of concern to voters. The 'economy' was well down the list. So why are these important topics crammed together into just one chapter? This is why: the problems of the health system, education, crime and so on are to a large extent all the same problem, which is the basic economic problem: low wages, insecure jobs, and mass unemployment.

Restoring high-wage full employment won't cure cancer. But it will reduce its incidence (because happily employed people smoke less and eat better) along with the incidence of just about every other sickness and disease, and will make the suffering that remains easier to cope with. And healthier children from stable households are easier to educate. The sociologist Ian Shirley has compiled a massive survey of studies of the effects of unemployment, and there is not much good news in it. Summarising the findings of more than 2,000 papers, he writes:

> there is a strong relationship between unemployment and a wide range of social problems, such as ill health, premature death, suicide, marital breakdown, child abuse, racial conflict, violence and crime.[1]

We do not yet (as far as I know) have such a large body of research into the ill effects of the modern corollary of unemployment — overemployment (both being the symptoms of a high-transaction cost 'competitive' economic system). Overemployment occurs when both parents have to work full time or more just to keep the family financially afloat, and I think we can expect that it is also bad for the physical and mental health of parents and children. It may be that those hospitals and schools which are having trouble coping with the demands being made of them would find their difficulties receding into manageability if good jobs at decent (family-supporting) wages were available for all. And of course causation goes both ways: a healthy, well-schooled population will be able to generate more of the social capital needed for decent economic performance.

So a well-functioning economy might be enough to alleviate the crisis in health and education. But these sectors — especially health care — have also been at the forefront of the rationalist reforms, and what has happened to them is of great interest and concern to students of the New Zealand economic revolution.

The escalation of health-care costs seems to be the result of a unique combination of near-limitless demand — *'Save my life, doctor, whatever it costs!'* — with a supply side typified in this century by a vast expansion in the number and expense of available treatments and procedures. Previously, people still got sick, but no one knew much about how to cure them. As John Kenneth Galbraith has put it, in the old days the medical profession just didn't have a lot to sell, and the problem of paying the local doctor was about on a par with the problem of paying the local grocer.

That's not so now, and the result — at least in a public health system — is some really tough decisions, both at the macro-level of deciding how much total funding to pour into health care, and at the micro level of allocating these scarce funds between limitless competing potential uses. Add to this problem the distinctive economic characteristics of health and sickness, and it should not surprise anyone that the application of economic rationalism to this sector has been such a disappointment.

To achieve the 'purchaser/provider' (demand/supply) split, treatments and procedures have all to be costed and valued, then contracts negotiated, drafted, signed and implemented.

With the best will in the world it is difficult for the health professionals to communicate to the lay managers the information needed to make these decisions and to draft and enforce these contracts: it needs a lot of managers, and a lot of the professionals' time. This means, of course, increased transaction costs, so that resources are diverted away from the actual productive business of helping people get well (or stay well).

And you may no longer be able to rely on that goodwill. This is the fundamental problem of rationalism, with its emphasis on 'commercialisation', which forces people to act as opportunistic profit-maximisers or cost-minimisers. In health care you have complex and hard-to-cost processes and technologies, and producers — the nurses, therapists, doctors — who know a lot more about those processes than either their customers (the patients) or their ostensible bosses (government, the health authorities, line managers). This means that the rest of us have to trust the professionals to behave honourably and not abuse the power of their information advantage.

But rationalism has no place for trust. Outputs and inputs are tightly specified and enforced contractually, with no discretion for people to behave well or badly. Unfortunately, because the information asymmetries are so fundamental, only a part of the process can actually be rationalised, so that for much of the time the professionals will be, in essence, unsupervised. How will they respond? As a simple motivating example for considering this, take a class of schoolchildren whose teacher is suddenly called away. 'I want you to carry on working quietly by yourselves,' says the teacher. 'You are on your honour to behave.'

If the teacher has previously run the class in such a way that the children have been encouraged and trusted to behave well — for example, allowing them to talk amongst themselves on the understanding that they are helping each other to do the problems, not just gossiping — then they might well accept that they are on their honour and behave accordingly. But if this teacher has ruled with a rod of iron, allowing no talking or autonomy, then the kids are likely to feel that 'honour' is a pretty hollow concept, and will begin to hoon it up just as soon as teacher is safely off down the corridor.

Even in a good class, kids are kids (not adult health professionals), and the teacher would be well advised not to stay away too long. But the point is, I think, generally valid: if you want to be able to trust people to behave well, you have to trust them all the time, not just when you can't exercise close supervision over them. This is true in families, in the workplace and in life generally. It is especially true in the health-care sector, where even medically trained managers will often — perhaps usually — not know enough about particular situations to be able to closely monitor and control the decisions of the people nominally reporting to them.

It seems to me that when we had a health-care system that functioned reasonably well, it was run on the basis of what philosophers call 'virtue ethics'. Instead of government trying to control complex outcomes directly through rationalist management, what we did was try to ensure that people doing the job were well-trained and honourable, and trusted them, basically, to make the decisions themselves.

This applied not just to minor matters like adjusting medications or discharging patients, but also — and *especially* — to the big, literally life-and-death decisions, like who gets kidney dialysis treatment and when the life support is quietly turned off on a terminally ill person (with family input here). How on earth else could such terrible issues be decided? You can't write these things into an operating manual — non-smoker gets preference over smoker, etc. — nor can they be referred upstairs to a manager. The allocation of resources just has to be made by the people involved, for which we must rely on their skill, experience and humanity, and if we are to do that safely, we must rely on them totally, not just in the matters which fall outside the purview of the rationalist/managerial control calculus.

There is nothing radical or extreme about this. There is still need for management structures (though not necessarily high-paid management), and for community and political involvement, especially in determining big-ticket decisions such as where a new hospital gets built. There is plenty of room for the sensible application of economic principles, especially in a publicly funded health system, where there is always a potential problem of people 'overconsuming' if they don't have to pay. The smart distinction here is between 'goods' and 'bads'. For most people, spending time in a hospital is a 'bad' — it isn't very pleasant and we would rather be at home in our own bed. So, having free hospital care should not encourage much wasteful overconsumption.

On the other hand, a consultation with your family doctor is, for many people, a 'good' — a reassuring, soothing experience. My own father, who was a fine general practitioner in Dunedin from after the war until he retired in the late 1970s, used to say that about half his work was 'psychological', and about half the pills he prescribed had nothing but chalk in them — they were placebos. He was not being flippant, though I suspect he was exaggerating. My father knew well (and many of his former patients have told me so over the years) the importance of 'The Doctor' as a sort of guru-counsellor-wizard in the lives of his charges. It made sense, then, because his time was limited, to have some sort of a price-based rationing system, and indeed for many years the standard fee for a consultation (throughout New Zealand) was fifteen shillings, of which seven shillings and sixpence (seventy-five cents) was paid by the state and 7s 6d by the patient.

What about poor people, for whom seventy-five cents would have been quite a significant sum? Well, my father (like other GPs) knew who could pay and who couldn't (doctors did house calls in those days), and would simply not send a bill to any of his patients he judged unable to afford it. Of course this smacks of 'charity', but so what? That's life: people dealing with each other on terms they have to sort out for themselves. Again, the real 'bottom line' is that the person in the position of greater power — in this case the doctor — is a decent, competent person. We just have to trust them.

Education differs from health care in that it has not experienced the blowout in costs due in the health sector to an ever-expanding availability of expensive methods of treatment. Education technology — the body of techniques for augmenting students' 'human capital' — may have changed significantly since Socrates and his slate, and then again it may not. If you are lucid, lively and care about your subject and your students, you will be an effective teacher. If you are missing one or more of these characteristics, you and your class will struggle a bit. I suppose one can point to some clear-cut improvements in educational practices: lefties like me are not now forced to write with the 'right' hand; no doubt children with 'special needs' are better understood and cared for than they used to be; children are no longer (I hope) beaten with straps and canes . . . are there some other advances I have missed? Probably, but it does seem that the three main functions of the incarceration of children in schools are timeless and not really subject much to improvement in their mundane necessity: (1) instilling numeracy and literacy (the '3 Rs'); (2) training for adult citizenship; (3) childminding.

Like the health sector, education has been exposed to the chilly winds of economic rationalism over the past decade, though not (yet) in nearly so virulent a form. The jargon — *contestability, accountability, purchaser/provider split, consumer sovereignty, outcome oriented* — has been wafted around the schoolyard and the quadrangle, to noisome effect. As always, the propaganda has an insidious but superficial appeal. In the school-system context it goes something like this:

> *Do you (the parent) want to be able to exercise genuine choice and control in the matter of where and how your child is educated rather than have the matter decided for yor by autocratic principals, bureaucrats in Wellington and the Teachers' Union?*

Gosh yes, I suppose I do. But consider this alternative pitch:

> *Do you (the parent) want your child and every New Zealand child, no matter where they live or what their social background, to have access to a public school system of uniformly high and consistent standards run by well-trained and dedicated professionals, or are you happy to have the matter controlled by the whims and prejudices of other parents and local politicians?*

New Zealanders of my generation and before grew up in a strong state-school system, and it worked well, not just at 'educating' us in the narrow sense of the 3 Rs but in forming our citizenship by giving us a shared experience and training in what are now called 'life skills'. Sure, there were sillinesses (like corporal punishment and army drills for boys) and outmoded biases in the curriculum (we learnt more about English kings than Maori chiefs), but these are things which can — and have been — improved gradually, without ripping the system apart.

Oscar Wilde supposedly once said that socialism would never work because it would take up too many evenings. He was probably referring to the gentle Fabian socialism espoused by his contemporaries the Webbs and Bernard Shaw, with their relentless rounds of committees, pamphleteering and meetings, but the great irony revealed by the New Zealand revolution is that it is actually 'capitalism' — more precisely, the ubiquitous propagation of decentralised markets — which is so squandering of our 'evenings'. These are the transaction costs of which the alarming blowout since the early 1980s is documented above in chapter 12. In terms of primary and secondary education, it literally is a matter of evenings: in so-called community-controlled schools, evenings during which tired parents and tired teachers try and hammer out detailed matters of school policy.

The alternative is schools largely controlled (as they used to be) by the professionals who teach in them. I find this quite acceptable, taking comfort from virtue ethics again. If the teachers are well chosen, well trained and decently paid, then we can trust them to make sensible and honourable decisions. This doesn't mean *no* parent or community input, or that schools should not respond to the special needs and opportunities of their community. In my home town of Wanaka, for example, the local high school — Mt Aspiring College — has developed (with much community involvement) what amounts to a highly successful export business, which offers a seventh-form year to children from all over New Zealand and the world concentrating on teaching them about the outdoors and orienteering skills. The young people even seem to have some fun.

What about the universities? This is the 'industry' that I personally care and know most about, but I am quite cautious about proposing cures for our problems. This is partly because we are not in crisis — we actually do a pretty good job still. We have been able thus far largely to resist the rationalist reformers, much to their frustration, unlike health care and primary and secondary education. Our problems are probably mainly macroeconomic in origin — students struggling to pay fees and survive; staff oppressed by budget squeezes which force up student/teacher ratios. In a high-wage full-employment economy students would be better able to support themselves; there would be fewer people attending university for lack of anything else to do; there would be more scholarships and private-sector sponsorship of education; there would be a bigger tax base from which to source government funding; there would be less need to divert resources from teaching and research to crisis management.

I am not convinced that 'society' needs more university education, or should devote more resources to the system as it stands. The academy seems rather to have lost favour with the general public, and this is reflected in a gentle but persistent erosion of our real incomes. Well, so be it. If that is really what you want, Jo Public, we academics can all go and work somewhere else if we don't like it. What I would never compromise on or accept is an attack on the basic values of the university — its great duty to seek knowledge and tell the truth, no matter how unpopular this is to the powers that be.

I certainly do not support the idea that, because there is a 'world market' for academics, we should pay 'internationally competitive' salaries to attract staff to New Zealand universities. If you want to live in New Zealand, you have to live like a New Zealander, for the sort of salary earned by other, less internationally mobile, New Zealanders of similar training and ability. It is indeed true that the academics business is international in scope, particularly in fields such as economics which have — rightly or wrongly — been largely homogenised into the pseudo-universal doctrine I have called 'McModel'.

Thus, for example, the top five New Zealand academic economists all work in universities in the United States, not in the country of their birth.[2] This is perhaps a pity; perhaps just inevitable given the way things are. It certainly does not — in my opinion — justify the current sneaky practice of offering secret salary 'loadings' to (often untried or second-rate) American academics applying for jobs in New Zealand, simply because, being Americans, they need more money than do folk from other countries, including our own.

As for the students — they seem to be under quite a lot of stress, both academic and financial. I have suggested that high-wage full employment would take the pressure off, but what can we do in the meantime? I used to be in favour of totally 'free' (i.e. no fees) tertiary education, but now feel that some contribution is sensible and fair. Attending university is more like visiting the doctor than entering hospital, and so the rationing function of fees is useful. It has been suggested that students be paid the equivalent of the unemployment benefit to attend university or other tertiary institutions. Since I am against the dole, I am not very keen on this idea either, though there should be a generous system of scholarships available to poor and disadvantaged students. As for student loans, having to borrow to buy groceries seems a sorry state of affairs in any walk of life. Starting one's career with debts of twenty or thirty thousand dollars, rather than being able to begin saving for a house or whatever, must be a pretty miserable prospect, especially for young people whose financial discipline has been eroded by the easy availability of money through the loan scheme.

All this might sound rather reactionary — favouring the interests of the comparatively affluent middle classes. But the middle classes *always* have an advantage in purloining resources from the welfare state, be this health care, schooling or tertiary education. Middle-class children are likely to go to better schools (private or public), have a more supportive learning environment at home, and have more financial support from their parents. If we paid all students a 'wage' to attend university (as they did in England), the middle classes would benefit the most, at the expense of the general taxpayer.

There is no 'solution' to this, but good primary and secondary schools for kids, and good jobs for parents, will take us a long way. I remember my own high school in the 1960s — King's, in the mainly working and lower middle-class suburb of South Dunedin — at which twenty of the forty boys in my seventh-form year, going on to university, had started five years ago in the lowest 'nonacademic' forms, and had been able to work their way up. Attending university is not the be all and end all for everyone — who will drive those buses? — but it is terribly important that young people with the potential to benefit from tertiary education get to realise it.

In this chapter I have developed two lines of analysis for the problems of health and education and what to do about them (I didn't get to housing and crime, but the same principles would apply there too.) One line, which we could call the micro-analysis, sees these sectors — especially health care — as case studies in the dogmatic application of simplistic economic rationalism to complex and sensitive real-world situations. The results: costs go up, output deteriorates and everyone gets upset and frustrated. The alternative is to rely on virtue ethics, on employing decent, competent people and trusting them to behave well.

The second line of analysis is the macro-theme of this book: that a lot of these problems are really secondary to the primary problem of not having decently paid jobs for the entire adult workforce. Perhaps it should be emphasised that this does not lead to a call for 'more economic growth'. We have had economic growth over the past quarter-century — by conventional measures per capita GDP is quite a lot higher now than it was then — but somehow we can't 'afford' the quality of health and education services that we used to manage. I suggest that it is where and how the GDP is earned that really matters. If we have ordinary people going off each day to well-paid, secure jobs that bring in enough to raise a family in decency, then we will find that these families can handle a lot of their health, education and other problems themselves, leaving the social and state institutions with a reduced and manageable public-health and education burden. Wouldn't that be a help?

Chapter 20
Virtue Ethics and Big Business

The upper echelons of large bureaucratic business corporations are the natural stronghold of the commercialist-rationalist ethos. Here the selfish-shit model of unrestrained opportunism reigns supreme, and it is not surprising that the most fervent private-sector propagandists for commercialism are the chief executives in the New Zealand Business Roundtable, whose world this is. They behave like that themselves and they expect the people they deal with to behave like that. Cocooned in their mirror-glass office towers, kow-towed to by toadies, they probably cannot comprehend the existence of an alternative.

But commercialisation has been a crock in its widespread imposition on the public sector in New Zealand, and *it doesn't even work where it is supposed to*, in the market or private sector. It is perhaps the major example of the proponents of 'more markets' not understanding how markets really work. The application of 'agency theory' has resulted — as we saw in chapter 12 — in the numbers of transaction workers (monitoring, measuring, managing) exceeding actual shop-floor transformation workers, with particularly spectacular growth in the managerial cadres.

But all this would be of no more than 'academic' interest if we really were stuck with the selfish-shit model as the only game in town. 'Show us your alternative,' the hard-nosed proponents of agency theory will demand. 'And make it a real working alternative, not some ivory-tower utopia.'

Well, I can do that. And, ironically, my real working alternative example is not an ivory-tower utopia but the ivory tower itself — the modern university. My favourite definition of the place where I have worked for most of my adult life comes from the great Clark Kerr, labour economist and long-time President of the University of California at Berkeley. Kerr said that a university is 'a collection of independent academic entrepreneurs united only by their common grievance about parking'.

No one is ever going to solve the parking situation (the only campuses without parking problems are in places no one wants to go to), but the first part of that definition hits the button exactly. The modern university is basically a complex, self-regulating network of thousands of students and staff, each with substantial autonomy about what they do and how they do it, though all somehow fitting together into a cohesive whole. It is quite an achievement. In the university most of the 'management' decisions are self-management decisions, and most of the rest are made by amateur managers — busy, responsible people who would rather be doing something else, back in their labs or on their word processors. That is good. We have actually broken the iron law of hierarchy, that 'managers' must be paid more than the people they manage.

I am always puzzled when people talk about the university as an ivory tower, supposedly remote from reality. We — students and staff — spend our days (and, often, nights) engrossed in studying the workings of the human and natural worlds. That seems pretty down to earth! And there is nothing cosseted about the environment we work in, either. On the contrary, it is ferociously demanding and competitive. Students are continually being assessed and graded, with no apologies or softeners: A, B, C, *Fail*! Academic staff have to compete for scarce research funds and then compete with their peers to get their results published. In a tough field like economics, the best journals only print one article in every ten submitted to them. That's a lot of rejection to get used to. Even the job-tenure system, which was designed to safeguard academic freedom, actually confers no more real rights than does the employment law at large, and it is harder to get — the four-year probationary system is tougher than its equivalents in the private or public sector.

Perhaps because of the stress and pace of campus life, we have had to get very 'real' about how we get our jobs done. Not for us the shiny uniforms of the Queen Street towers — blue or grey suits for boys, black for girls: in the university the only dress code is that there is no dress code — just wear whatever you are comfortable in. Sexist, racist, bullying behaviour is simply not tolerated. There is a sensible informality. I am on first-name terms with everybody I know at the University of Auckland, from Terre who looks after our tea room to Kit the former Vice-Chancellor, and including of course the students.

What is our secret? We work on the basis of 'virtue ethics', mentioned in the last chapter as being about good people behaving well, about taking care to appoint honourable and competent personnel, and then trusting them to get on with the job. We don't need phalanxes of managers to monitor and control us because most of the controls are self-administered, or dealt with by our peers.

Now contrast us with the bloated bureaucracies of the private sector, where the law of hierarchy reigns rigid. In chapter 12 I compared the University of Auckland with Fletcher Challenge Ltd, which is of similar size in human terms, but which is organised on quite different lines, with a massive managerial superstructure of more than two thousand employees paid more than $100,000 a year in 1996. So expensive, and is it all really necessary? At the top of the pyramid, the CEO of Fletcher's received $1 million in salary and bonuses; not, I suggest, because he was in charge of 25,000 workers, but because he was in charge of four — the four senior managers just below him in the hierarchy over whom the chief must of course be paid a decent premium, and who themselves must get their 30–40 per cent premium over their own subordinates, and so on and so on down the ladder. Contrast with our own Vice-Chancellor, who has to handle about 25,000 staff and students on a salary one-sixth as much.

I certainly don't want to pick on Fletcher Challenge, who may be no worse than average, and who did train one of the best managers in the country — All Black coach John Hart. And it is probably unrealistic to expect the corporate behemoths to achieve the university's high levels of operating efficiency. But there might be something useful to learn from us; and, surely, no one in their right mind would want us to become more like them!

Unfortunately, this is not so. The rationalists are rattling the gates of the academy. Our efficient, humane virtue-ethics system is threatened by commercialisation. Internally, an insidious sneaking managerialism has seen, for example, the ratio of administrators to producers (teaching and research staff) in the commerce faculty creep up from 2/50 to 20/150 over the past decade, and whole new layers of 'upper' management have been added in the university. Just one item — central registry salaries — was budgeted to increase by nearly $1 million over two years, enough to fund twenty frontline workers. And externally we have to face the public-sector 'reformers', unrepentant at the mess they have made of the health and school systems — both fields in which virtue ethics are essential for success — who now want to have a go at tertiary education. A Green Paper has been issued. It is written in the clichéd Treasury-speak that is the *lingua franca* of what I call The Kremlin — the closed-shop Wellington policy establishment, to whom the concept of virtue ethics would be virtually ethereal. Certainly this paper gives no sign of any appreciation of how an institution like a university functions. Instead, the stale routines of agency theory are run out yet again. There must be a principal — an owner — because the theory requires it. So it is simply asserted that the state 'owns' the university. This is wrong — no one owns the university, because everyone does. Then, for the 'owner' to exercise control, they propose that university councils be appointed by government, instead of the present, correct, trusteeship system of representation by all the stakeholders. The theory needs a measure of output or performance, so the Green Paper resorts to banal buzzwords: 'dynamic', 'innovative', 'competitive', etc. It would all be quite funny if it weren't deadly serious, and if it weren't terribly off the mark.

We have to stop this. More, we need to push back. Trusting good people to behave well is not an 'ivory tower' ideal. It is a smart, moral, low-cost way of getting things done, and we should be looking to extend its reach, not just defend existing bastions. And here is where a bit of realism about markets and the private sector helps. Of course the university doesn't have a monopoly on morality. There are plenty of good people behaving well out there in the corporate world. If there weren't

— if everyone was purely opportunistic — no amount of management monitoring would make the system function effectively (cf. Nigeria and Russia). But the policy push in New Zealand has been explicitly in this direction, and if you impose systems of control that assume people are opportunistic, then you will encourage them to be so. That is scary, but it also implies the chance of rebuilding a virtue-ethics-based system: people's behaviour, even their natures, are not exogenously given; they — we — do respond to our environment.

So, focusing specifically on the big-business sector, what could be done? I have three suggestions: responsible regulation, stronger competition policy, and having a go at executive pay. On the first of these, we must be unafraid to intervene, to have our government willing to 'regulate' business. In New Zealand we have retreated to something officially known as 'light-handed regulation', which more accurately is 'no-hands' regulation since it eschews any activist intervention in markets, relying on competition laws and the courts. The theory, of course, is that anything that interferes with the free competitive-market equilibrium can only make things worse, since the free-market outcome is, by assumption, the best of all possible worlds. But if markets really aren't perfectly competitive — a possibility that agency theorists above all should appreciate, given their obsession with imperfect information — then the laissez-faire market outcome is not necessarily optimal or efficient. Moreover the absence of explicit regulatory interference is actually an implicit regulatory position. It rubber-stamps the outcome that favours the most powerful player in the market.

The long-running dispute between Telecom New Zealand and Clear Communications about the terms on which the smaller company should pay for access to the Telecom network is cited around the world as the exemplar of what can go wrong when government bails out of regulation. In essence, Telecom, as the stronger incumbent, said to Clear: 'We've got the ball and we aren't going to play with you unless you guarantee we won't lose!'[1] With no industry referee to turn to, Clear had to resort to the courts. Result: a prolonged and massively expensive battle right up to the level of the Privy Council in London, which has really resolved nothing. Even a quite obtuse regulator could have done better than this for the industry and its customers, if not for the lawyers and consultants who feasted mightily in the process.

And the regulator need not be obtuse at all. Well-crafted regulations act as coordinating devices, providing focal points for sensible, mutually beneficial social and economic interaction. There are many obvious examples — the rules of the road, for example. Such regulations may be at their most effective when they don't seem to be having an effect at all. Thus, there will be few collisions at an intersection well controlled by traffic lights, but we would not conclude from that fact that the lights are redundant.

So, I suggest, should we interpret intelligent economic regulations. Of course, to the convinced rationalist, 'intelligent regulation' is an oxymoron. In their morally and scientifically impoverished view of the world, regulators — governments in general — are at best a clumsy impediment to market forces, and at worst are thoroughly 'captured' by the special interests of those they are supposedly regulating. From a world-view that extols opportunism as the basic building block of the economy, it is hard to envisage how public servants (or anyone else) could behave decently and in good faith, even though the slate from New Zealand's regulated decades is conspicuously clean of any trace of corruption or bribery in the state bureaucracy.

But, in the decent economy, laws and legislators, regulations and regulators are not the enemies of business or of the general populace any more than the referee is the enemy of the players on the sports field. A fair ref will disappoint individual players about as often as they are pleased by the decisions; a good 'preventative' referee will keep the game flowing fast and smoothly, so that at the end of it all 'sport was the winner on the day', as the current cliché has it.

The body of law that was being relied on to sort out the Telecom/Clear dispute is called competition law — part of an apparatus of laws and interventions known generally as competition policy ('antitrust' in America). Though clearly not suited to dealing with situations involving elements of natural monopoly (such as Telecom's network, which requires more activist regulation), competition policy has, in many countries for a very long time, been a valuable tool for fostering and protecting a pluralistic market system.[2] It is really all about rights and freedom — the right of everyone to participate in the market economy on reasonable and fair terms. On this basis competition policy has worked rather well for a century or more, but it is now under threat, especially in New Zealand. What has happened is that rationalist economists tacked something called the 'efficiencies exception' or the 'public benefit test' onto the body of competition law and practice. This, in essence, introduces cost-benefit analysis to competition policy. A takeover that would restrict competition and raise prices, say, should be allowed if the *net* sum of its likely costs and benefits is positive, even if this net gain is the tip of an iceberg of *transfers* of income or wellbeing between one group — e.g. consumers, and another — e.g. the shareholders of the merging firms.

This criterion may not sound so exceptionable — it is certainly quite orthodox economics — but it conflicts bluntly with the traditional competition-law doctrine on which it has been superimposed. It is a classic struggle between the due process and the outcome-oriented models of public policy. Due-process antitrust simply states that restricting competition is wrong, so don't do it. Underpinning this is a belief that a good society is an open society, which includes open access to participation in the economy, but this 'outcome' judgement is not called into question in every case. This approach seems — and, in the literal sense, is — irrational to the orthodox economist, who wants each case tried on its merits.

An analogy would be with corporal punishment. The due-process approach is that beating children is wrong, so don't do it. The rationalist economist would say that you can't assume the validity of any general rule; that there may be some children who benefit from being beaten and some who don't, depending on the child and the circumstances — the costs and benefits should be weighed up in each case.

The conflict between justice and efficiency (process and outcomes) has frustrated rationalists, and the New Zealand Business Roundtable (who else!) has called for the replacement of competition policy with efficiency policy. I think we can see this is a thinly disguised Trojan Horse. Once the due process requirements that competition not be lessened and dominance not be abused had been rubbed out, it would be extremely difficult to proscribe any practice or takeover, because the burden of proof would be on those who would interfere with willingly undertaken business agreements, and such proof would seldom be forthcoming — the data and forecasts that go into efficiency analyses are almost always sketchy and speculative.

Thus, a solely 'efficiency-based' policy would quickly become a rubber stamp for anything-goes laissez-faire, which of course would be just fine as far as the Business Roundtable is concerned. Much better, in my view, to go the other way: to abandon the notably unsuccessful attempt to graft rationalist efficiency criteria onto the corpus of traditional antitrust, and turn our attention to strengthening the latter. There could be ex post monitoring — perhaps by an agency independent of the Commerce Commission, which is responsible for the initial determinations — with the right to break up mergers or practices that turned out to be anti-competitive. The Commission could be empowered to be proactive, undertaking its own studies of industries and markets, using a beefed-up Commerce Act to break up anticompetitive arrangements and aggregations of market power. For example, is the consumer or the general business interest served by allowing liquor manufacturers, such as breweries, to own their downstream retail outlets, as is permitted currently in New Zealand, though not in some countries? Should we let the supposed imperative of economies of scale (which so often turn out to be illusory and/or swamped by the inflation of administration expenses when firms get too large) dominate considerations of pluralism and competitive markets? To use another example from the beer business, why not require Lion Nathan (the old New Zealand Breweries) to spin off its acquired South Island breweries — Speights and Canterbury — back into independent, regionally based ownership? Perhaps our small total market size means we need smaller firms, not larger, the better to fit into the markets and communities they serve.

Smaller firms have flatter hierarchies, and pluralistic and diverse markets generate less of the monopolistic and oligopolistic slack from which bloated bureaucracies are funded.[3] But if we really want to do something about the great management rip-off that soaks up billions of dollars in excessive and largely useless salaries and bonuses, we need to attack the problem at source. This is the third of my proposals for dealing with the big-business bureaucracy problem. It entails (a) culling the incentives that fertilise the weed-like growth of managerialism, and (b) strengthening the virtue-ethics-based principles that allow us to trust people to handle things for themselves. Here are some specific suggestions:

- *Break the iron law of hierarchy.* We have to stop management being the easy way of getting rich for people who aren't clever enough to get into medical school and who don't have the gumption and creativity to set up on their own. Treat management like any other trade — those especially good at it get paid more than their colleagues, but with no presumption that all managers should be paid more than the people they manage. That is, treat management — administration, really — as a useful service occupation, attracting people with an aptitude for that sort of thing. The university remains a serviceable model of how this system can function. It gets the incentives aligned correctly: aimed towards getting the job done with a minimum of fuss rather than padding and prolonging procedures for the sake of a more important bureaucracy.
- *Let the public sector set an example.* Pay increases of parliamentarians should be tied to changes in the average wage; not to the cost of living and certainly not — as at present — to the out-of-line increases being enjoyed by private-sector upper-management classes. Public servants should be treated similarly. Does it make any sense at all that the boss of our little central bank should be paid more — $360,000 in 1996 — than his American counterpart, the Governor of the mighty Federal Reserve, one of the most important jobs in the world? No, it doesn't make sense: in fact it is grotesque.
- *Outlaw incentive payments.* A big part of Dr Brash's 360K pay cheque was 'earned' as a result of him meeting certain targets written in to his contract. The problem with these

incentive schemes is not that they don't work but that they do, *at the inevitable cost of underfulfilment of other valuable goals not in the contract.* Thus, Dr Brash got paid for squeezing down the consumer price index, at a big cost in profits and jobs that aren't part of his brief. Private-sector CEOs are in a good position to wrack up the share price or quarterly profits or whatever is in their contract, to the detriment of the long-term viability of their company.

- *Outlaw share-option schemes.* A particularly unsavoury form of incentive payment is the granting to senior managers of 'options' to buy shares at a set price. This is of course a one-way bet: if the share price rises then cash in; if it doesn't, then nothing is lost. If managers want to get seriously rich, they should start their own ventures, not plunder their employers.
- *Install two 'Kiwi Share' directors on the boards of every public company and corporate body.*[4] These directors would be appointed by a statutory body and paid (by the company) a set fee — say, $25,000 a year. They could be distinguished retired business people and others of genuine achievement and ability (i.e. not chosen with an eye to political correctness). They would be charged with promoting the interests of the broader community as well as the long-term sustainability of the company and, in particular, both would serve on their company's remuneration committee — the subcommittee of the board which determines the pay of the executive directors and other senior managers. You might be surprised what a difference this would make.[5]
- *Don't allow nonexecutive directors to receive additional payments from their company.* In 1996 two nonexecutive directors of Brierley International Limited received substantial sums on top of their quite substantial director's fee ($50,000) for 'work undertaken beyond their duties as directors of the company'. Mr R.H. Matthews (Chairman) was topped up to the tune of $350,000; Sir Roger Douglas, the former Minister of Finance and failed pig farmer, scoffed another $140,000. As a (small) shareholder in BIL, I would be keen to know exactly what duties Sir

Roger, in particular, performed. This sort of thing obviously isn't illegal in New Zealand, but it should be. There is the clear possibility of a conflict of interest, especially when — as is the case with both Matthews and Douglas — the directors also serve on the remuneration committee determining the pay of the other directors who have employed them for those unspecified additional duties.

Such proposals as these will, of course, raise protests. It will be argued that corporate life is indeed highly competitive so big firms must indeed be efficient or they would not survive. There is some truth in this but not enough. As the proponents of agency theory should be the first to appreciate, those 'agents' who actually make up organisations have plenty of opportunity to divert resources in their own private interests. What I have suggested is a two-pronged attack on bureaucratic bloat, relying partly on sharpening the market, regulatory and internal governance structures that constrain opportunistic behaviour, and partly on strengthening the alternative to agency theory — the virtue-ethics-based system of trusting people to act responsibly and to manage themselves. It would be really interesting to see what would happen if management became just another service activity, worthy but not extraordinarily well paid. Would the great costly pyramids of hierarchy gently subside?

It will also be argued that the extraordinarily high salaries paid to top management are not extraordinary at all: there is an international market for executives and this is the going rate. We have to cough up if we want to be 'competitive'. This is an argument that New Zealanders need to confront and reject. It is true that there is a class of carpetbagging professional managers who wheel around the world at the whiff of a higher salary and a more generous stock option. Some of them are even New Zealanders. But cultural and social attitudes still result in striking differences in management remuneration and these differences should be taken seriously.[6] They remind us that in an autonomous society what people get paid is not just a 'market' decision, but a reflection of what is believed to be worthy and dignified for people with their skills and responsibility.

If we must put the matter in terms of incentives or individual motivations, then see it as the difference between 'extrinsic' and 'intrinsic' work motivations.[7] The first applies to workers whose interests are purely personal, and who therefore must be motivated to contribute to the common weal through the extrinsic incentives of cash and perks. This is the landscape of agency theory, with its shirking, distrust, monitoring and hierarchies. Intrinsically motivated people, on the other hand, get satisfaction from the job itself: they find it interesting; they value their personal and team relationships on the job site; they are fulfilled by the very act of participating in a joint purposive enterprise. Such people tend to be difficult to manage, but of course they do not need so much management: they can be relied on. This is the world of virtue ethics, where we trust good people to behave well. In reality, of course, both sorts of motivation are present in varying proportions in different people and in different circumstances, and we must take account of that. But we must also realise that they are at odds. There is no doubt that a healthy and successful economy is utterly dependent on intrinsically motivated people getting things done, and it seems increasingly clear that the deliberate imposition of extrinsically based incentive schemes, widespread in New Zealand since 1984, has been corrosive of intrinsic motivation at considerable moral and economic cost.

Chapter 21
The Do-it-Ourselves Economics of Decency

How should we live? What are the terms of the social contract that determines how we deal with each other? How do we know what the social contract is? There is an old proverb: do unto others as you would have them do unto you. But what if — as George Bernard Shaw pointed out — they have different tastes? It's a lot easier to behave well by others if you know what they like, and it is easier to know what they like if it isn't too different from what you like. And of course it is easier to behave well if you wish other people well. Social discourse is oiled by the understanding or empathy that we have with the goals and attributes of others, and supported by sympathy with those goals; by basically wishing others well.

The new economics emphasises empathy and sympathy as being as important to economic affairs as these qualities are to just about everything else that matters in life. This hardly seems a revolutionary idea, but it is nowhere to be found in the rationalist rule book that has dominated economic policy in New Zealand since 1984. This — to reiterate — actually has no meaningful use for the concept of 'society' or social behaviour. The economy is simply the aggregation of the individuals in it, each operating as a ruthless little maximiser of personal self-interest in a framework of institutions which, ideally, consist of little more than a set of laws protecting private-property rights.

The rationalist model is morally impoverished, but also (and partly because of its amorality) it is hopelessly wrong about how economies — *market* economies — function and flourish. It is not just how hard individuals work or how much capital they have that determines how productive they will be. Production — purposive economic activity — is almost always a cooperative activity involving others, and the terms on which individuals cooperate are the key to the success or productivity of their ventures.

Economic enterprises are never certain, and in the surprises and unforeseen turns of events that are the handmaidens of uncertainty, situations are always arising in which one party has the opportunity to take advantage of another. If you expect others to behave opportunistically, you have only two sensible choices of action: you cannot deal with them at all — more generally, retreat to safe positions — or you can devote time and resources to monitoring your associates so that they are unable to get away with cheating you. Both choices have big costs. Retreat to opportunism-proof positions results in prisoner's-dilemma situations in which both parties are worse off than if they behaved better with each other. It is when one party is willing to trust the other to 'leave a dollar on the table', and the other has the forbearance to do so, that the real work can get done. This is as true for great and risky capital-investment projects as it is for the day-to-day processes of the work site.

The alternative to spending more on monitoring others is no more attractive than succumbing to the prisoner's dilemma. Monitoring directly diverts resources from productive activities and, more insidiously, it fosters the sort of behaviour that it is supposed to prevent. People who are systematically not trusted will eventually become untrustworthy. Yet, dressed up as 'agency theory' this is the basis of what could really be called an epidemic of managerialism that has swept through New Zealand, resulting in the apparent paradox of rampant bureaucracy accompanying supposedly more-market reforms. There is in fact no paradox — cohorts of managers are intrinsic to a system based on narrowly 'rational' or opportunistic behaviour.

This is not loose anecdotal talk. The numbers show what has been happening almost frighteningly. In chapter 12 I reported that, by 1996, as many people in the economy were occupied in 'transaction' activities (basically, coordinating and supervising exchange) as were in the business of 'transformation' (of producing the actual goods and services themselves).

The Do-it-Ourselves Economics of Decency 217

This tells us that getting our sundry economic acts together is no trivial task. It must be taken seriously. Of course there is nothing wrong or inferior about being a transaction worker. They are an absolutely necessary complement to the division of labour. But *so many* clerks, accountants, lawyers, guards, insurers, managers? The fall in transaction productivity implied by these figures dwarfs even the most optimistic of efficiency improvements claimed by the rationalists to be the consequence of deregulating and opening up the economy to the international market.

We had, in the New Zealand of a generation ago, a system based on high-wage full employment sustained by the general observance of an unwritten but well-understood social contract between workers, employers and the state. It was indeed a market economy, but one in which trust and forbearance, based on empathy and sympathy, did not just temper the excesses of markets but actually allowed them to function with a remarkable lack of fuss, in terms of all those monitoring, managing, guarding and accounting activities required to excess in a more opportunistic society. It was extremely successful in terms of exchange efficiency (most notably in needing no reserve army of unemployed workers to facilitate exchanges in the labour market), if supposedly lacking in what economists call allocative efficiency — the promised fruits of the more-market reforms.

And, as each year goes by, those promised efficiency improvements themselves seem less and less plausible. Compared with any reasonable counterfactual — performance in the OECD, performance in Australia, performance right here in New Zealand before 1980 — our narrow economic outcome (GDP growth) has been mediocre. The economists and politicians who don't see this are simply in a state of denial. *Wake up, pinch yourselves: the revolution has failed.* Now that is too bad, but it is also really interesting. We can learn something useful. And what we can learn, taken seriously, could change in their entirety the terms of the economic-policy debate in a way that transcends the old left-vs-right, government-vs-market dichotomies.

First, the role of government. Our expectations must be quite modest here. The economic environment is not something to be 'got right' by the appropriate choice of policies and institutions.

The economy is us, the people who participate in it. It is something we create and recreate all the time and it performs well or poorly depending on how we perform — on how we behave. Each of us depends on others and they depend on us.

But although the state can't do it all for us, we cannot do without the state. Good government is a big brother (or sister) in the protective, not the Orwellian, sense. We need government to stick up for our interests in the world; to tell the IMF and the OECD and the Americans politely but firmly where to get off: 'Thanks for your advice, but we are running our own show now.' Above all, New Zealand governments should be protecting and fostering our economic sovereignty, giving us the space within which we can sort out our own affairs. This certainly doesn't mean supplanting the market, but it means saying firmly that our own markets are more important to us than other people's markets. Those bonds of empathy and sympathy, of knowing and wanting to do unto others according to their tastes — the social capital — are best built up by people of fairly homogeneous experiences and aspirations — in our case the people of New Zealand — being able to deal repeatedly with each other in a secure economic setting. That is why I have urged that we import and export less, and develop production for the domestic market; and why we should not hesitate to exercise controls over foreign investment in our economy. This is not xenophobia or isolationism; it is just getting the proportions more aligned with our own best interests. Other countries should do it too — we will all be happier as a result.

So suppose the state is doing its bit. How do we do ours? How do we generate all this decent behaviour that is so important? I don't think I have a particularly sentimental view of human nature and there are certainly a lot of jerks out there. But I think that most of us do have a moral sense, and even the jerks — apart from a few irremediable hard cases — can be induced to behave better under the right circumstances.

Within our country, there are a number of factors that foster empathy and sympathy, that build up the social capital of trust and forbearance. Having everybody in work matters, so that people's life experiences have this big thing in common. And working for a decent (family-raising) wage, which we used to believe was an essential clause in the social contract but which is pretty tattered now. This has to mean a fairer distribution of earned income. It is hard to feel empathy or sympathy for those who earn large multiples of the average wage, apart from our heroes of the stage or sports field. And we have learnt that it is no use trying to redistribute income after it is earned — we have to get it right at source.

A big help can be what economists call externalities. Behaving well is not just its own reward, it rewards others too, and makes them more likely to act decently. It is self-reinforcing. Each time you behave honourably to others increases their estimate of the general likelihood of honourable behaviour, and reinforces the moral code that such behaviour should be the norm. (Conversely, of course, the amoral, opportunistic behaviour forced on us by economic rationalism is also self-reinforcing, for the same reasons.) This is why I stress the value of many small changes — programmes, policies, changes in attitudes — none of which will do the trick by itself, but which are mutually reinforcing and together add up to something really worthwhile.

There are some difficult issues to be faced. New Zealand is now a multicultural society, and that may make it more difficult to build up our social capital. We must not become a nation of strangers. When the economy was dominated by Pakeha males (like me), empathy and sympathy were easier to develop. But we now have, in particular, women and Maori wanting to participate economically in ways which differ morally and culturally from those of the white men, which means we need to work a bit harder to find that common ground. Of the two great metaphors for the absorption of immigrants or, more generally, for dealing with 'otherness', I prefer the (American) melting pot to the (Canadian) cultural mosaic, for cultural as well as economic reasons, but I know everyone won't agree with this. I don't actually believe these 'problems' have a 'solution', but we must find ways of working through the issues in a good spirit.

Another controversial trend is the 'rights' movement, an outgrowth of American individualism which has gained some ground in New Zealand — rights to 'privacy', rights to 'equal' opportunity, rights to recognition of 'special' needs. There is nothing cut and dried about the issues here, either, but I would just note that the behaving-well ethos depends rather more on shouldering duties than on claiming rights — or, put another way, on the willingness to temper one's own egotistic individualism with recognition of the interests of others. People get upset about, say, the top-heavy management bureaucracies that are one obvious handmaiden of excessive individualism; perhaps they are less keen to go easy on claiming their rights, especially when these are seen as hard-won correctives to very real historical and social injustices.

A third rather tricky distinction is (in Herman Daly's words) that between 'community and communities', or, as I put it, the difference between being willing to trust strangers and only trusting people you know. Not everybody has figured this out yet. There has been a lot of talk about 'building stronger communities' and fostering neighbourliness and local self-help, sometimes in the hope that this will somehow supplant the welfare state.

Though not a particularly neighbourly sort of chap myself, I do not decry this quality in others. But more folksy neighbourhoods aren't going to solve our social and economic problems and may actually be a hindrance. Geographical communities, with their mistrust of outsiders, can be as inhibiting to commerce as can exclusionist cultural or racial communities. To achieve a decent standard of living we have to cast our nets rather further, which means, crucially, being willing to trust and do business with new people — strangers — sustained by a spirit of community-at-large which is inclusive not exclusive. I see the natural domain of community to be the nation state, specifically our nation state of Aotearoa New Zealand, but I do recognise that in a healthy, diverse, pluralistic society and economy people will operate over both wider and narrower communal bands.

We have the problem of the fixation — shared by nearly all our political parties — on the crude materialist goal of increasing growth in measured gross domestic product. Growth is eventually unsustainable; it must always run into limits. The very idea of a flow variable like GDP 'growing' is inherently absurd. We could say that a tree grew by so many feet last year and it would mean something, in that the extra volume of wood is likely to be permanent. The tree is unlikely to shrink, so that we could expect this year's growth will be on top of last year's. But we wouldn't say 'the Clutha river grew by so many cusecs last year'. Flows come and go; they are perpetual flux. And even trees must stop growing some time.

Because of the damage done in its name, it might be better if we didn't even try to measure gross domestic product, or at least paid it a lot less attention.[1] It is a very gross measure of wellbeing indeed. If a family spends more on childcare and takeaway food because they have been forced by economic circumstances to take on an extra job, then GDP goes up. If the relationship eventually breaks up under the strain, then the lawyers' fees for the separation agreement increase GDP. If the children of the relationship become troublesome as a result of the break-up and require counselling or correction, then GDP rises again.

Instead, we should focus on the more basic, process-oriented indicators of how well we are living. Indicators of moral, mental and physical health such as nutritional intake, infant mortality, marriage break-up, crime, suicide rates, and the consumption of alcohol, tobacco and other drugs: these are worth some attention. In the cause of sustainability, it would be smart to keep a tally of the condition of the stocks of physical and environmental resources. Have we left the soil or the air or the fish stock in at least as good a condition as we found them?

And we should ask what sort of a standard of living the people are managing to achieve for themselves. Gross domestic product as a measure of the sum total of economic activity conceals the much more important matter of the distribution of income. Distribution is important because income is such a relative concept. How well off we feel ourselves to be can largely depend on our economic position relative to others. This means that much of any measured increase in GDP is futile, because it cancels out — one person's increased income just means that others have to achieve similar increases not to be worse off. And it seems much that is done in the name of increasing GDP — such as New Zealand's liberalisation programme — actually harms material wellbeing because it worsens economic relativities (apart from its ineffectiveness at actually increasing growth, as noted).

We must, literally, work our way out of the present deteriorating situation and into something that is sustainable. This means everybody taking responsibility for making their own contribution to the economy, and also taking some responsibility for helping others to contribute too, in an economic environment or space that gives us the room to make decisions that, in all senses, are decent. There is really no big constraining economic problem in a highly developed, civilised country like New Zealand. *Just about everyone can earn themselves a comfortable living if we get the processes right.* There is no shortage of 'capital' in the financial sense. All we really need is plenty of power tools (meaning machines that extend the human capacity for physical effort), which we have. The rest is social, cultural, moral: how we work together and treat each other; how we live.

There is an excellent metaphor that brings all these issues down to the personal level of how we see ourselves: it is the metaphor of the consumer-taxpayer versus the producer-citizen. Our more-market revolution has explicitly and deliberately been pressing New Zealanders into the mould of (greedy) consumers and (grudging) taxpayers, with everyone concerned about what they can get for their money. Producer-citizens, on the other hand, are essentially focused on giving, on making things for others, on playing an honourable part in the economy and society. Really, few would argue about which model has the moral edge. What I see as really interesting and important is that the producer-citizen society is economically superior as well.

So how does this very book stack up in the producer-citizen stakes? It does of course represent one Kiwi economist's earnest attempt to contribute to our economic and social future, so you can't fault me for intent there. And it is done in a different way. Books on the New Zealand economy have tended to be one of two types: the manifesto or the moan. The manifesto type is a confident blueprint for success — do this, that and these forty-three other things and our future is assured. The moan, on the other hand, bewails everything that has happened without coming up with much in the way of useful ideas about what to do about it all. One book prescribes, the other proscribes. I have tried to write another sort of book. True, I have been fiercely critical of rationalist orthodoxy — well, it does cry out for fierce criticism. But my purpose in so doing has been basically creative rather than destructive; to establish the possibility of an alternative, and show that the gross mistake of trying to force us into the image of selfish individualism implies a better way based on a more complete fulfilment of our social and cultural mores.

However, I have resisted the temptation to prescribe rigid terms for that alternative. I could scribble down a manifesto as glibly as any economist or politician, and it would be worth as much as anyone else's: very little. If, as I argue, it is process that really matters — how we behave — then we have to develop those processes for ourselves, by the ways we deal with each other. Perhaps some readers will be frustrated by the lack of a tidy blueprint in these pages, though there are plenty of specific policy suggestions. I would just gently remind such people of the harm done to most of us by their willingness to submit to the know-it-all, top-down prescriptions of Robert Muldoon, of Roger Douglas and Ruth Richardson, and of Treasury and their suffocating insemination of the Washington Consensus of globalisation and laissez-faire. It is 'bottom-up' that does it, folks.We have to create the decent economy for ourselves, by our engagement in it as producers and citizens.

But what about the book *qua* book as an item in the marketplace? Does it represent a satisfactory engagement in the decent economy by its citizen-producer author? In fact most of the themes and theories I've expounded are illustrated in the book's physical production, though not always completely satisfactorily. It is a home-grown effort by a home-grown New Zealander, which is good, but of course it takes a lot more than a manuscript to make a finished product. Quite early on I started looking for a publisher. Naturally, I wanted a New Zealand firm to do it. I thought first of Longacre Press, a small partnership of three feminist women in Dunedin. I knew something about them and liked what I knew. They were based in my part of the world — Otago — and I was keen to do my little bit to help that rather hard-pressed regional economy. They had done a terrific job in producing and marketing my friend the painter Grahame Sydney's book *Timeless Land*, having persuaded quite a large number of people, including me, to fork out quite a lot of money for numbered, signed copies, and then selling even larger quantities of the regular edition.[2]

So I sent some draft chapters (four, I think) and arranged a meeting with them in Dunedin, which duly took place and was very pleasant, for me at least. However, I didn't get a contract to deliver a complete manuscript by a certain date. My first book, written when I lived overseas, had been accepted by Macmillan of London (Keynes' publisher, which is why I went to them) on the basis of a few sample chapters, and I hoped I would get that again. Longacre were interested, but were not sure that a book on economics was the right thing for them and they wished to see a complete draft before making a decision about publishing it.

Of course this was fair enough, but I was a bit disappointed and considered other options. A few years ago my first choice would have been Bridget Williams Books, in Wellington. Unfortunately, Bridget had just been taken over by Auckland University Press, which is certainly a classy and successful operation. But I worried that publishing with the press of your own workplace is rather the cosy option, smacking of parochialism rather than patriotism, to be seen in terms of the 'community not communities' distinction that I believe is important for economic development. I should be trying to build new networks, not relying easily on the old.

However, having failed at Longacre, I thought again of AUP. After all, I am a loyal corporate citizen of this university, and to contribute to its mana with a successful book would in itself be most pleasing. I let Elizabeth Caffin, who runs the press, persuade me against my scruples about inbreeding, and sent her the portfolio of draft chapters. Same result as Longacre: polite enthusiasm but no contract without seeing the whole book. So I gave up. I suppose I could have continued looking — though I certainly wasn't going to give my work to any other university press (possibly excepting Otago) — but this was all transaction activity, subtracting from my real, transforming work of actually writing, and it was to that I returned my energies. I would sort out a publisher later on.

Then, in November 1997, I found myself in Dunedin again, at the launch of Iain Gallaway's memoirs, *Not a Cloud in the Sky*. Iain, a long-time family friend, is himself a redoubtable performer at the podium, and it was a somewhat daunting honour for me to give one of the celebratory speeches. But it turned out well enough and the evening was great fun. Present was Iain's editor and publisher, Ian Watt of HarperCollins, the New Zealand subsidiary of the huge multinational publishing house formed by a merger of two of the largest publishers in the United States and Britain. A couple of weeks later I received in Auckland a letter from Ian. He recalled the Gallaway evening and mentioned that he had read with interest a *Listener* article by Bruce Ansley, which had given a sympathetic account of the new economics of decency and related matters. 'Have you considered writing a book? Should we talk about it?' Ian asked.

Had I considered writing a book? Should we talk? By this time the draft manuscript was close to completion but I didn't send it, choosing again four or five sample chapters. In my covering letter I explained that I really wanted a publisher who was prepared to take a punt on me, willing to trust me to produce a serviceable literary commodity on the basis of the samples and what else they knew about me. I also said, as I had to the other publishers, that it would be essential for the book to be printed in New Zealand.

I received a prompt note of acknowledgement from Ian Watt, and in due course HarperCollins decided to publish. I did tell Ian that my preference had been for a New Zealand-owned publisher, hoping of course that he would say something in reply that would quiet my conscience at having said 'yes' straightaway to the first person who actually offered to take my book, no matter that the profits from it — which I expect will be considerable — would eventually flow out of the country. He didn't really soothe me, but told me that the smaller HarperCollins subsidiaries, such as those in New Zealand and in Canada, operated with a rather proud independence from the mighty parent company in the United States, and of course all the editing and marketing would be done in New Zealand. Nor was printing it here going to be a problem.

So there we are. Have I behaved decently? The carping reader might accuse me of hypocrisy in espousing do-it-ourselves and self-sufficiency and then signing up with a giant multinational corporation owned by Rupert Murdoch, no hero of mine. Those of a more generous disposition might say that publishing always has been an international affair, that the writing, editing, designing, printing, distribution, marketing and most of the reading of the book will be done in New Zealand, and that all this episode shows is that Hazledine is not a fanatic.

With my deadline nigh, let me finish with a final survey of the ground covered. We started with the economic rationalists, the purveyors of McModel, the one-size-fits-all global prescription for 'free' trade and open markets. Many of those who push rationalism are really in it for reasons of the crudest cupidity — to feather their own nests. But there are others who sincerely believe that laissez-faire individualistic free markets do deliver the goods — more goods than any other system. A generation or two ago that proposition was vigorously challenged by socialists: capitalism was intrinsically inefficient; only with state ownership and central planning could the mighty Prometheus of technology be unbound. The communists did have about a quarter-century of history on their side, but nobody really talks like that any more.

Nowadays the orthodox challenge to laissez-faire is much more timid. It accepts the axiom that the open-market system is efficient in narrow economic terms of maximising GDP, but it worries about the side effects: alienation, extremes of wealth and poverty, deterioration of spiritual values. These are indeed valid concerns in themselves, but I am suggesting that the recent economic history of many countries and of New Zealand in particular supports a deeper, more fundamental challenge. Rationalism, laissez-faire, globalisation — call it what you will — is not just bad in its side effects and its spin-offs; it is bad economics, even bad *market* economics. Decency, trust, behaving well are not just leisure-time activities, to be indulged in after the real work has been done: they are essential to work itself, to a prosperous and stable economic system.

Potentially, this perspective is tremendously liberating. It means that we aren't faced with a nasty trade-off between efficiency and equity, between the size of the economic pie and the fairness of its division. It is tempting to say that we can have 'more' of both, but that is old-speak, the crass language of rationalism with its emphasis on narrow quantifiable outcomes. Rather, try instead: get the processes right and the outcomes will look after themselves. A nation of producer-citizens all contributing to, and sharing in, an environment of mutual trust and forbearance — that is the good economic process. We can achieve this, but we will need to believe that it is possible, we will need to give ourselves the space to do it in, and we will need to do it ourselves.

Endnotes

Chapter 1

1. This chapter is adapted from my contribution 'Is there an economic alternative?' in Alan Lee (ed), *Business Reporting: A New Zealand Guide to Financial Journalism*, Wellington, New Zealand Journalists' Training Organisation, 1997.
2. 1960–95 data on a quite wide range of economic variables are published in Paul Dalziel and Ralph Lattimore, *The New Zealand Macro Economy: A Briefing on the Reforms*, Melbourne, Oxford University Press, 1996. I updated these statistics to 1996 and backdated them to the 1950s, using the same Statistics New Zealand sources. This book is also valuable for its lucid commentaries on the reforms and preceding events, in particular because these are written as the jointly agreed output of one who is quite critical of the reforms (Dalziel) and one who is broadly in favour (Lattimore).
3. In fact, per capita real government expenditure is now twice as high as it was in 1962.
4. More accurately, there was a job for every adult male *whether he wanted one or not*. A crucial but little-appreciated aspect of the old full-employment regime was that it was the result of workers being expected to work as well as employers being expected to offer jobs. What it was *not* was jobs working for the government. Full employment was essentially a private-sector affair.

Chapter 2

1. Another benefit, perhaps not unexpected, has followed from the protection given to the woollen carpet industry. Even now, with free trade, the domestic market shows a strong preference for wool over synthetics, and this strong market base has helped the domestic industry do well in the high-value international niche market for woollen carpets.
2. Marcia Russell, *Revolution*, Hodder Moa Beckett, 1996, p. 69.
3. *loc cit.*
4. Full-time equivalent jobs are calculated as the total number of full-time (more than 30 hours per week) jobs plus one-half the number of part-time jobs. The figures cited are from the database of Dalziel and Lattimore, updated by the author to 1996 using Statistics New Zealand data.
5. As I write this, the real Albanians are rioting in their streets. It seems that most of the adult population fell for a pyramid investment scam, and lost their savings.
6. It is a bit worrying that a large number of the Treasury officials responsible for setting up the new deregulated financial markets very quickly jumped ship in the mid-1980s to seek their fortunes in the industry which had been largely created on their advice. Perhaps there should be a statute of limitations on this sort of thing.
7. I owe this phrase to Bob Stephens' review of *Welfare and Inequality: National and International Perspectives on the Australian Welfare State* (Melbourne; Cambridge University Press, 1994), in *New Zealand Economic Papers*, December 1994.
8. Those who need a bit more persuading before they can bring themselves to see the similarities between the Muldoon and Douglas

et al. regimes should know that the average per capita growth rates for the two decades 1976–86 and 1986–96 are 1.0% and 1.1%, respectively.

Chapter 3

1. Alec Nove, *The Soviet Economy*, London, George Allen & Unwin, 1965 (rev. edn). Nove also recounts the bolt factory story, and is the likely source for our Stage One lecturer's account of it.
2. Another story from Nove, which I hope is true, demonstrates that the Soviets did know something about incentives. The engineer in charge of building a new railway bridge had to stand underneath it when the first train went over.
3. Douglas Stone and William T. Ziemba, 'Land and Stock Prices in Japan', *Journal of Economic Perspectives*, vol. 7, no. 3, 1993.
4. 'Luxury of world's poorest man', Robert Guest, *Sunday Star-Times*, 24 December 1995.
5. *Economist*, 13 November 1993.
6. Jane Kelsey, *The New Zealand Experiment: A World Model for Structural Adjustment?*, Auckland, Auckland University Press, 1995, p. 157.
7. 'A bumpy ride through the single car market', the *Observer*, 30 July 1995.
8. 'The fading of Japanophobia', the *Economist*, 6 August 1994, p. 25.
9. Joseph E. Stiglitz actually puts the GM losses at $US100 billion — or two years' New Zealand GNP at the time. See *Whither Socialism?* Cambridge MA, MIT Press, 1994, p. 276.
10. See Graeme Wells, 'Fiscal Policy', in Brian Silverstone, Alan Bollard and Ralph Lattimore (eds), *A Study of Economic Reform: The Case of New Zealand*, vol. 236 of *Contributions to Economic Analysis*, Amsterdam, North-Holland Elsevier, 1996, p. 228.

Chapter 4

1. One book that debunks much trade orthodoxy (though from a firmly American perspective) is Paul Krugman's *Peddling Prosperity*, New York and London, W.W. Norton & Company, 1994.
2. Sources for these figures (and other interesting material on trade, Japan and US policy) are Peter Drysdale, 'The Question of Access to the Japanese Market', *Economic Record*, September 1995, and Gary R. Saxonhouse, in a 'Symposium' on Japan's trade regime in the *Journal of Economic Perspectives*, 1993.
3. For an insider's list, see Jeffrey E. Garten, 'Is America Abandoning Multilateral Trade?', *Foreign Affairs*, November/December 1995.
4. John McCallum, 'National Borders Matter: Canada-U.S. Regional Trade Patterns', *American Economic Review*, vol. 85, no. 3, June 1995, pp. 615–24.
5. See Paul Krugman, 'Dutch Tulips and Emerging Markets,' *Foreign Affairs*, vol. 74, no. 4, July/August 1995. The illustrative calculation is mine, done using the standard 'allocative efficiency triangle' method. With a distortion of 10 per cent and an assumed elasticity of 1, the inefficiency as a proportion of the value of the transaction is 0.1 x 0.1 x 1.0 x 0.5 = 0.005 — or one half of 1 per cent.
6. Jeffrey D. Sachs and Andrew Warner, 'Economic Reform and the Process of Global Integration', *Brookings Papers on Economic Activity*, vol. 1, 1995.
7. The now huge Korean automobile industry was built up in a domestic market 100 per cent protected from Japanese imports. See Dani Rodrik, 'Getting Interventions Right: how South Korea and Taiwan grew rich', *Economic Policy*, vol. 20, April 1995. Two excellent survey/synthesis papers on the evidence by Sebastian Edwards are

'Openness, Trade Liberalization and Growth in Developing Countries', *Journal of Economic Literature*, September 1993, pp. 1358–93, and 'Openness, Productivity and Growth: What Do We Really Know?', *Economic Journal*, vol. 108, March 1998, pp. 383–98.

8. Since writing this I have come across a remarkable statistic. If all 30 of China's provinces are treated as separate economies (and with average populations greater than 40 million they would be larger than most countries), the 20 fastest-growing economies in the world since 1978 have all been Chinese provinces! This is a World Bank statistic, cited in Joseph Stiglitz, 'More instruments and broader goals: moving toward the post-Washington consensus', World Bank 1998 WIDER Annual Lecture, 7 January 1998.

Chapter 5

1. Francis Fukuyama, *The End of History and the Last Man*, New York, Free Press, 1992. See also the earlier article 'The End of History?', *National Interest*, 1989, pp. 3–18.

2. On the Washington Consensus, see Paul Krugman, 'Dutch Tulips and Emerging Markets', *Foreign Affairs*, vol. 74, no. 4, July/August 1995. In the New Zealand context, see Jane Kelsey, *The New Zealand Experiment: A World Model for Structural Adjustment?*, Auckland, Auckland University Press, 1995.

Francis Fukuyama — an American with a Japanese father — became a US State Department analyst after *The End of History* was published, before returning to his position at the Rand Corporation Think-Tank.

3. One of the easiest ways to get published in economics is to write about how much and where other economists publish. The most recent of such studies is Richard Dusansky and Clayton J. Vernon, 'Rankings of U.S. Economics Departments', *Journal of Economic Perspectives*, vol. 12, no. 1, Winter 1998, pp. 157–70. Their top ten departments are, from the top: Princeton, Harvard, MIT, University of Pennsylvania, Northwestern, New York University, Boston University, Yale, Stanford, University of California at San Diego.

4. Though no money goes with the Clark Award, it is so highly valued that one Young Turk, Joseph Stiglitz, is said to have given up one of the most honourable jobs in economics — the Drummond Chair in Political Economy at Oxford — to scurry back to a US university before his fortieth birthday in order to qualify. He got it.

5. See David Kreps' contribution to the Winter 1997 issue of *Dædalus* (the journal of the American Academy of Arts and Science). For a review article of this special issue and of two New Zealand books (Kelsey; Easton), see Tim Hazledine, 'Economizing on Morality', *Landfall*, November 1997.

6. John Maynard Keynes, *The General Theory of Employment, Interest and Money*, London, Macmillan, 1936, p. 383.

7. The speech by Joseph Stiglitz cited above is a constructive analysis of the limitations of the old Washington Consensus and the prospects for a more balanced approach to economic policy making. Significantly, Stiglitz moved from a brilliant academic career to his present position as Senior Vice-President and Chief Economist of the World Bank, historically a quintessential Washington Consensus institution.

8. Eisuke Sakakibara, 'The End of Progressivism', *Foreign Affairs*, vol. 74, no. 5, September/October 1995, pp. 8–12.

9. Though one could hardly claim that industrialisation in China or

anywhere else has been less environmentally and ecologically harmful than in the West.

Chapter 6

1. And a few other things, such as no increased demand for things as a result of them becoming half as expensive to produce as before. These simplifications do not affect the point of the example.
2. A sector accounting for 50 per cent of initial output increases its production by 50 per cent giving an increase in total output for the economy (given no increase in thing-sector output) = 0.5 x 0.5 = 0.25
3. (0.125 / 0.75) x 0.60 = 0.10
4. Lee Rainwater, 'Poverty, Living Standards and Family Well-Being', Joint Center for Urban Studies of MIT and Harvard, Working Paper No. 10. Cited in Lester C. Thurow, *Dangerous Currents*, New York, Random House, 1983, p. 202.
5. Thurow, *op. cit.*, p. 203. The study cited is by Richard Esterlin, 'Does Money Bring Happiness?', *Public Interest*, vol. 30, Winter 1973.
6. 'A ploughman does not envy a king: but he envies another ploughman who has a shilling a week more than he has.' Sidney Smith, see below.
7. The seminal modern work on this, still very much worth a read, is the late Fred Hirsch's *Social Limits to Growth*, London, Routledge & Kegan Paul Ltd, 1977.
8. Even the cost of installing and 'debugging' robots before they start to break down — highly labour-intensive work — has been estimated at 'between one and three-quarters to five times the cost of the robot'. ('The Robot Makers Stub Their Toes', *New York Times*, 4 March 1984).
9. 'The kindergarten that will change the world', *Economist*, 4 March 1995, p. 67. A later article in this magazine ('Roboflops', 19 October 1996) reports that in Japan factory workers outnumber industrial robots by 50 to 1; in the US the ratio is 300 to 1.
10. Wit is a notoriously perishable commodity. Who today, for example, would find at all amusing Smith's nostrum that 'The only consequences of a university education are the growth of vice and the waste of money?' For this and other *bons mots* I am indebted to Smith's biographer, Hesketh Pearson, and his *The Smith of Smiths*, London, Hamish Hamilton, 1945.
11. Paul Johnson, *The Birth of the Modern* (New York, HarperCollins 1991, p. 179), from which this account of McAdam is taken.
12. John Deeks, *Business and the Culture of the Enterprise Society*, Westport, Connecticut and London, Quorum Books, 1993.

Chapter 7

1. George Psacharopoulos, 'The Contribution of Education to Economic Growth: International Comparisons', in John W. Kendrick (ed.), *International Comparisons of Productivity and Causes of the Slowdown*, AEI/Ballinger, 1984. Organization for Economic Cooperation and Development (OECD), *Economic Surveys: New Zealand 1993*, Paris, 1993.
2. Andrew Weiss, 'Human Capital vs Signalling Explanations of Wages', *Journal of Economic Perspectives*, vol. 9, no. 4, Fall 1995.
3. Victor Fuchs, 'Economics, Values, Health Care Reform', *American Economic Review*, March 1996.
4. Sorting is not the same thing as 'credentialism', which is employers taking advantage (reasonably enough) of an oversupply of graduates to require tertiary training for jobs which don't really need it — janitors with BAs, for example. Credentialism is perhaps a more

serious phenomenon in the United States (where about one adult in five has a university degree), than in New Zealand, where fewer than one in ten do. The proportion of American college graduates taking jobs that do not call for a degree is reported to have nearly doubled over the last two decades, to 20 per cent (*Economist*, 15 January 1994, p. 35).

Credentialism is of course another example of the private returns to education exceeding the social returns. An individual faced with a credentialist job market is smart to get a degree, but everyone would be better off if the practice could be dispensed with (this being an example of a 'prisoner's dilemma' situation).

5. 'Bottom of the class', *Economist*, 13 January 1990, p. 57.
6. Paul Miller, Charles Mulvey and Nick Martin, 'What do Twins Studies Reveal About the Economic Returns to Education? A Comparison of Australian and U.S. Findings', *American Economic Review*, vol. 85, no. 3, June 1995, pp. 586–99.
7. James J. Heckman, 'Is Job Training Oversold?', *Public Interest*, Spring 1994.
8. For example, Daniel Bell and Marc Porat, cited in the *Economist*, 28 July 1984.
9. 'Training up America', *Economist*, 15 January 1994.

Chapter 8

1. This is a slight variation on the version told by Avinash K. Dixit and Barry J. Nalebuff in *Thinking Strategically: The Competitive Edge in Business, Politics, and Everyday Life*, New York, W.W. Norton & Company, 1991, pp. 11-13.
2. John von Neumann and Oscar Morgenstern, *The Theory of Games and Economic Behavior*, Princeton, Princeton University Press, 1944. The speed and power of von Neumann's mind was so dazzling that one person who knew him suggested that he represented a new, higher level of human evolution. Despite this, mainstream economics was not quickly impressed by game theory, which was set up in direct opposition to standard neoclassical (perfect competition) theory, in which there are no interpersonal interactions because each agent is so small and each market so large. The leading neoclassicist, Paul Samuelson, is purported to have said of *The Theory of Games* that it was 'written by a mathematician who knew no economics, and an economist who knew nothing'.

An interesting account of the personal and intellectual origins of game theory is given by Robert J. Leonard in the June 1995 issue of the *Journal of Economic Literature*.

3. So called not because it was discovered by a Professor Folk, but because no one appears to have discovered it; it just emerged, part of the folklore of the field.
4. What follows is based on the discussion by Colin Camerer and Richard Thaler, 'Ultimatums, Dictators and Manners', in *Journal of Economic Perspectives*, Spring 1995, who give further references.
5. *The Theory of Moral Sentiments* (1790, p. 160), quoted by Amartya Sen, *On Ethics and Economics*, Oxford, Basil Blackwell, 1987, p. 87.
6. The virtue ethics process is described in chapter 20.

Chapter 9

1. 'American Academic Culture in Transformation: Fifty Years, Four Disciplines', *Daedalus*, Winter 1997.
2. John Cassidy, 'The Decline of Economics', *New Yorker*, 2 December 1996.
3. Tim Hazledine, 'Economizing on Morality', *Landfall*, vol. 194, Spring 1997, pp. 282–91.

Endnotes 233

4. Coleman credits Jane Jacobs with first use of the term in her classic *The Death and Life of Great American Cities* (New York, Random House, 1961).
5. See Tim Hazledine, 'Unbalanced Growth in the Welfare State', *Scottish Journal of Political Economy*, vol. XXIII, no. 3, November 1976, pp. 221–34, on middle-class capture of the welfare state.
6. This concept came to me through Francis Fukuyama's second — and much better — book, *Trust: The Social Virtues and the Creation of Prosperity*, London, Hamish Hamilton, 1995.
7. At Anderson's Bay our school song was: 'Musselburgh monkeys, Tainui rats,/ When you come to Andy Bay, please raise your hats.'

Chapter 10
1. Ian Ayres and Peter Siegelman, 'Race and Gender Discrimination in Bargaining for a New Car', *American Economic Review*, vol. 85, no. 3, June 1995, pp. 304–21.
2. Ayres and Siegelman cite a study by the Consumer Federation of America which found that 37 per cent of respondents believed the sticker (list) price on a car was not negotiable at all, with twice as many blacks as whites, and somewhat more women than men, believing this.
3. Though not impossible — I once flew across the Atlantic as 'Ms C. Ross', using the return half of a ticket given to me as a birthday present by Ms Ross.
4. Michelle Krebs, 'Saturn Comes to a Crossroads', and 'G.M.'s Satellite: A New Spin', *New York Times*, Sunday 8 October 1995.
5. In New Zealand, the Korean car company Daewoo uses a quite similar system, with salaried 'territory managers' rather than commissioned salesmen, and a no-haggle price (though how does the trade-in price get set?). Daewoo have done well in increasing their sales in a declining new-car market, and have found that men as well as women like to escape from the tackiness of the car salesyard.
6. The actual proportions were 62 per cent and 44 per cent.
7. For example, Robert J. Shiller, Maxim Boycko and Vladimir Korobov, 'Hunting for *Homo Sovieticus*', in *Brookings Papers on Economic Activity*, 1992, vol. 1, pp.127–81. One question asked by these authors in both Russia and the United States was: 'A salesman tries to please you — do you suspect he is thereby acting foolishly?' The split of answers Yes/No was about 50/50 in Russia and 25/75 in the US. But Shiller *et al.* seem to misinterpret these answers, concluding that 'attitudes that serve in a market economy are even more prevalent amongst easterners'. My argument is that willingness to trust others is an indispensable factor in achieving a successful market system.
8. Actually, negative-sum, because of the resources (time and energy) used up in the haggling process itself.

Chapter 11
1. See Bob Edlin, 'Will selling the ECA to the Aussies help or hobble them?', *Independent*, 9 August 1996.
2. Up to 1954, the New Zealand Arbitration Court was obliged by law to determine a basic wage for adult males that 'should be sufficient to maintain a man, his wife and three children in a fair and reasonable standard of comfort'. See Paul Dalziel and Ralph Lattimore, *op. cit.*

Chapter 12
1. Adam Smith, *Inquiry into the Nature and Causes of the Wealth of Nations*, Oxford, Oxford University Press, 1976 (originally published 1776), book I, chapter 1

2. Apparently the phrase 'invisible hand' appears only three times in Smith's writings, and one of these occasions refers to the guidance of celestial objects. See Emma Rothschild, 'Adam Smith and the Invisible Hand', *American Economic Review*, vol. 84, no. 2, May 1994, pp. 319–22.
3. In 1967, as a twenty-year-old student, I blew my life savings on a gorgeous but rough old Austin Healey 100/4. The price I paid — first-time buyer of a powerful sports car — for full comprehensive insurance was about $24/year, around $260 in 1997 dollars. (I might add that the insurance company made maximum profit on my premiums.)
4. John Joseph Wallis and Douglas C. North, 'Measuring the Transaction Sector in the American Economy 1870–1970', chapter 3 in Stanley L. Engerman and Robert Z. Gallman (eds), *Long-Term Factors in American Growth, NBER Studies in Income and Wealth*, vol. 51, University of Chicago Press, 1986. For New Zealand, see Tim Hazledine, 'The New Zealand Economic Revolution after Ten Years', University of Auckland, Department of Economics, Working Paper No. 161, November 1996.

Chapter 13
1. In fact, in each of John Siegfried's Rich List studies, a panel of experts is used to determine whether industries are to be classified as 'competitive' or 'non-competitive'. For the New Zealand study, we had the help of six highly experienced local economists.
2. Seventy of the 144 individual and family entries in the *National Business Review*'s 1997 Rich List live in the Auckland area.

Chapter 14
1. Marilyn Waring, *If Women Counted*, London, Macmillan, 1989, p. 279.
2. Euston Quah, *Economics and Home Production: Theory and Measurement*, Aldershot, Ashgate Avebury, 1993; reviewed in the *Journal of Economic Literature*, June 1995.
3. 'Why sex workers do it', *Next*, January 1996, p. 42.
4. In Arjo Klamer, *The New Classical Macroeconomics: Conversations with the New Classical Macroeconomists and their Opponents*, Brighton, Sussex, Wheatsheaf Books, 1984, p. 48.
5. Lucas also wears his economic principles with some dignity. Under the terms of his divorce settlement with his first wife, she was to receive half the $US1 million Nobel prize if he won it, on the very reasonable grounds that her nurturing of him and their family had enabled him to do the work for which he was very likely to be ennobled. This agreement, also reasonably, had a time limit, and was to expire, I think, in 1995 or 1996. When asked if it was unpleasant to have to hand over half the huge prize to his ex-spouse, Lucas just smiled and said: 'A deal's a deal.'
6. Paraphrased by Jerry Z. Muller in 'Another Wealth of Some Nations', *International Herald Tribune*, 15 October 1992.
7. Nancy Folbre, 'Children as Public Goods', *American Economic Review*, vol. 84, no. 2, May 1994, pp. 86–90.
8. *Economist*, 21 December 1985, p. 43.
9. 'The Family still rules, OK', *Sunday Star*, 24 October 1993, p. A4.
10. Using the term 'public' not in its technical economist's sense of a good which one person can consume without affecting the consumption of others, but to describe services which have a significant public or social content in either their provision or consumption.
11. The 'Chicago' version of this

maxim is: 'The bad things in life are free' (attributed to Frank Knight).

Chapter 15
1. Barry Eichengreen and Charles Wyplosz, 'The Unstable EMS', *Brookings Papers on Economic Activity,* 1993, vol. 1, pp. 51–124.
2. Barry Eichengreen, James Tobin and Charles Wyplosz, 'Two Cases for Sand in the Wheels of International Finance', *Economic Journal,* January 1995.
3. Kelsey, *op. cit.*, p. 106.
4. See review of *Studies in International Taxation,* in the *Journal of Economic Literature,* June 1994, p. 703, for evidence of widespread and massive shifting of tax burdens by multinationals.
5. My parents' first new car, a 1947 Chevrolet Fleetmaster, was built in Canada — something which greatly disappointed me when my father told me, since as a small boy I was a dedicated Americanophile.
6. GATT is the General Agreement on Tariffs and Trade — a post-war series of rounds of tariff-cutting treaties signed by all the industrial trading economies.
7. See Brian Easton, *NZ Listener,* 14 December 1996.

Chapter 16
1. With transport, distribution and mark-ups, a 16 per cent tariff on imports translates into about 8 per cent of the retail price, for this product.
2. A technical note: it is *differences* in tariff rates that are responsible for most of the allocative inefficiencies predicted by orthodox theory (small though these are).
3. Adam Smith, *op. cit.*
4. Amartya Sen, *Poverty and Famines: An essay on entitlement and deprivation,* Oxford, Oxford University Press, 1981.

Endnotes 235

Chapter 17
1. Anne Else, *False Economy: New Zealanders face the conflict between paid and unpaid work,* Tandem Press, 1996.
2. Take the case of two young university graduates, each earning $35,000 per year, living together on one salary and saving all the other — say, $25,000 a year after tax. If that money gets put into something like a house-renovation project into which the couple can inject some of their youthful excess energy (Susan and Rob's 'sweat equity'), they should be able to realise a 10 per cent annual return, which would convert the original savings into $68,000 after ten years, or double it after seven years (which is about how long Susan and Rob spent both in the labour force).
3. Dalziel and Lattimore, *op. cit.*, p. 72.
4. *op. cit.*, pp. 74–5.
5. I owe this startling insight to my former colleague Keith Rankin.
6. A rule of thumb used by superannuation advisers is that you need about 80 per cent of your previous income to maintain your standard of living after retirement. Given that most people retiring are on higher-than-average earnings, this figure is consistent with weekly costs of being employed of about $150.

Chapter 18
1. I owe this phrase to Bob Stephens' review of *Welfare and Inequality: National and International Perspectives on the Australian Welfare State* (Melbourne, Cambridge University Press, 1994), in *New Zealand Economic Papers,* December 1994.
2. As noted in chapter 9, unemployment (and sickness) benefits were 55 per cent of average earnings for a married man with children in 1962, versus about 42 per cent today.
3. My account of epidemics and their

social manifestations is based on Malcolm Gladwell, 'The Tipping Point', *New Yorker*, 3 June 1996.
4. *op. cit.*, p. 38.
5. See Dalziel and Lattimore, *op. cit.*, p. 48, table 6.1. By far the biggest social expenditure in the government accounts is superannuation, which took nearly $5 billion in the 1994/5 fiscal year.
6. Susan St John, 'Delivering Financial Assistance to Families: An Analysis of New Zealand's Policies and the Case for Reform', Department of Economics Policy Discussion Paper 18, University of Auckland, December 1994.
7. Every additional 100,000 people working generate nearly $2 billion in extra taxes (half income tax, one-quarter GST, the rest company and excise taxes). Though under true full employment some people who are now forced to work to help keep a family financially afloat would not need to, there are probably at least 200,000 people out there — current beneficiaries, registered unemployed, discouraged workers, reluctant students — who could and should be working and paying taxes.

Chapter 19
1. Ian Shirley, 'Unemployment: Its Realities and Human Costs', Massey University, 1992.
2. Although we at Auckland have been lucky enough to see quite a lot of the most eminent of these expatriates, the Yale econometrician P.C.B. Phillips, who is Distinguished Alumnus Visiting Professor in our economics department.

Chapter 20
1. This is the meaning of the famous 'Baumol-Willig Rule' that carried the day with the Privy Council in London. For a discussion of this and related regulatory issues, see Michael Pickford, 'Information Disclosure, the Baumol-Willig Rule, and the "Light-Handed" Regulation of Utilities in New Zealand', *New Zealand Economic Papers*, vol. 30, no. 2, December 1996, pp. 199–218.
2. The competition legislation of Canada and the United States (known there as 'antitrust') dates back to the end of the nineteenth century. For an opinionated account, see Tim Hazledine, 'Rationalism rebuffed? Lessons from modern Canadian and New Zealand competition policy', *Review of Industrial Organization* (1998), vol. 13, pp. 243–64.
3. Preston McAfee and John McMillan, 'Organizational Diseconomies of Scale', *Journal of Economics & Management Strategy*, vol. 4, no. 3, Fall 1995, pp. 399–426.
4. An extended and interesting discussion of alternative governance structures for public companies is provided by the economist and management consultant John Kay in his book *The Business of Economics* (Oxford, Oxford University Press, 1996). See Part III, 'Corporate Personality: Shareholders and Stakeholders'.
5. My colleague Mike Ross reports the findings of an American study to the effect that having 'patrician' nonexecutive directors typically reduces CEO pay by 20 per cent ("Tis the season when well-paid CEOs get defensive', *National Business Review*, 20 June 1997, p. 15).
6. For an illuminating set of studies on the determinants of and international differences in management-remuneration systems, see the Special Issue on Managerial Compensation of the *International Journal of Industrial Organization*, vol. 15, no. 4, July 1997.
7. Bruno Frey, 'On the relationship between intrinsic and extrinsic work motivation', in the special issue of the *International Journal of Industrial Organization*.

Chapter 21

1. This is aside from the inadequacies of GDP at achieving what it is supposed to, which is measuring the flow of economic activity. Such were discussed in chapter 14 and include: neglect of non-marketed work and failure to account for externalities, including activities which represent 'illth' rather than wealth creation.

2. The 'limited' edition sold for $399, the regular edition for $99. The only difference was that the first came in a cardboard slipcase and was signed by Grahame Sydney and his two coauthors, Brian Turner and Owen Marshall.